Chicago Public Library

Form 178 rev. 11-00

PRAISE FOR *EMPIRES OF PROFIT*

"A gem of a book. The language sparkles with insights into the core dilemma of multinational companies: how to combine international profit with local politics. Shareholders will benefit if business schools require student executives to read this book."
— John Mitchell, Associate Fellow,
Royal Institute of International Affairs,
author of *Companies in a World of Conflict*

"Daniel Litvin injects judgment, balance, and good storytelling into the overheated globalization debate: there is learning here for companies and critics alike."
— Mark Goyder, Director,
The Centre for Tomorrow's Company

"Daniel Litvin is a star of his generation, and his book is sure to transform the debate on multinationals."
— David Lipsey, Labour Peer and
Chair of the Social Market Foundation

"Daniel Litvin reminds us that the issues surrounding the current debate about corporate responsibility are neither completely new, nor as simple as many would like to believe. His book will help anyone interested in the debate over globalization make wiser, better-informed choices — and this is a great service."
— Aron Cramer, Vice President
of Business for Social Responsibility

EMPIRES
of
PROFIT

EMPIRES
of
PROFIT

Commerce, Conquest and Corporate Responsibility

DANIEL LITVIN

TEXERE

New York • London

Published in 2003 by

TEXERE LLC
55 East 52nd Street
New York, NY 10055

Tel: +1 (212) 317 5511
Fax: +1 (212) 317 5178
www.etexere.com

In the UK

TEXERE Publishing Limited
71–77 Leadenhall Street
London EC3A 3DE

Tel: +44 (0)20 7204 3644
Fax: +44 (0)20 7208 6701
www.etexere.co.uk

This publication is designed to provide accurate and authoritative information in
regard to the subject matter covered. It is sold with the understanding that the
publisher is not engaged in rendering legal, accounting, or other professional
services. If legal advice or other expert assistance is required, the services of a
competent professional person should be sought.

TEXERE books may be purchased for educational, business or sales promotional
use. For more information, please write to the Special Markets Department at the
TEXERE New York address.

Designed and project managed by Macfarlane Production Services, Markyate,
Hertfordshire, England (e-mail: macfarl@aol.com)

Library of Congress Cataloging in Publication Data is available.

ISBN 1-58799-116-0

Printed in the United States of America

This book is printed on acid-free paper.

10 9 8 7 6 5 4 3 2 1

For my parents and my brother

Contents

Acknowledgments

Many individuals and organizations have provided me with invaluable insights and advice – and spurred me on with general enthusiasm for the subject of *Empires of Profit*.

The Royal Institute of International Affairs hosted two study groups to discuss early drafts of the book. Attended by those with an interest and expertise in the field, these meetings helped me refine my narrative and arguments. I am grateful to the Sustainable Development Programme of the RIIA for supporting my work in this way, and to all those who attended the meetings.

TEXERE, my publishers, have been superb. Thanks in particular to David Wilson, my editor, and to Jenna Lambie. Thanks also to Bill Hamilton, my agent, for taking my initial idea for the book from conception to reality.

I owe a long-term debt of gratitude, too, to my former employers – both *The Economist* (where I spent six years as a journalist) and Rio Tinto (where I was employed as policy advisor). Both organizations, in different contexts, provided me with an opportunity to begin to explore and understand some of the issues dealt with in this book (with regard to Rio Tinto, see also page xvii).

Many individuals in a variety of countries gave generously of their time, advice or other assistance. Among them:

Emeka N.A. Achebe, Anthony Adair, Robin Aram, Jeff Ballinger, John Bray, Marcelo Bucheli, Rachel Crossley, Alan Detheridge, Oronto Douglas, Aidan Eardley, Marwa El-Ansary, Ibrahim El-Missiri, Daniel Franklin, Bennett Freeman, Adele Harmer, Jenny Geddes, Noke Kiroyan, Bernice Lee, Marcus Leton, David Lipsey, Alizah Litvin, Mark Litvin, Melvyn Litvin, E. Croft Long, John Micklethwait, John Mitchell, Indera Nababan, Naoko Nakamae, Pandji Putranto, Ian Read, William Redgrave, Nick Robbins,

Tammy Rodriguez, Andre Rogowski, Norman Selley, Shaun Stewart, Ruth Tatton-Kelly, Simon Wake, Steve Waygood.

To all these people, and many others, I owe thanks. Given the controversial nature of some of the issues examined in the book, I also owe it to them to emphasize that all errors and opinions in *Empires of Profit* are mine alone.

Preface

Giants really do stalk the world, and most of creation trembles.

Article on multinational companies in *New Internationalist* magazine.[1]

This book aims to shed new light on one of the great issues of our time: the spread of western-style capitalism across the world, and the forces of local resistance it may provoke. The focus of its attention is on giant multinational companies, the most prominent, controversial symbols of western capitalism, and some of their forays and conquests in developing countries from historical times to the present.

Rather than examine the economic impact and performance of such corporations, the book describes instead their interactions with local societies and governments. That is, it is about what happens when these huge companies and the host societies and governments meet – about the often profound impact on the countries concerned, and about the multinationals' attempts to grapple with the problems, frictions and sparks generated by the interaction. While a fascinating subject, this has so far been little researched in a way that explores the parallels between the past and present – a surprising fact perhaps, given the intense discussion the issue generates today, and the rich lessons from the imperial era that can be learnt by modern-day multinationals.

Out of the tens of thousands of possible examples of western companies in developing countries through history, the chapters that follow concentrate on just a handful of the larger, more powerful and more extraordinary. The purpose is to document these several giants' behavior dispassionately and in detail as would, say, a zoologist studying a certain species of animal, or an anthropologist a particular group of humans.

Why? One of the aims of the book is simply to provoke interest in the subject. For, in doing so, it is hoped that the reader will be persuaded that multinationals' political behavior in developing countries is as intriguing and worthy of understanding as that more traditional subject of historical and political inquiry – the evolution of states and the empires that they governed directly. Underneath the cloak of boring balance sheets and management jargon, which companies like to pretend describes their activities, lie institutions as influential and imperial in their own way, and also at times as mismanaged and fuelled by crude ambition, as anything the field of politics and government has to offer. This is why the book consists, not of a dry analysis, but of a series of narratives focusing on some particularly unusual, ruthless, or colorful characters: a set of stories that would be regarded as far fetched were they fictional.

Alongside the stories of coups, assassinations and adventure, the evidence contained in the book also generates a serious and unexpected finding about multinationals. This is that, for all their might, for all the vast economic resources they command, these organizations so crucial to the spread of western-style capitalism have invariably struggled to understand, predict, and shape the social and political environment in which they operate in developing countries – even though the nature of this environment may underpin, or undermine, their commercial success in the long run. Time and time again, in a pattern which is too pronounced to be coincidental, the western (and, in one example, Japanese) multinationals have exercised their power in unplanned, unsophisticated or self-defeating ways.

Their problem in this respect, it will be seen, has been caused in part by the limited understanding at home about the situation faced in developing countries. Throughout history, this short-sightedness has afflicted not only the companies' external critics but also their own bosses based in their home headquarters, who have often attempted to direct things from afar. The companies have also tended to focus their attention, and their best brains, on narrow economic issues – such as how best to market their goods or to boost profits from year to year – rather than the social and political environment in which they do business, even though neglecting this, or failing to understand it, has often damaged their interests in the long run. Many multinationals today still think of this non-economic context as merely a "public relations" issue; or instead they categorize any problems as "political risk", suggesting they are simply beyond their control.

The problem has not simply been due to poor management. Judging by the examples in the following chapters, there may be inherent limits to the capacity of large multinationals to manage social and political issues in developing countries effectively, a problem that applies as much to their explicit attempts to behave ethically (as with the current fashion for "corporate social responsibility") as to their efforts to protect their assets from local political attack. For the social situations they face on the ground are often too complex – involving as they do ingrained suspicions of foreign firms, unavoidable ethical and political dilemmas, and ever-shifting local power structures – to be susceptible to any managerial fix, however carefully planned.

Multinationals are often compared to giants. But whether or not "creation trembles" at their feet, what has so far been little understood is that they are inherently clumsy, partially sighted giants, which often wield tools too blunt for the job at hand.

Raging arguments

Before the story-telling can begin, a few preliminaries need to be addressed. First, it is worth setting what follows a little more in the context of current events, and in particular the heated debate in the west between the pro- and anti-globalization lobby – that is, between those who view the spread of markets and multinationals in the developing world as a positive process, and those who see it as destructive. The book does not take sides in this argument. It is not an overall moral evaluation of multinationals, but rather a set of observations about their behavior. Nonetheless, its message is relevant to fervent believers on each side of the debate, for it challenges many of the preconceptions of both camps.

Enthusiasts for globalization, including many of the multinationals themselves, have tended to view capitalist expansion in much of the developing world as an inexorable process in which western firms – being clever, capable entities – would be able to overcome any local political problems without great difficulty. This

optimism underpinned a rise in foreign investment in the developing world from some $20 billion a year in the early 1980s to over
$200 billion a year by the late 1990s, a vast surge of money mostly
flowing to a handful of economies in Asia and Latin America. By the
end of this period there were over 53,000 multinational companies
worldwide,[2] and though the bulk of their trade took place between
rich nations, it was their perception of the potential for capitalist
economic growth in countries such as China that excited them most.

By 2002, the time of finishing this book, the general enthusiasm
of the "pro-globalizers" had been dimmed by a number of events.
Financial crises at various prominent American firms, such as Enron
and WorldCom, for example, led for a time to public concerns about
the ethical standards of other large corporations (though the focus
here was on such companies' overall financial trustworthiness, rather
than their political interactions in developing countries). The
terrorist attacks on 11th September 2001, meanwhile, provided a
terrifying example of the potential for backlash against America, and
against the western capitalist system in general, from less-developed
parts of the world.

For the globalization enthusiasts, the book provides an extra
reason for introspection, for the evidence it contains of a series of
botched political maneuvers by apparently sophisticated multinationals indicates that foreign investors in developing countries
may face a more volatile, less controllable future than many had
originally assumed. A "clash of civilizations"[3] between the west and
other regions (a theory which became popular after 11th September)
may be avoided but, if the past is any guide, localized episodes of
backlash are inevitable in the future.

As for the anti-globalization activists, a common assumption
which is challenged in the following chapters is that multinationals
face a set of clear, black-and-white ethical choices in developing
countries, and that – being powerful entities – they tend to be in
control of local social and political situations. This outlook is shared
not just by those who took to the streets in anti-capitalist riots in
Seattle, Genoa, and other wealthy cities in the late 1990s and early
2000s but also by the many millions of peaceful citizens in the west
who perceive a direct link between big, apparently controlling
companies and a host of ills in host countries: child labor, low wages,

human rights abuses, and the perpetuation of corrupt and repressive regimes, and so on.

The book does not take direct issue with these complaints, but its observation of past patterns of western criticism of multinationals indicates that a broader perspective is required. Throughout history, it will be seen, critics have tended to focus on particular issues which happen to chime with the western concerns and anxieties of the time, rather than reflecting the entirety of the situation in the country itself. In this way, the criticisms have often obscured the complexities and ethical ambiguities faced by companies, as well as allowing some genuinely bad corporate behavior to go unnoticed.

One of the on-the-ground problems faced by multinationals in the modern era is thrown into particular relief by the stories from history: it is that any political maneuvers on their part may be interpreted by governments of developing countries as "neo-colonial" interference in their affairs. Furthermore the multinationals, for all their undoubted power, have usually been less capable of manipulating social outcomes, for either good or evil, than their critics have suspected. It is precisely these difficulties which have bedeviled attempts by modern multinationals to achieve positive results from their "corporate social responsibility" programs, as the last section of the book explains.

The structure of the book is broadly chronological and split into four parts, each focusing on consecutive waves – or repulsions – of foreign investment in poor countries. "Empires I" deals with the ruthless multinationals associated with the British Empire, the first major economic power of the industrial age, while "Empires II" covers equally domineering multinationals associated with two later imperial powers, America and Japan. "Backlash", the third part, focuses on the period of decolonisation and rising nationalism in developing countries after the Second World War. "Resurgence", the final part, brings the story up to the present day: it considers the renewed rush of investment into developing countries in recent decades and the risk that the currents of backlash may emerge again.

These stages in the ongoing saga of globalization are not totally distinct – they sometimes overlap and share features. However, the "Empires – Backlash – Resurgence" division broadly represents three eras each with a distinct geo-political climate. Each part of the book begins with a brief introduction, and then examines two or three powerful multinationals from that particular era. This narrow focus is to permit a close-up look at some of the interactions between the company and the society concerned in a way which, it is hoped, is both interesting and revealing.

Although the term "multinational" company ("transnational" company is sometimes used interchangeably) only gained common currency in the second half of the twentieth century, its definition is simply a company operating in more than one country. Therefore, it is applied in this book to such historical entities as the East India Company as well as to its modern equivalents. Another, perhaps obvious, point is that the book's focus on multinationals means it does not deal with another important channel for western capital in the developing world: investments in such financial instruments as stocks and bonds. Because such "short-term capital flows" involve less face-to-face interaction with local societies than does investment by multinationals, they are a less tangible symbol of the spread of western capitalism, and create less starkly visible clashes of culture. This is not to say that the study of such flows through history would not make an interesting subject in its own right.

Strict disciplines

The particular subject of this book – the social and political machinations of powerful multinationals in developing countries through history – does not appear to have been tackled in this way before (at least not to this author's knowledge). As a final point of context, it is worth noting why this may be the case. At first sight, it would appear odd, given that the theme is relevant to a large number of intellectual disciplines – economics, international relations, history, business history, anthropology and management theory, to name a few. Certainly, there exist scores of excellent books, journals, articles and diaries dealing with specific aspects of its subject matter, or exploring overlapping topics, and these have been plundered as source material for the chapters that follow. A selection of the most useful are contained in the bibliography.

Perhaps it is precisely because the subject examined here crosses a number of academic disciplines, that few writers have tackled it in this way. While historians, for example, have written most about the individual episodes dealt with in the book, they have rarely approached these episodes from the perspective of multinational management. While economists and business historians have long debated, and attempted to model and track, the behavior of multinationals and their investment strategies, the focus of this set of scholars has been mostly on the economic, rather than the political and social, intricacies of the phenomenon. One exception to this is Raymond Vernon's book *In the Hurricane's Eye*[4] which highlights some of the political tensions faced by multinationals, though it delves only partly into the history of the issue.

The work of anthropologists is also relevant here. These particular social scientists have long been fascinated by the impact of modern market forces on pre-capitalist societies, but they have rarely looked at the inner workings of the multinationals which help bring about such changes. There is also a growing body of recent writing on globalization – the best-selling example of which is probably Naomi Klein's *No Logo*[5] – but such works rarely focus on the rich lessons offered by history and are often written as an explicit rallying call.

This book is not intended as a call to arms, or at least not for or against any specific companies. On that point, and given the sometimes controversial topics covered in the book, I should point out that I have received no financial support from any multinational or campaign group for this book. All research trips have been at my own expense. To avoid possible conflicts of interest, I have avoided writing about organizations for which I have worked or advised. These include Rio Tinto, the mining firm, at which I spent two years as policy advisor. Like other big resource multinationals, such as Shell (see Chapter 8), Rio Tinto has been involved in some complex, hotly-debated local situations in developing countries over the decades. The focus of my work at the company was to help formulate internal guidelines on human rights and also anti-corruption principles for the company's managers.

This experience awakened me to the issues and dilemmas faced by such big organizations on the ground. But this book is not in any way about Rio Tinto. In any case, it has proved unnecessary to relate my personal experience when – as the following pages aim to show – a bounty of fascinating material exists on other multinationals.

Empires I

INTRODUCTION

This is the first of the historical parts of the book. But it is worth opening it with a brief glimpse into the present, for in recent times in two former colonies of the British Empire, foreign multi-nationals have come under fire – and history may have a part to play in these outbursts of anger.

One of the former colonies is India. Early in 2001 it happened to be McDonald's, the American burger firm, that incurred the wrath of locals. For the majority of India's 1 billion population who are Hindu, the cow is held to be a sacred animal. So when rumors arose that McDonald's had been "secretly" lacing its French fries with beef fat, local fury drowned out the protestations of the company's managers that they had done no such thing. Religious activists burst into one McDonald's branch in Bombay and defaced its signs with cow dung; at another branch, a crowd of over 500 smashed furniture and an ice-cream machine. "We don't want McDonald's in India", raged a Hindu religious leader.[1]

India's ruling classes are suspicious to a degree of all sorts of foreign firms, not just McDonald's, and this is in spite of periodic promises by the government to open up the economy further. In the late 1990s and early 2000s, India's largest foreign investment – a $2.9 billion power plant in the state of Maharashtra in which Enron, the now-bankrupt American firm, had a controlling stake – became mired in legal and political wrangles, and was a target of anger for nationalist politicians opposed to western multinationals.

The other former British colony is Zimbabwe, where attacks on foreign firms have been orchestrated from the very top. In 2000, Robert Mugabe, the country's president who fought in its war of independence, threatened just ahead of parliamentary elections to expropriate all foreign-owned mines. The threat was not carried out – or at least had not yet been at the time of writing – but it made western managers nervous indeed. Another aspect of Mugabe's strategy to reassert the economic power of black Africans around the same time was the occupation of white landholdings in Zimbabwe by "war veterans". Some white landowners were being attacked and intimidated. "The white man has not changed", proclaimed Mr Mugabe, in a speech to his supporters. "I appeal for him or her to repent."[2]

On one level, modern-day factors are sufficient to explain these flashes of anger in both India and Zimbabwe. But history has shaped the political landscape of both countries and also the inherited outlook and attitudes of those launching the attacks. For these two nations were not only influenced in their early stages by multinationals but were also brought into being by them – through violent interactions with the native societies. The multinationals concerned – the English East India Company and the British South Africa Company – were among the most powerful companies associated with the British Empire, the first empire of the modern capitalist age, and the period covered by this part of this book.

A curious demonstration of the relevance of history is that the trigger for the fury of modern Indians against McDonald's – suspicions about the use of animal fat – was also what helped spark a violent revolt against the power of the East India Company in 1857: Hindu soldiers employed by the company suspected that the cartridges they were being asked to use had been greased with animal fat. Many English were massacred as a result. Robert Mugabe's attacks on foreigners and whites harks back even more directly to the past, for it was the British South Africa Company in the 1890s which established the inequitable pattern of land distribution which still persists in Zimbabwe.

But the stories of these two companies – which are the subjects of Chapters 1 and 2 respectively – do not just help explain some of the current resentment against multinationals in India and Zimbabwe. More generally, they also illustrate dilemmas and difficulties faced by corporate managers that are equally relevant today.

The story of the East India Company shows how commercial success may suck a multinational into local political machinations and disputes in a developing country, even if the company's bosses intend to avoid such entanglements. The story of the British South Africa Company illustrates an inherent conflict between the fast-moving processes of global competition and the fine-grained, gradual approach which is necessary if companies want to work successfully with local cultures. These are profound challenges, even for the best-intentioned, most "ethical" companies – and both the East India Company and the British South Africa Company failed to deal with them in a way that served even their own commercial interests.

A sketch of the landscape

Before describing the actual experiences of these multinationals, however, some scene setting is in order. How did such vast organizations evolve? What sort of political and economic situation gave birth to them? And what can be said of the cultures of the countries with which they were about to collide?

Of course the East India Company and the British South Africa Company were not the first, and far from the only, multinationals of the imperial era. It was only in terms of the scale of their power and influence that these two stand out. Throughout the colonial period, what motivated western powers to establish spheres of influence in poorer parts of the world was the lure of profits as much as a desire for political control, even if conquest was not always undertaken through formal corporate structures. The Spanish and Portuguese conquered much of South America in search of gold, for example. The settlement of North America and the eviction of its native people was also partly driven by commerce, with the Hudson's Bay Company, incorporated in England in 1670, coming to play a crucial role in the development of modern Canada. And in the seas around Asia and Africa, European merchants and companies competed fiercely, and often by means of open warfare, for control of trading networks. Before the English East India Company came to dominate routes to Asia, these were controlled by the Portuguese, and later by the Dutch.

The Dutch East India Company, founded in 1602, provides a revealing foretaste of the methods applied, and the problems faced, by its British counterpart. A symbol of the pre-eminence of Dutch trading power in the seventeenth century, which was built on the supply – innocently enough – of salted herrings to Europe, the Dutch company's expansion was driven by ambitious managers such as Jan Pieterszoon Coen. Like the British manager Robert Clive who features prominently in the next chapter, Coen was adept at manipulating and co-opting native rulers, and if necessary, exterminating their subjects. With his help, the company gained control of the lucrative spice trade in much of South East Asia. As with the English East India Company, the directors in the firm's headquarters in Europe often had trouble restraining over-enthusiastic employees on the ground. As one manager based in Batavia (now Jakarta) put it in 1706: "The Directors in the fatherland decide what matters, as it seems best to them there; but we do here, what seems best and most advisable to us."[3]

The scale of the power of the East India Company in its later years, and also of the British South Africa Company during its period of expansion, had its roots in the industrial revolution which convulsed Britain from the mid-eighteenth century onwards. The relationship between industrialization and empire is complex, and is a subject still debated by historians. But it is clear that the same factors that drove domestic economic growth – British technological superiority, including military technology, and the development of domestic financial markets – facilitated and helped finance imperial expansion. Industrialization also led to dramatic changes in the structure of British society and these shifts in turn helped shape domestic attitudes to capitalism and its prime symbol, large corporations.

The growth of British cities and the emergence of a discontented urban proletariat, for example, worried conservatives and churchmen, while exciting others, such as Karl Marx, who saw in it the possibility of revolution. A once rural society accustomed to the natural rhythms of agricultural work welcomed the wealth brought by industrialization, but not the social alienation and rigid work disciplines of factory life. Popular attention focused on the worst abuses of companies, such as the employment of women and children in unsafe mines and factories, and governments began to regulate these issues by the mid-nineteenth century.

Attitudes to big companies were also influenced by deeper ideological currents, which even today underlie many arguments about capitalism. For centuries in Europe, for example, warnings had been issued about the apparent ethical dangers of market exchange and profit-making: it was St Paul who proclaimed that the love of money is "the root of all evil". The Greek philosopher

Aristotle was also skeptical about the morality of profits and trade. So Marx's message was not new in this respect.[4]

Another set of long-term ideological currents worth noting here are western attitudes towards indigenous people – that is, towards the locals in Africa or Asia or Latin America with whom multinationals would come into contact. Throughout history, there have been two principal, and contrasting, images of such people in western debates, both of them simplifications of the underlying reality. One perspective of them has been as uncultured savages, living a life which is "nasty, brutish and short" (in the words of Thomas Hobbes), and hence in need of a dose of western civilization and progress. The alternative view of them has been as Rousseau's "noble savages", living a simple, utopian life in harmony with the natural world, and hence deserving of protection from western, capitalist forces.

It was the first outlook that dominated western attitudes at the time of both the East India Company and the British South Africa Company. However, it should be emphasized that many Britons during this era were simply oblivious to ethical issues raised by the impact of western commerce on native people. The acquisition of foreign territories tended to be welcomed at home with a sense of pride in the growth of empire, excitement at the exotic commodities – such as tea or silks – they made available to British consumers, and optimism (which sometimes turned out to be misplaced) about the benefits they would bring to the domestic economy. But the welfare of the natives in the African or Indian colonies was often neither here nor there.

The major exception to this was the popular campaign against the slave trade, which succeeded in its goals in 1834 with legislation to abolish slavery across the British Empire. This was among the most significant ethical movements in historic times to call for regulation of private enterprise in poorer parts of the world. However, it achieved its victory centuries after the trans-Atlantic slave trade had begun, and by that time seven million or more Africans had been shipped, in appalling conditions, to the New World.

Unsuspecting hosts

If British society, from which the two multinationals sprang, was absorbed largely by domestic concerns, the two societies at the receiving end were even less aware in advance of the likely consequences of impact. On the Indian sub-continent in the centuries before (and indeed for some time after) the arrival of the English East India Company, attentions were largely focused on titanic local power struggles. This was the period of expansion of the Mughal Empire, which by the 1700s covered most of modern-day India. The Mughals were Muslim invaders from the north. Stage by stage, they overran and repressed the Hindu and other kingdoms into which India was divided at the time. As rulers, however, they in large part tolerated Hindu culture and practices, and allowed many Hindus to hold high office. A delicate cultural synthesis developed which underpinned for a time the stability of the Mughal empire.

At the point of first contact the Mughals had more reason to pity than to fear the English traders, for theirs was an empire far mightier, more sophisticated, and in some ways more artistically advanced, than the English state of the early seventeenth century. The Mughal emperors often accumulated vast wealth from their conquests, which they would spend not just on buying continued political support but also on exquisite buildings, art and poetry. One such emperor was Shah Jahan, who ruled from 1628 to 1658, and whose name means "emperor of the world". He kept a harem of 5,000 women but was nonetheless sufficiently distraught at the death of his wife that he had built in her memory the Taj Mahal, which is believed to have taken 20,000 workers 20 years to construct. It is little surprise that the English later began to use the word "mogul", derived from the ancient Indian empire, as shorthand for a person of great power. In fact, the European traders – starting with the Portuguese, and followed by the Dutch and the English – at first failed to interest the Mughals in anything but bullion, for Indian goods were superior to anything the foreigners had on offer. One resource which the Mughals lacked and the English had, however, was a powerful navy, and this was later to prove decisive in the English multinational's expansion.

South Asian society under the Mughals was also advanced economically, another reason why the eventual English conquest may have seemed improbable at the time. Though the region's economy was predominantly agrarian – as it continues to be today – it also formed a hub for various trading networks, and may have possessed around a quarter of the world's manufacturing capacity. Banjara trading caravans, which carried food and goods between regions, were sometimes said to stretch for 20 miles or more.[5] Arguably these were the early shoots of a home-grown Asian version of capitalism; certainly they were to be significantly modified, if not cut short, by the English East India Company.

The African societies which were to collide with the forces of the British South Africa Company in the late nineteenth century were far less economically developed than the Mughal Empire. They were, however, more politically variegated. These societies will be described in more detail in Chapter 2. For the moment, the political landscape of southern Africa at the time might best be described as a confusion of African kingdoms and European imperial outposts. The Africans and Europeans were sporadically fighting each other as well as warring among themselves.

The slave trade had – and was still having – major and varied effects throughout Africa, devastating many areas, while enriching those who helped control it. The rise of an aggressive Zulu kingdom in the southeast of what is modern-day South Africa in the 1820s also triggered a period of political dislocation. Known as the Mfecane or "crushing", this Zulu expansion forced neighboring peoples to migrate large distances to the north, shaping the tribal composition of the lands throughout the region, including those which would be taken over by the British South Africa Company in the 1890s.

For the majority of sub-Saharan Africans the institutions of British imperialism and capitalism could not easily be anticipated or comprehended, for their own frame of reference was very different. Though they had some experience of trading, they were mostly subsistence farmers or hunter gatherers, and their political structures sometimes extended no further than their clan group.

The ways in which the Africans tried to resist imperial incursion on their lands sometimes seemed irrational to the British, who expected the natives to be grateful for the opportunity to become "civilized". In the case of the Xhosa people of southern Africa, the form of indigenous resistance played directly into the invader's hands. The Xhosa had been fighting the British for many decades without much success, and in 1857 turned to millenarian prophecies in the hope of salvation. They slaughtered all their cattle and destroyed all their crops in the belief that this would raise their ancestors from the dead who would help drive away the whites. The tactic failed, and their lands soon fell under British control. By contrast, the religious beliefs of the Matabele and Shona people actually assisted them in their struggle against the British South Africa Company. Their spirit mediums helped incite a violent rebellion against the company's rule in 1896. In this case, the multinational would have done well to study in advance the tribal systems of belief, however irrational these may have seemed.

This, then, is a first taste of the cultures encountered by the two western multinationals covered in this part, and of the conflicts that arose as a result. Because the cultures themselves were so complex, the interactions between them and the companies would be doubly so. The corporate managers would encounter political problems as intricate, unexpected, and difficult to solve as those faced by modern multinationals. The one main difference – which will shortly become apparent – is that when the going got particularly tough, or when peaceful means did not achieve the results they wanted, these early companies could employ a tactic not available to their modern counterparts: open warfare.

ONE

The corruption of the Moguls
The English East India Company

It is well known to all, that in this age the people of Hindoostan, both Hindoos and Mohammedans, are being ruined under the tyranny and oppression of the infidel and treacherous English.[1]

Declaration by mutinous Indian soldiers, 1857.

The Government in which they [the East India Company] have borne a part has been not only one of the purest in intention, but one of the most beneficient in act, ever known among mankind.[2]

John Stuart Mill, 1858.

This is the story of a multinational so powerful and feared in its time that opposition to it helped to define India's very sense of nationhood. Run from offices in Leadenhall Street, in the City of London, the English East India Company started life in the seventeenth century as a humble trading concern, but grew over time into a major territorial power. By the early nineteenth century its reach extended not just across India, but Burma, Singapore and Hong Kong, covering a fifth of the world's population. Even today, some Indian politicians cite the ruthless exploits of the company to help justify their hostility to foreign investment. But the story of the company provides more than just a means of understanding certain ideological currents in modern India. It provides a dramatization, on a colossal scale, of one of the principal challenges facing modern multinationals: how to manage their political interactions with host governments.

It is worth setting some context on this point. In the modern world, companies have two broad options when dealing with this challenge, both of them fraught with difficulties. The first is to try to avoid interfering in political issues. This is the approach which most multinationals claim to have followed over the last few decades, for it appears to respect local sensitivities. But how achievable is it in practice? Can powerful companies really avoid becoming politically embroiled in some way, especially when the governments of many developing countries are weak and unstable? Can bosses in home-based corporate headquarters really be sure about what their managers on the ground are up to?

The second option is for multinationals to recognize that they have political influence, and to try to wield this influence responsibly. In regions where state capacity is lacking, they even may opt to fulfil some of the roles of government. Over the last few years, this approach has started to be accepted by some multinationals as a result of pressure from western campaign groups and the "corporate social responsibility" movement. It will be dissected further in the last part of this book, but the challenges it presents are perhaps obvious. How can companies apply political pressure without evoking resentment? Who decides which political outcomes the company should try to achieve – the company itself, western campaigners, or local people? Do companies have the capacity to act as quasi-governments? Putting to one side the ethical issues, can they remain profitable while doing so?

In fact, the story of the East India Company can be divided into two overlapping stages which coincide precisely with these two approaches; and with both it reveals their inherent problems. The first stage, which covers the period from the company's establishment in 1600 until the 1750s, shows employees in India struggling to keep to the stated corporate policy that they should engage only in peaceful trade. Instead they became heavily embroiled in local politics, often contrary to the instructions of their bosses in London. Such was the failure of headquarters to understand and control the situation on the ground that the company took its first steps towards the invasion of an entire subcontinent in an unplanned, almost accidental way.

The second stage, which covers the invasion of the rest of India from the 1750s onwards, shows the multinational forced to become consciously involved in political administration, with all the financial risks and dangers of cultural imposition that that entailed. The climax of the story, as will be seen, was an explosion of violent anger against the company in 1857.

There are many differences between the East India Company and modern multinationals: in today's world, for example, most corporate headquarters exercise tighter (though far from absolute) control over local managers; also, with rare exceptions (such as companies that hire mercenaries), today's multinationals cannot call upon their own armies to protect their assets. But it is the timeless elements in this ancient multinational's story – and in particular, the general difficulties faced by headquarters in managing intricate and volatile political situations from afar – that are highlighted in this chapter.

Given that the history of the company spans many centuries and continents, various interesting subplots have had to be excluded for the sake of brevity. These include Stamford Raffles' exploits in Singapore and the company's involvement in the controversial opium trade with China. As with other chapters in this book, the aim here is not to attempt a moral evaluation of the company and of its impacts on the indigenous society, but rather to comprehend the nature of its political interactions. The history of the company also spans a change in the political constitution of the home country: in 1707 England and Scotland were united to form Great Britain. This is why, in different parts of this chapter, officers of the company are described as either "English" or "British", depending on the period concerned.

The hapless nawab and the restless manager

The best vantage point from which to understand the first stage of the company's history is right at the end of that period, in 1756, just as the company was about to make the transition from trading concern to territorial power. For this allows an important question to be posed: what exactly made the company turn away from the path of political non-intervention? The answer was not any new management directive from London but rather a set of confused and difficult local circumstances.

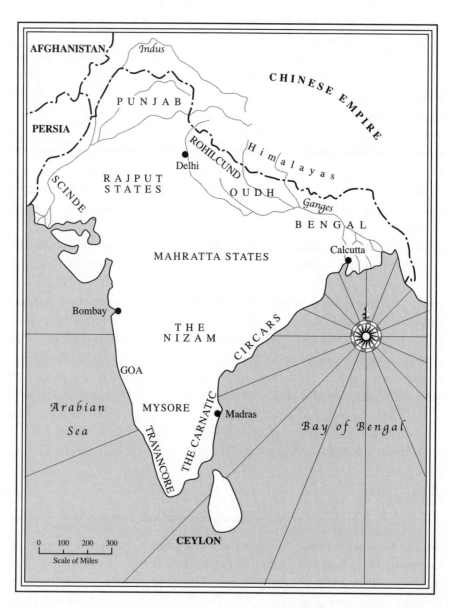

AFGHANISTAN

Indus

CHINESE EMPIRE

PERSIA

PUNJAB

SCINDE

RAJPUT
STATES

ROHILCUND

Delhi

H i m a l a y a s

OUDH

Ganges

BENGAL

Calcutta

MAHRATTA STATES

Bombay

THE
NIZAM

THE CIRCARS

GOA

*Arabian
Sea*

MYSORE

Madras

THE CARNATIC

Bay of Bengal

TRAVANCORE

0   100   200   300
Scale of Miles

CEYLON

INDIAN SUB-CONTINENT 1760s

As often at key moments in history, it might appear that individuals made all the difference. In this case, the leading local characters were Siraj-ud-daula, a headstrong nawab, or Mughal regional governor, and Robert Clive, an ambitious company official who later came to be known as Clive of India. These egocentric young men were both bruising for a fight. The scene of their confrontation was Bengal, the province of the Mughal empire governed by Siraj, where over the decades the company had gained a major commercial foothold, trading in cotton, silks, spices, and other goods. Prior to the first major acquisition of Indian territory, at which point taxation also became a source of profits, the company made its money by trading in a broad range of commodities, typically buying them in the East and shipping them back to England, though trading within Asia and other regions offered many profitable sidelines too.

Of the innumerable opponents of western companies through the centuries, Siraj counts as probably the most hapless. From the start, the British were contemptuous of his brusque manners, and on various occasions had barred him from their factories and country houses: "this excessively blustering and impertinent young man used to break the furniture, or if it pleased him, take it away",[3] fumed one European observer.

Indian, as well as British, historians describe Siraj as wilful and immature. As a child he had been spoiled by his grandfather, the then nawab of Bengal. As a young adult, he was insecure about his position in the febrile world of Bengal politics. The previous nawabs of Bengal had maintained an uneasy co-existence with the local branch of the company, one of them likening the Europeans to a hive of bees "of whose honey you might reap the benefit, but that if you disturbed their hive they would sting you to death".[4] But the 23-year-old Siraj found it difficult to suppress his irritation with the multinational's activities in his territory.

He had a number of specific complaints. For a start the British were strengthening their fortifications in Calcutta, which was the company's base in Bengal, without requesting his permission. This appeared ominous to Siraj, who had heard reports that nawabs further south in India had come under the control of French forces. The British had also apparently given refuge to a corrupt official from his own regime who had embezzled over 20 million rupees. Siraj had written to the East India Company's governor in Calcutta to complain about these matters, but the responses he found terse and unapologetic.

Siraj's short-lived revenge directly against the company occurred in June 1756. With an army of some 50,000 he approached Calcutta. The British were taken by surprise by his attack, and were heavily outnumbered. After a few days of fighting they began to panic: many of them fled in boats, while the rest surrendered. Siraj, his confidence inflated by the ease of his victory, boasted that he could govern the British with a pair of slippers. Meanwhile, his guards were dealing with the prisoners. Acting on their own initiative they held a group of the British in a stiflingly hot punishment cell. Dozens, perhaps over 100, prisoners died overnight. There is no evidence that Siraj himself ordered or sanctioned this outcome. No matter: the episode became known to the British as the "black hole of Calcutta", providing a convenient symbol of the nawab's alleged barbarity, and a justification for the company to hit back at him without mercy.

From the company's commercial perspective, the problems with Siraj were not disastrous, but nor were they possible to ignore. The company operated three major commercial outposts, or presidencies, in India – one on the west coast at Bombay, one at Madras, near the southern tip of the sub-continent, and the one at Calcutta. And Calcutta was becoming an increasingly important source of profits. In 1717, Frauksiyar, the Mughal emperor, had granted the company the right to trade in Bengal without paying customs duties. This was in return for a mere 3,000 rupees a year. In the intervening years, Calcutta had become a relatively wealthy city, with opulent merchants' houses springing up outside the company's fort.

Siraj was not the only threat to the company's local interests. Other European traders, particularly the French, were eager to increase their presence in the region. In addition, there was a continuing threat from the Marathas, an aggressive Hindu confederacy from the west which had tried on numerous occasions to invade Bengal. Indeed it was these concerns rather than a desire to snub Siraj which had prompted the company to renovate its Calcutta fortifications. Equally, however, Siraj's behavior could not now be tolerated. His pragmatic predecessors had provided the company's Calcutta presidency with an unusual degree of political stability and this had allowed trade to blossom. Siraj's aggression was putting this profitable co-existence under threat.

Clive's opportunity

Robert Clive, the other key personality in the local confrontation, was no less unstable a character than Siraj. Even as a child he was unruly: while at school in England he and a gang of his mates had threatened to vandalize local shops unless the shopkeepers paid them money. "He made progress in mischief, but none in scholarship", according to his headmaster.[5] Prone to bouts of depression and also intensely ambitious, Clive was sent by his family while still a teenager to work for the company in India. His father, a minor Shropshire landowner, hoped that Clive's business dealings overseas would help augment the family fortune.

Clive began his corporate life as a lowly clerk, copying documents in the Madras presidency. But he found greater excitement and enjoyment once he transferred to the company's military forces and distinguished himself in battles with the French in India in the early 1750s ("Be sure to encourage Ensign Clive in his Martial Pursuits",[6] noted his employers in their records). On a brief return to England, he made an abortive attempt to contest a parliamentary seat. But while in London he did succeed in bending the ears of the company's directors, persuading them that the French remained a menace in India. He returned to the sub-continent charged with dealing with that threat. This had became more explicit with the outbreak in 1756 of the Seven Years War, which pitted the French against the British in Europe itself.

News of Siraj's capture of Calcutta emerged shortly after Clive arrived back in India. From the perspective of his career, the timing was fortunate. He was dispatched to Bengal with an army of some 2000 troops, including both British and Indians. "This expedition if attended with success may enable me to do great things. It is by far the grandest of my undertakings. I go with great force and great authority",[7] he wrote to his father. And so the scene was set for a historic confrontation.

Powerful underlying forces

But it will help to pause there, for it would be a mistake to suggest that what brought the company's period of political non-intervention to an end was simply that two aggressive characters happened to pop up locally. Personalities are important. But also at work were various underlying phenomena which, over the decades, had made the headquarter's policy of keeping out of politics and local conflicts increasingly out-of-step with the reality on the ground. Sooner or later a major disagreement would have erupted between the company and local rulers, even if Clive and Siraj had not been around to throw fuel on the fire; and this is where similarities to the situation faced by some modern multinationals can be pinpointed. One underlying force, for example, was the decline of the Mughal empire in the first half of the eighteenth century. This had made the political environment in which the company operated increasingly unstable, factious, and unpredictable – a situation found in many developing countries today.

The emperor Aurangzeb, who ruled from 1658 to 1707, had helped sow the seeds of the Mughal decline. Even by the standards of other Mughal rulers, Aurangzeb was particularly aggressive. He had fought against three other princes for the throne, and kept his father an effective prisoner for eight years in his Agra fort. A zealous Muslim, his policies towards Hindus were more explicitly repressive than those of his predecessors – he banned Hindus from high office and destroyed many of their temples. Aurangzeb may have simply stretched the central authority of the Mughal dynasty too far. Waging wars at almost every edge of the empire, he doubled the size of the Mughal army, a cost which was ultimately borne by the peasantry. For 26 years, until his death at the age of 90, he fought a war against the Marathas in the south. He shifted his entire court, administrative system, as well as vast armies, to the region in order to focus his energies on the conflict. But while his imperial troops laid waste to large areas, they failed to pin down their enemies who harried them in endless guerrilla attacks.

Threats to the empire grew after Aurangzeb. The Marathas' own territory expanded outwards during the eighteenth century towards the imperial capital of Delhi and also towards Bengal (the map near the start of this chapter gives some idea of how far their territory extended by the 1760s). In the Punjab, armed Sikh bands were gaining influence. From the north and west came the Afghans and Persians. In 1739 a Persian ruler, Nadir Shah, led an attack on Delhi, massacring 30,000 and taking away bullion and jewels worth some £30 million. The center of the empire was starting to collapse, leaving in its place just its chaotic substructure – several hundred regional kingdoms, some small, some large, and of which Siraj's kingdom of Bengal was just one.

The decline of the empire brought not just risks for the company, but also temptations for its local managers. The wealth and political power of the emperors had derived from an elaborate system for raising revenue from the peasantry and for buying-off those in positions of influence. Peasants would be expected to give up perhaps a third or a half of the cash value of their harvest (the proportion varied according to the success of the harvest and the greed of the emperor concerned). The wealth flowed upwards, some of it kept by regional barons, such as the nawab of Bengal, and much of it reaching the court of the emperor himself. It was a ready-made system of revenue collection which – once the central authority of the Mughal empire began to erode – appealed to company officials eager for new sources of profits.

London distractions

Another factor underlying the embroilment of the company managers in local politics, as already mentioned, was a lack of control from the top bosses in London. Admittedly the London directors knew well that local political conflict could be bad for business. The one time prior to Clive's arrival that the company had experimented with openly aggressive tactics, which was under the governorship of Sir Josia Child in the 1680s, it had suffered humiliation: its soldiers were beaten back by forces allied to the emperor Aurangzeb. To restore its trading privileges the company had had to grovel to the emperor, and pay him £15,000 in compensation. But in spite of their mostly peaceful intentions, the directors had little grasp of the situation on the ground, and the years-long time lag involved in communication with India made it difficult to monitor the behavior of local employees. Above all, they had their minds focused on what they considered to be more important issues.

One of these was commercial competition from other European powers. This was a fear which had been active since the company's inception. In fact, it was concern that the Dutch might corner the market in sea-borne trade with the East Indian spice islands that originally led a group of London merchants to petition the court of the English Queen Elizabeth I for the company's first charter in 1600. The resulting market competition with the Europeans was literally fierce. Off the coasts of India, the company's ships fought battles with Portuguese traders, whose influence in the region was beginning to wane. It proved more difficult to dislodge Dutch control over the spice trade, and the London directors had been shocked when in 1623, the Dutch tortured and killed ten Englishmen at Amboina, an island which forms part of modern-day Indonesia. At a later stage, as has already been noted, it was fear of competition from the French that inspired the directors to send out Clive on his second, fateful trip to India.

Then there were the time-consuming issues of corporate finance, structure, and administration. As one of the earliest joint-stock corporations, the East India Company allowed investors to pool risks over the long term, rather than sharing out the returns or losses at the end of each hazardous, two-or-so years journey to the East. Its administrative system was sophisticated, and focused on maximizing returns. The company's principal executive body, the Court of Committees, consisted of a governor, a deputy governor, and 24 directors. Detailed records were kept of products and prices. Given the uncertainties and complex logistics of long-distance trade, it made economic sense to set up warehouses and ports of call along the sea route and in India. These were the first territorial footholds of the company, but the London directors only envisaged them as trading outposts and not – as they would eventually become – centers of a vast political empire.

There were also economic cycles in domestic markets to contend with. The company's profits plunged during a trade recession in northern Europe in the 1620s and 1630s, a problem compounded by outbreaks of the plague in England. But it retrenched its operations, cutting back on warehouses, and on the number of voyages to the East, and thus survived until the next economic upturn.

Perhaps the greatest concern of all for the London directors was maintaining the charter from the English – and later the British – crown. This was key to the company's financial credibility. It gave it a statutory monopoly over trade to the East, preventing other English merchants from intruding on its business. It also gave the company permission to export bullion. The company devoted a great deal of effort and money in order to retain such privileges, and not just in terms of its official tax payments to the crown. For instance, it slipped a payment of £20,000 to King James I in order to dissuade him from granting a charter to a rival group of Scottish merchants; and during the reign of Charles II, the company's ships would return to London with samples of exotic birds and animals for the king's menagerie in St James's Park. But maintaining the terms of the charter was not always easy.

In the late seventeenth century, the company's profitability and rampant bribery was attracting increasing envy from commercial rivals and criticism from politicians. A crisis struck in 1698 when the crown was persuaded to shift the monopoly of eastern trade to another company. But the wily directors of the East India Company snatched triumph from the jaws of bankruptcy. They lobbied successfully for a stay of execution on their firm, and then launched an effective merger with the upstart trading house by buying up much of its stock.

Amid all these domestic concerns, one problem in India which did attract the directors' attention was the growth of corruption among the company's managers. For ambitious employees, or company servants, as they were known, the attraction of a foreign posting was as much the opportunity it offered for private enrichment, as the official salary. Employees ran their own accounts with Indian merchants. They took kickbacks on contracts, and sometimes engaged in smuggling. This not only cost the company money; it was also beginning to tar its image at home. Some company servants became so wealthy that on returning to Britain, they bought country estates and parliamentary seats. They became known as "nabobs", a corruption of nawab, the title of the Mughal governors, and attracted sneers from the English aristocracy for their conspicuous, *nouveau riche* style of consumption. "We can never expect a faithful Discharge of the Trust reposed in our servants if they allow themselves to be corrupted by Duallys [Divali] Bribes or New Years Gifts",[8] complained a missive from the London directors in 1740 – though like other London instructions on such issues, it is likely to have been ignored by employees in India.

A meshing of local cultures

The fact that the attention of the London directors was mostly elsewhere allowed interactions between local employees and local people to evolve of their own accord, and this is perhaps the most important underlying factor which made some sort of political conflict in India inevitable. Not all of the effects of this hands-off approach were negative. Sometimes local employees exhibited a degree of sensitivity to Indian culture which would be sorely lacking towards the end of the second stage of the company's history. Employees learned the local languages, befriended Indians, and shared in local pleasures, including smoking the hookah, and listening to poetry. A number of employees married Indian women.

Enlightened local managers had the freedom to pursue their own policies. In the late seventeenth century, for example, one manager of Bombay, Gerald Aungier, insisted that local disputes should be resolved according to customary laws, and promoted religious toleration of Hindus and Muslims. Enlightened approaches were possible on other issues too. One historian has traced the emergence of the environmental movement in the west to the experiences of the managers of the East India Company and those of other early trading companies. Sent to establish trading posts on beautiful, Eden-like islands, such as St Helena, company servants witnessed the destructive effects of sudden development, and some tried to institute conservation policies to save trees and the natural habitat.[9]

The other aspect of the hands-off approach from London, however, was that it encouraged employees to pursue commercial opportunities in ways which seemed to them to be most likely to achieve success – and that inevitably drew them into issues of local politics and power, especially as the company grew in size and influence. For example, it did not take too long for local employees to realize that demonstrations of military prowess could help the company secure trading concessions from the reluctant Mughals. In

1609, the first London emissary to the Mughal court, William Hawkins, failed to extract firm concessions from the then emperor, Jahangir. This was in spite of Hawkins' diplomatic and cultural skills, including his command of Turki, the language spoken by the emperor (though he did secure something of a consolation prize from Jahangir, who fixed him up with a wife and a troop of 400 cavalry). But a decade later, the second major emissary, Sir Thomas Roe, had more luck, in part because in the intervening years the emperor had witnessed English ships successfully fight Portuguese galleons off the coast of India.

This evidence of a shift in European power relations impressed Jahangir. Not that he was overly concerned about the Europeans: compared with his own, elephantine empire, these traders appeared to be of no great significance. But they did have control of the shipping lanes, whereas the Mughals' military might was land-based. They also could be useful as a source of extra revenue. Consequently, Jahangir gave permission for the English to trade and build warehouses on his domains.

As the company began to develop its trading posts, a form of interaction emerged with the local Mughal governors which involved a combination of diplomacy, bribery, and threat. If a dispute which threatened the company's trade in the area could not be resolved by compromise or paying off the nawab, the English ships typically would threaten a blockade of the port. The risk then was that the nawab's land forces might attack the company's personnel and warehouses. In practice, these disputes were often resolved without open warfare, as Indian merchants, who had a financial interest in the continuation of peaceful trade, were often eager to act as mediators.

The increasing involvement of the company's servants in local economies was also drawing them closer into the Mughal empire's politics. Maximizing the returns from bribery, for example, required company servants to manage carefully the political situation. Given the federal nature of the Mughal state, an agreement from the emperor granting the company specific trading privileges often would not be sufficient to persuade the local Mughal governors to co-operate. These nawabs demanded payments of their own, and would sometimes threaten the company with the use of force to raise their take.

The many company officials moonlighting as private traders also would strike political deals of their own with local officials. And in the area where the political authority of the company was uncontested by Mughal officialdom – on the seas – employees found all sorts of ways to raise revenue, including selling "safe conduct" passes to Indian ships or, in effect, running a maritime protection racket.

In Bengal, the local economy and the company's interests were becoming particularly intertwined. Company servants based in the Calcutta presidency were involved in trade in silks, cotton and agricultural products in inland areas of Bengal, as well as in the overseas trade with Canton and the East Indian islands. Hindu bankers were lending money to the English and other European traders, and some wealthy Indian merchants were moving into the European compounds. In turn, company servants were selling Indian traders the right to exemption from customs duty, which the company had been granted by the emperor in 1717.

For all these reasons, the confrontation between Clive and Siraj was the culmination of a long-standing process, rather than just a coincidental collision between two volatile personalities. By the time of the collapse of Mughal central authority, the company's servants were already up to their knees in political intrigue in Bengal and other provinces. Imperial decline simply sucked them in further. Insecure nawabs and Hindu provincial rulers sought alliances with the French and British to strengthen their hand with their own rivals. In turn, the French and British, by then at war with each other in Europe, themselves sought alliances with these potentates to further their own military ends. The London directors, of course, just wanted to protect the company's commercial interest. But what they had failed to predict was that achieving this on the ground now involved an extraordinary degree of political maneuvering. From this perspective, asserting political control through open warfare was a logical next step for local managers – and the provocation offered by Siraj presented the ideal excuse.

Siraj and Clive: the showdown

At last the story of the confrontation itself can be rejoined. In fact, the first main fight between Siraj and Clive – which was a battle over

Calcutta in January 1757 – was to prove far from decisive, or indeed glorious: Clive's forces became lost in fog at one point. The young nawab eventually agreed to Clive's terms of peace more out of nervousness of the damage the British might inflict rather than actual force of arms. The terms did little more than restore the status quo: the company's trading privileges were reaffirmed, Calcutta was returned, and Siraj remained as nawab. In Clive's mind, however, Siraj was a continuing threat to the company's interests. In particular, there was a risk that he might strike a deal with the French. But how could his behavior be constrained?

Conveniently for Clive, Siraj's power base at that time was particularly insecure. His aunt was intriguing against him, and among those who resented his arrogant behavior was Mir Jafar, his chief general, and Jagat Seth, the leading local banker (whom Siraj is said to have struck on the face and threatened with castration).[10] In such an environment it was not long before a conspiracy emerged to depose Siraj and to replace him with Mir Jafar. Clive learned of the plot, and persuaded the East India Company's local management group in Calcutta, known as the Select Committee, to support Mir Jafar.

If the battle of Plassey, at which Clive and Siraj had their final showdown, had been decided on numbers alone, the nawab would have won, and Indian history would have taken a different turn. Siraj's forces numbered some 50,000, whereas Clive's army was only several thousand strong. And the nawab's hordes looked impressive from a distance. One of Clive's men wrote, "what with the number of elephants all covered with scarlet cloth and embroidery; their horse with their drawn swords glittering in the sun; their heavy cannon drawn by vast trains of oxen; and their standards flying, they [the enemy] made a most pompous and formidable appearance".[11]

Clive's eventual victory was not a testament to his military skills and courage but rather to his political maneuvering in advance of the battle. In fact, both Clive and Siraj at various points were quivering with nervousness in their compounds. Clive happened to be changing out of his monsoon-drenched clothes when one of his commanders, acting without orders, launched one of the principal attacks of the battle. What proved crucial was that Mir Jafar, Siraj's army chief, had an understanding with Clive that he was to be the next nawab, and hence took care not to launch too energetic an assault against the British. Siraj simply fled from Clive's advancing forces, taking with him a servant and a favorite concubine.

Though Clive appears to have been content to let Siraj live as a prisoner, Mir Jafar was eager to ensure his own ascendancy was uncontested. Soon after the battle of Plassey, Mir Jafar's men captured Siraj. The young man pleaded for mercy, or at least for time to wash and say his final prayers. "His merciless executors flung a pot of water over him, and dispatched him with their swords. His remains were exposed on an elephant round the city", according to one contemporary account.[12]

With the unfortunate young nawab thus removed from the scene, the pattern for the immediate future began to emerge in Bengal shortly after Plassey. Mir Jafar became the new nawab, and – in a fitting piece of symbolism – Clive led him to the throne on his investiture. The company, and certainly the London directors, had no explicit plan to interfere in, let alone take over, his governorship. But power brought temptations on a local level.

In Mir Jafar's fractious court, company servants were offered bribes for their support for this or that ambitious Indian politician. On an official level, the Calcutta arm of the company demanded payment from the nawab for its role in the coup, and for its continuing military support, and in return was given the right to raise tax revenue from various districts around the city. When the nawab's territory was threatened by fresh invasions – including from an army led by the Mughal crown prince, and soon-to-be emperor, Shah Alam – Clive's forces helped repel them. As a tribute to his services, Clive was himself given a *jagir*, or the right to land-tax revenues, to the value of £28,000 a year.

"Bengal is an inexhaustible fund of riches, and you may depend on being supplied with money and provisions",[13] Clive wrote to the company's governor of Madras, offering to milk the territory further for the multinational's benefit. The Calcutta arm of the company soon began to demand the rights to raise revenue – and thus in effect territorial power – over more areas of Bengal. Mir Jafar naturally became annoyed about the company's insatiable appetite, and once he began to prove un-cooperative, it was a natural step for the local company managers to replace him – which they did, by force of arms, in 1760, and appointed in his place his more pliant son-in-law, Mir Kasim.

That year, Clive returned to Britain, an exceptionally wealthy man, and lauded by many as a hero, a conqueror of "oriental despots" (as the Mughals were often then described by the British). But for a short while, he faced a threat from within the boardroom. Laurence Sulivan, the high-minded London chairman of the company, wanted to make the multinational's internal management systems more transparent. Among other things, he was concerned that the degree of corruption among employees in India was damaging profits. He made a particular issue of Clive's income from the *jagir*, which he tried to get stopped. When Clive was later called to account before a British parliamentary committee, he explained his acceptance of gifts from the nawab thus:

> Consider the situation in which the victory at Plassey had placed me! A great prince was dependent on my pleasure; an opulent city lay at my mercy; its richest bankers bid against each other for my smiles; I walked through vaults which were thrown open to me alone, piled on either hand with gold and jewels! Mr Chairman, at this moment I stand astonished at my moderation.[14]

Clive was not in a mood to admit fault. Instead, in a bitter campaign, he tried, and failed, to oust Sulivan from the company's senior management team. What saved his career this time was that a fresh crisis had erupted in Bengal.

The new puppet nawab, Mir Kasim, had not proved quite puppet enough. He had taken exception to the rapid growth of private trade by the British in Bengal. In his view it was intolerable enough that the company's official business was exempt from customs duty. It was too much to expect the same privileges for "unauthorized trade." The company's local servants had a different view of the matter, naturally, and another war had broken out. Mir Kasim had struck an alliance with emperor Shah Alam and the Wazir of Awadh, a well-armed local potentate. Once again, the multi-national's considerable interests in Bengal were under threat. On hearing the news, the panicked London directors opted for a short-term fix to the problem: setting aside Clive's alleged misdemeanors, and without giving him any precise instructions, they sent him back to Bengal again to sort out the mess.

This time Clive took care to ensure that the company's dominance of the province was unassailable. Mir Kasim's forces were destroyed, and emperor Shah Alam was brought to book. Not only was a new, even more deferential, nawab installed, but the very mechanisms of revenue raising were now placed in the control of the company. Henceforth the company would collect the tax and allocate a share to the nawab which it deemed appropriate, rather than vice versa. In Clive's mind there was no other option: "either the princes of the country must, in a great measure, be dependent upon us, or we totally so on them".[15] A grand ceremony at Allahabad in August 1765 confirmed the transfer of power which had already taken place: Shah Alam appointed the East India Company as *diwan*, or revenue collector, for the provinces of Bengal, Bihar and Orissa.

This, then, was how the East India Company embarked on the territorial conquest of the Indian subcontinent. It was not because corporate headquarters had devised a strategic plan to do so, but rather precisely because the London directors had failed to control developments on the ground, and because they did not predict the organic process by which Bengal's unstable political environment drew managers into local disputes and furnished them with opportunities for political power. Whether later multinationals would cope better with such unexpected local processes will be an interesting subject for subsequent chapters.

Stage two: total domination

The second stage of the company's history now begins. Political control of Indian lands had become an inescapable fact, and the company's territorial expansion now proceeded at an extraordinary pace. This presented fresh challenges for its managers, in particular in dealing with the costs and complexities of political control, and the moral controversies that swirled in its wake. Just as the first stage illustrates how a multinational's policies against political interference can be subverted on a local level, so this second stage illustrates that explicit intervention can prove equally difficult to administer, and – if handled badly – can be even more explosive.

Each of the successive annexations of Indian territory from the battle of Plassey onwards is a story – like that of Clive's takeover of Bengal – of British officers and managers playing off one Indian ruler against another, and of superior British military technology. Each of the wars was justified in terms of protecting British interests and those of the company, even if sometimes they only served the interests of army commanders and local employees.

To give just a sample of the wars during the period: in 1799, the Marquis of Wellesley, the then governor-general in India, and a man who disdainfully described the company's directors as those "cheesemongers of Leadenhall Street", defeated Tipu Sultan of Mysore, a fierce Muslim ruler from the south of India. In the west, the Maratha empire was beaten back and then finally annexed at the hands of a 120,000-strong British force in 1817–1818. In the Punjab, the death of the charismatic Sikh ruler Ranjit Singh, who had sought a peaceful co-existence with the company (and who was joined on his funeral pyre by his four wives and seven concubines), led to a period of unrest, prompting the British to annex the territory in 1849. By this late stage, British control extended over most of the sub-continent.

One unfortunate consequence of Clive's original victory was to send a signal to the company's ambitious employees that great rewards could be reaped from individual initiative. Even the company's governor in Madras, Sir Thomas Rumbold, took to extorting money from his local nawab, which helped him accumulate a personal nestegg of some £750,000 during his two years in office in the late 1770s.

The company's army developed a life of its own too. It was more meritocratic than the British army, whose upper ranks were controlled by aristocrats, and hence appealed to ambitious, less well-heeled sorts who saw Indian wars as a vehicle for making their own fortunes. What was once a small security force, grew rapidly: the unit in Bengal, for example, trebled in size from 1763 to 1805 to 64,000 troops.[16] As with the army's other units, it was commanded mostly by British soldiers, while the rank-and-file were predominantly Indian. As the size of their forces grew, the officers began to resent interference, even from the company's managers in India. They began to see the army itself, rather than the company, as the focus of their loyalties.

Why couldn't the London directors now take control of the situation? The dispatches on political matters which they received from local managers not only took many months to arrive but tended to provide a justification of actions already taken. As before, few managers in London understood the political situation in India sufficiently to assess what they were being told. They were credulous of tales of imminent wealth from new conquests. In the words of James Mill, a nineteenth-century historian, the company's proprietors were "impatient for a share of the treasures which the imagination of their countrymen, as well as their own, represented not only as vast but unlimited".[17] As in the past, the directors' instructions to conduct trade by peaceful means were often ignored by managers who thought they knew better. To their credit, in 1769 the directors did send out a three-man "Supervisory Commission" to India, but their ship sank on leaving Cape Town for the sub-continent, taking the commissioners down with it.

The costs of power

Political control of Indian territories brought two practical problems for the company. The first was developing an effective system of administration. Running the intricate Bengal tax system, for example, depended on understanding the methods of revenue assessment and collection which had developed under the Mughals, as well as unpicking the web of economic relations between Muslims and the different castes of Hindus. Unsurprisingly, the company at first failed to meet its revenue targets. A terrible famine in Bengal in 1770 made matters worse for the company financially, as well as wiping out as much as a third of the province's population. This disaster had been brought on by the failure of the monsoon the year before. But the company did little to soften its impact on the local people, and some company servants were accused of profiteering from, and hoarding, food.

A few years later an attempt was made to auction off the right to collect taxes to local overlords, or *zamindars*, for five-year periods. One reason the company did this was its belief that this group of *zamindars* represented the ancient landholding class, akin to the aristocracy back in England. This assessment was flawed. The *zamindars* had evolved as a specifically Indian institution – they were more like merchant intermediaries between peasants and the Mughal nawabs than benign hereditary landholders. Perhaps predictably the scheme was marred by corrupt deals between *zamindars* and individual company servants, and parts of the countryside were simply plundered. Some historians reckon that the company's overall tax demands on the Bengal peasantry turned out to be even more crippling than in the Mughal period. The company experimented with a variety of revenue-raising systems in its growing territories across India, and some were less harsh than that in Bengal. But with all its schemes, it grappled with a similar problem: how to graft British methods of administration and notions of property rights onto a social system with its own, very different traditions and power structures.

The second practical problem was the huge costs of political control. What appeared to be Clive's triumph in Bengal was in fact just the start of a century-long period of financial problems for the company. Clive's estimate that the tax from the provinces he had secured would add £4 million to the company's revenues had helped send the stock soaring back in London. But there was an obvious flaw in his reasoning, and indeed that of the many subsequent managers who expanded the company's reach further in India. They failed to include in their calculations an accurate estimate of the vast administration and defense costs of their new territory. For example, the £600,000 revenues from land ceded to the company in 1760 were not even enough to cover the cost of the war a few years later in Bihar. Without recognizing the circularity of their strategy, the local managers resolved to try to make up the shortfall by seeking more territory.

Financially, the company began to reel from crisis to crisis. Profits continued to flow from many of its trading activities: the British as a nation became hooked on tea which the company imported from China (just as the Chinese became hooked on the opium which the company's agents sold them). But the costs of war, territorial administration, and internal corruption soaked up these revenue streams, and forced the company severely into debt. In the early 1770s, and repeatedly in subsequent decades, it faced a real threat of bankruptcy.

The company was too significant a tax-payer at home, and too important to Britain's strategic interests, for the government to allow it simply to go bankrupt. Instead, the government helped prop up the company, while also interfering more in its workings. In stages, its monopoly privileges were withdrawn and its activities constrained by red tape. It was thus forced to endure a slow strangulation. The noose was slipped over the directors' heads by the Regulating Act of 1773: the state lent the company £1.4 million to bail it out, but fixed its dividend payments, reformed its internal voting procedures, created the post of a governor-general for the whole of India, and established a Supreme Court to deal with legal disputes on the sub-continent. The India Bill of 1784 set up a Board of Control to regulate relations between the company and native powers. This was an attempt to stop the company's warmongering, or at least to put the state in charge of that activity – though even with state regulation, it proved difficult to rein in local commanders, such as Wellesley, whose minds were set on conquest.

The state's intervention in the company's affairs was motivated not just by a desire to prevent its bankruptcy. By dint of its size, the company had become a symbol for reformers, a feature in the intellectual landscape of eighteenth-century Britain against which emerging moral and political movements could position themselves. For the time being, politicians and activists tended to be concerned above all with domestic aspects of the company's affairs. Admittedly, Edmund Burke, the political thinker, voiced concern about the effect of the company's activities on the inhabitants of Bengal, insisting that the "prosperity of the natives must be previously secured, before any profit from them whatsoever is attempted".[18] But even Burke did not oppose British rule in India *per se*. And some of the angriest complaints were about the nabobs, or *nouveau riche* company servants returned from their foreign postings. Some commentators argued that they were bringing corruption and other "Asiatic principles of government"[19] back to Britain with them.

Clive, the greatest nabob of all, again faced a wave of criticism once he had returned to England. In 1773, politicians tabled a motion in parliament condemning his acceptance of the *jagir*, which he had illegally acquired, they said, "to the evil example of the servants of the public, and to the dishonor and detriment of the state". Responding to these attacks was to be one of Clive's last public actions. He made a defiant speech in parliament defending himself against the charges, and the motion was defeated. But though his political skills were not diminished, the ambitious company manager was increasingly ill from a gall bladder problem, and was suffering from the mood swings that had plagued him periodically during his life. He also appears to have become addicted to opium which doctors had originally prescribed as a pain-killer. Perhaps another problem was that life back in England offered few excitements compared with the power he had once commanded in Bengal. In November 1774, Clive died at the age of 49; his family tried to hush up the circumstances of his death, but it appears that he slit his throat.

Meanwhile, the company's activities became the subject of further political debate at home. The many competitors and customers of the company who had a commercial interest in the curtailment of its monopoly were given intellectual succor by Adam Smith's *The Wealth of Nations*. This 1776 tract became famous as an argument for free trade, even though it was not quite as hostile to the concept of monopoly as many assumed. In 1813, when the company's charter came up for renewal, it was stripped of all its monopoly and trading privileges, except over the tea trade with China. And in 1833, even this business was thrown open to the free market. By this stage, the company's principal activity – dull compared with its earlier exploits – was the administration of its Indian territories. The strangulation was almost complete.

A moral imposition

From the 1820s onwards, political administration in India had begun to present even greater difficulties for the company's managers, for attention was increasingly focusing on their behavior on the sub-continent, and they were coming under increasing pressure to influence the everyday life of Indians according to British "ethical" standards of the time. This is the period of the company's rule perhaps most intriguing in the light of the pressures faced by modern-day multinationals to help shape political outcomes in developing countries. Ultimately, as we will have seen in this story's bloody finale, the managers failed to find the right balance between imposing standards from the outside and respecting local sentiment. This is what helped squeeze the last breath from the company.

It is not that sensitivity to local culture was unknown in the second stage of the company's history. Under the rule of governor-general Warren Hastings between 1774 and 1785, for example, company regulations were translated into local languages, and Hindu and Muslim laws were translated into English so that they could be administered by British judges. Hastings set up the Asiatic Society of Bengal which conducted research into Indian civilization and literature. "To rule effectively, one must love India", he argued.[20]

What changed in the 1820s was that new, self-confident ideas about the responsibilities of government were taking hold in Britain. Three different groups – liberals, utilitarians, and evangelicals – all argued for a more direct role for government in raising the welfare of citizens. Liberals and utilitarians thought that the way to achieve the "greatest happiness for the greatest number" was through the application of the rule of law, education, free trade and other practical measures. The evangelicals saw Christianity as the key. Though often thwarted at home, all three movements were eager to apply their ideas in India, through the offices of the East India Company.

Old hands in the company warned about the risks of upsetting the natives, but reformers under the new governor William Bentinck were convinced that God, or at least civilization, was on their side. One such Victorian reformer was Charles Trevelyan, an overly serious young company servant. His brother-in-law wrote of him: "He has no small talk ... His topics, even in courtship, are steam navigation, the education of the natives, the equalization of the sugar duties, the substitution of the Roman for the Arabic alphabet in the Oriental languages."[21] In fact, his brother-in-law was Thomas Babington Macaulay, another senior official in India, who was equally zealous in his attempts to anglicize the company's rule. Macaulay drafted a penal code which later became the foundation for modern Indian law, and persuaded the governor to make English the official language of the sub-continent (in his opinion "a single shelf of a good European Library was worth the whole native literature of Arabia and India").[22]

The company's limited funds – which were being drained by military expansion – prevented the reformers from implementing many of their social and economic schemes. But the governor did ban two indigenous practices: *suttee* – the burning of widows on the funeral pyres of their husbands; and the activities of the *thags*, bands who practiced ritual assassination and robbery (and who bequeathed the word "thugs" to the English language). Though disowned by many Hindus, both practices symbolized for the British the barbarity of the culture they wanted to reform.

Meanwhile British missionaries spread across the subcontinent. For much of the company's history they had been banned from India, again for fear of upsetting local sensibilities. But the British parliament had granted them permission to begin their work in 1813 after lobbying from a number of evangelicals, including William Wilberforce. Perhaps best known for his righteous campaigns against the slave trade, Wilberforce's views on India were less advanced:

> Are we so little aware of the vast superiority even of European laws and institutions, and far more of British institutions, over those of Asia, as not to be prepared to predict with confidence, that the Indian community which should have exchanged its dark and bloody superstitions for the genial influence of civil order and security, of social pleasures and domestic comforts, as to be desirous of preserving the blessings it should have acquired?[23]

There are major differences between these nineteenth-century reformers and the western campaigners of today, for modern groups mostly preach respect, rather than disdain, for indigenous cultures. Nonetheless they have a few things in common: both have tended to focus on particular issues – whether Christianity or environmental protection – which resonate most strongly with western audiences; both have often focused, too, on the behavior of western multinationals as a means of achieving the outcomes they desire in developing countries, even though the companies may not always be capable of fulfilling their goals. This is an observation that is developed further in the last part of this book. For now it is enough to recount how the efforts of the nineteenth-century campaigners in "reforming" the East India Company's behavior contributed to an explosion of local anger.

A cast for the finale

If the confrontation between Clive and Siraj encapsulated the problems of the first stage of the company's story, the characters of Bahadur Shah and William Hodson best represent the final stage. Bahadur Shah, the last of the Mughal emperors, was 82, frail, and senile by the time of the 1857 rebellion. He reigned from his palace in Delhi, as a guest of the British rather than as their host. The British had refused to recognize his favorite son as his heir. He was given an allowance of 100,000 rupees a month, barely enough to maintain his properties or his dependants, some of whom lived in hovels within the palace walls. The hobbies of this unambitious, white-bearded old man included his pets – doves, nightingales, and a favorite old elephant – as well as literature and calligraphy. He was well versed in Urdu and Arabic, learned in Sufi philosophy, and spent much of his time composing Urdu poems, known as ghazals.

William Hodson was a 36-year-old English cavalry officer who commanded a team of Indians who spied for the army. A public schoolboy, he had been educated at Cambridge University, but was no intellectual: "a constitutional tendency to headache very much stood in the way of any close application to books", according to his brother. Earlier in his career he had been suspected of embezzling regimental funds, and of killing an Indian soldier because of an unpaid debt, but he had continued to advance in the army. His fellow officers in India were in awe of his fearlessness in battle and the way in which he relished a good fight. As one contemporary noted, "when it was time to charge, he would shout, 'Come along, lads, the fun's begun!' waving his spear in the air".[24]

For the company, one of the first bizarre signs that trouble was brewing across India was that indigenous officers and villagers began sending each other chapattis, flat round breads, and lotus flowers. These were sent like chain letters, from village to village, regiment to regiment, fresh chapattis and flowers being procured along the way, the phenomenon spreading as much as 100 miles a day. Rumor had it that a strange slogan – "everything has become red" – was also being whispered from Indian to Indian. "There is a most mysterious affair going on through the whole of India at present", wrote home a British doctor to his sister in 1857.[25]

Some twentieth-century Indian nationalists have suggested that the spread of chapattis and lotus flowers was a form of psychological warfare against the company, and a means by which the Indians could communicate to each other their readiness to revolt. Alternatively it may be that they believed this was the way to appease Hindu gods to prevent another outbreak of cholera – even now, the explanation for the phenomenon is not universally agreed. At the time, some of the British in India may have been unnerved, but few thought that it presaged any outbreak of violence.

Had the company a more effective system by which to gauge local opinion, it ought to have been apparent that resentment was mounting. Hindus' suspicions about the activities of the Christian missionaries had been aggravated by the Religious Disabilities Act of 1856, which had undermined Hindu inheritance laws. Indian rulers were smarting under the "doctrine of lapse", a policy instituted under the most recent governor, Lord Dalhousie. This gave the company *carte blanche* to annex states in which rulers had no natural heirs. There was discontent on an economic level too. Many peasants had been displaced by land reform and their cottage industries undermined by the company's interventions. Matters had been made worse by an international trade depression in the 1830s and 1840s.

It was within the company's army itself, however, that sensitivities were most bruised. Many of the Indian soldiers in the army – known as sepoys – were high-caste Hindus, or Brahmins; others were Muslim. To both, the attitude of their British commanders, swelled by home-grown theories of their own racial superiority, had become increasingly high handed. Brahmins had been forced to travel to fight wars abroad, against religious taboos which forbad sea voyages. They also had been given sheepskin jackets to wear, when their religion forbad them contact with leather. The trigger of the mutiny itself – as mentioned in the introduction to this part of the book – was a suspicion on the part of the sepoys that new rifle cartridges they were being asked to use were greased with beef fat (which was offensive to Hindus) and also pig fat (which was offensive to Muslims). Though the suspicion was unproven, it seemed to them to be part of a general attempt by the company to Christianize the army.

Violent ends

The violence of the "Great Mutiny", as it came to be known, commenced in Meerut, near Delhi, in May 1857. Hindu and Muslim sepoys, infuriated that their colleagues had been imprisoned for refusing to use the new cartridges, shot dead their British officers. Gathering support along the way, they then moved on to Delhi, where British officers and families were again murdered or forced to flee. Seeking a figurehead for their anger, the mutineers swarmed into the palace and proclaimed Bahadur Shah as emperor of the revived Mughal dynasty. The old man was bewildered at first, scolded the soldiers for their unruly behavior, and only reluctantly agreed to lead them. "I am not in a condition to join anyone", he complained.[26]

The British understood the symbolic importance of Delhi, as capital of the ancient Mughal empire, and launched a counter-attack rapidly. They moved towards the city, hanging or firing from the mouth of cannons (a form of execution originally devised by the Mughals) any local people suspected of supporting the mutineers. They then camped on a ridge outside Delhi, and besieged the city for several months. It was too soon to launch the final onslaught: the city itself was thought to contain over 30,000 sepoys. On the ridge, amid the flies and the putrefying bodies of executed Indians, William Hodson and his fellow officers waited impatiently for their attack on Bahadur Shah.

The rebellion spread across north-west India, and atrocities on both sides inflamed feelings of racial hatred. For the British, the massacres at Cawnpore – in which several hundred white women and children are believed to have been murdered – symbolized the evil forces which needed to be quelled. The man allegedly responsible for the massacre was Nana Sahib, a Hindu prince and the adopted son of a Maratha monarch, who had been refused a pension by the company. An over-excited account of the mutiny published in London in 1858 gave graphic descriptions of the horrors allegedly committed by crazed Indians, which apparently included forcing English parents to eat the flesh of their children. "These awful stories (and some even worse are whispered) will not be forgotten as long as England exists."[27] Less well reported at the time was that once the British had beaten Nana Sahib's forces they tortured his men, defiled their caste, and forced them to lick dried blood from the floor, before hanging them.[28]

Within the besieged city of Delhi, Bahadur Shah found it difficult to control the mutineers, who had taken to looting the shops of merchants and terrorizing civilians. They seemed more interested in personal enrichment than war. Once, when Bahadur Shah requested that an attack be launched on the ridge, the troops who had been sent out returned shortly after, moaning about heavy rains and flooding. Increasingly depressed, Bahadur Shah tried to strike a secret deal with the British, but they rejected his offer.

The assault on Delhi, when it finally occurred on 14th September 1857, was messy, involving days of bloody street fighting. Many of the British soldiers became drunk on liquor which they found in the city, and – according to their own letters and diaries – killed civilians and ransacked their property for loot. Bahadur Shah fled with some of his family to the tomb of the Emperor Humayan, which was just outside the city. The enthusiastic William Hodson asked his commander if he could lead the pursuit, and caught up with Bahadur Shah at the tomb. He persuaded the old emperor to surrender by guaranteeing his safety. The next day Hodson also coaxed two of Bahadur Shah's sons and a grandson out of the same hiding place. But rather than leading them to safety, he shot them dead, taking their swords and signet rings. This summary execution raised a few eyebrows among his superiors, but also a fair deal of praise from his colleagues. "I cannot help being pleased with the warm congratulations I received on all sides for my success in destroying the enemies of our race", he wrote in a letter.[29]

Bahadur Shah, meanwhile, awaited his trial at the hands of a British military court. He was kept in a small, dingy room in his palace, and was displayed as a curiosity to various British visitors. They observed him smoking his hookah, being cared for by a few, old female servants, and rambling incoherently about his dreams and poems. One journalist described "a dim-wandering-eyed, dreamy old man, with feeble hanging nether lip and toothless gums".[30] Hodson's wife saw the old emperor too, and wrote that she was "almost ashamed to say that a feeling of pity mingled with disgust".[31]

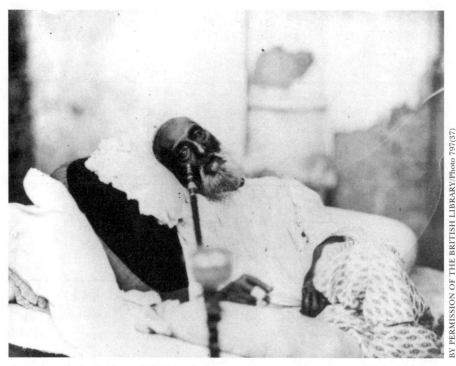

Bahadur Shah, the last of the Mughal emperors, in 1858, following his capture by
the British. Once a figurehead of the Indian rebellion, in captivity he was
described by a visiting journalist as "a dim-wandering-eyed, dreamy old man".

Though the rebellion spread quickly, and sputtered on for over
a year, the company's army was able eventually to crush it entirely. In
spite of the spread of the chapattis, the mutineers had no consistent
strategy and nor were they co-ordinated in their actions. These
consisted of a series of localized outbreaks of anger, rather than a
nationalist rebellion in any modern sense. Many sepoys continued to
serve with the company's army.

The rebellion brought about the end of the company's rule in
India, but not British rule, which was to continue for almost another
century. The reason why it triggered the company's demise was that
it forced the British government to make explicit what had long been
apparent. The company was no longer a commercial enterprise, its
trading activities having faded away long ago, but a quasi-
government agency which ruled over India. Many politicians in
London were criticizing the company for failing to anticipate the

rebellion. Certainly, by crushing the mutiny with the force of a sovereign power, it had confirmed the extent of its suction into the politics of India. The British government needed now to make the lines of command more explicit.

John Stuart Mill, the utilitarian philosopher and an East India Company employee, wrote a petition for a stay of execution on his employer – part of which is quoted at the start of this chapter – but his pleas went unheeded. The India Bill of 1858 brought to an end the company's role in administering India, and put a British Secretary of State in charge instead. The company had been effectively abolished, though it continued to exist as a legal entity until 1874.

If the first stage of the company's history had illustrated how a powerful multinational could so fail to control the political interactions of its local managers that it embarked on a series of unplanned territorial conquests, this second stage has shown how a company's conscious attempts at political intervention could provoke equally unintended results: in this case, its own demise. The struggles of another British imperial multinational in dealing with indigenous politics will be examined next.

Curiously, while the end of the "Great Mutiny" brought about the death of the company, it did not signify quite the last gasp of Bahadur Shah. The trial of the former Mughal emperor lasted two months. He was charged with rebellion and complicity in massacres during the uprising. Unsurprisingly, his British military judges found him guilty, and they sentenced him to exile in Rangoon. But, in spite of the senility witnessed by his captors in Delhi, Bahadur Shah survived in exile for four years, and continued quietly to compose ghazals until his death in 1862.

In the twentieth century, Indian nationalists resurrected a few lines of poetry attributed to him from the height of the rebellion:

As long as there remains the least trace of love or faith in the hearts of our heroes, so long, the sword of Hindustan shall be sharp, and one day shall flash even at the gates of London.[32]

Faint echoes of the sentiment can be heard today in modern Indians' suspicions of foreign multinationals.

TWO

A warlike tribe
Cecil Rhodes and the British South Africa Company

*I should like to lay out about 2,000 more Matabele
as we have not killed enough of them.*

Army officer fighting for the British South Africa Company, 1893.[1]

If the conquest of India by the East India Company was extraordinary in terms of its scale and speed, then the corporate takeover by Cecil Rhodes of swathes of southern Africa is in some respects
even more jaw-dropping. In the space of less than ten years, Rhodes
and his company had either invaded or brought British imperial
authority to bear over a region covering modern-day Botswana,
Zimbabwe, Zambia and Malawi – an area over three times the size of
France. Even more so than with the East India Company, this was a
corporate-led expansion which involved brutality, racist attitudes, and
the ruthless crushing of indigenous cultures. The story of Rhodes in
Africa helps set the context for the "backlash" described in the third
part of this book. It also offers an illustration of the reasons behind the
continuing suspicions of foreign multinationals in this region. Even in
modern times, as noted before, African leaders such as Robert Mugabe
have drawn political support by stoking the lingering local appetite for
revenge against their country's former white oppressors.

As with the previous chapter, however, this story does not merely
provide insights into current attitudes. Rhodes in Africa also
provides an illumination of a key problem faced by modern

multinationals. Put to one side the racist, violent aspects of the British South Africa Company's behavior (for the methods of today are far less brutal), and what remains is a challenge which is as relevant to modern-day multinationals as it was to British imperialists in the 1890s – and which is sometimes dealt with in as reactive, and unplanned a manner by today's corporations as it was by Rhodes.

If companies are to thrive, they must respond to the fast-moving forces of competition. Sometimes they have just days or weeks to make major, strategic decisions – such as whether to invest in, or pull out from a country. Given their large financial resources and the limited time of their managers, it may make sense for them only to invest in lumps of tens or hundreds of millions, or even billions, of dollars. To consider smaller-scale projects or minor details would distract managers from broader issues of strategy. In this sense, multinationals are like elephants – fast-moving, powerful, but not built for dainty footwork.

Societies and cultures, by contrast, are intricate and fine-grained phenomena, and they evolve at their own pace. As anthropologists have discovered, understanding communities can require years of patient study, and even then, the conclusions drawn still will be no more than an outsider's best guesses. How can even the best-intentioned companies reconcile these conflicting time-frames and perspectives, let alone the very different ultimate goals the host societies may have? How can firms work in co-operation with local cultures, and yet still on a practical level succeed in global markets? Put another way, how can an elephantine multinational proceed delicately in this area?

The final chapters of the book will describe how some modern multinationals are grappling (and often struggling) with this challenge. The story of Rhodes and his British South Africa Company illustrates a multinational in a rush, simply trampling as it went the local societies it encountered. But it also shows how the company's failure to comprehend the perspective of indigenous people actually damaged its own interests, for it failed to predict a violent rebellion which erupted against its rule in 1896–7. If the company's managers had been better able to understand indigenous concerns and beliefs, they would have spotted early on the rumblings of discontent. Inevitably the company's response was to crush the rebellion, though – as will be seen – Rhodes made a brief, and curious, attempt to seek a more enlightened approach.

The focus of this chapter will be on the experiences of the British South Africa Company during the 1890s, and particularly on its invasion, and the subsequent rebellion, of the Matabele and Shona tribes. Rhodes' life was peppered with political dramas, and his companies, of which the British South Africa Company was only one, continued to play a key role in the region's development (or arguably lack of development) for many decades after his death. But the episode retold here was the most significant clash between a company and indigenous society in that era, and in that part of the world.

A man in a hurry

Why did Rhodes and his company want control of these tribal lands? And why the rush? The answer lies partly in Rhodes' character and in his unique management style, partly in the politics of white power in the region, and partly in the global strategies of European imperial nations. As for the Matabele and Shona, the indigenous tribes whose societies will be explored later in the chapter, they had little clue about the giant forces encircling them. But that was not to last.

Historians and psychiatrists have frequently debated what drove Rhodes. Was he motivated more by profits, by power, or by a desire to expand the British empire? Certainly, his drive was unrelenting. The son of a clergyman from Hertfordshire, England, he left for southern Africa at the age of 16 to recuperate from an illness. He appears to have suffered from an atrial septal defect, a condition commonly known as a hole in the heart, and was struck by a number of heart attacks during his 48-year life span. Some have argued that it was the knowledge that he might die at any moment which fueled his desire to achieve. "He is often compared to Napoleon, and Napoleon felt he always had to be doing something, until at last he got land at S. Helena",[2] commented a suspicious British government official in 1895.

Rhodes began his business life as a farmer in southern Africa, though shortly afterwards became involved in diamond mining, which was booming at the time. An indication of his vigor was that,

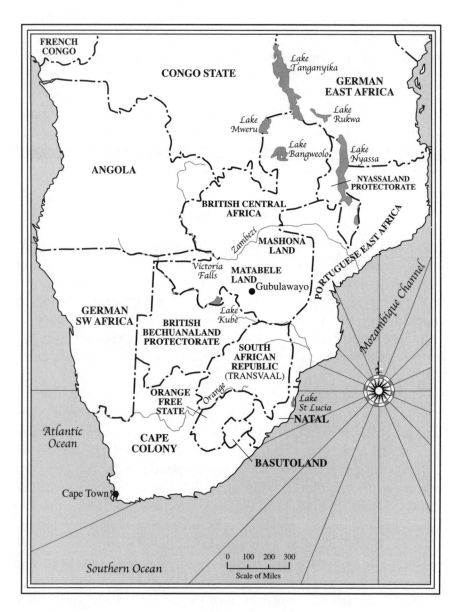

SOUTHERN AFRICA 1890S

in between stints running his diamond business in southern Africa, he found time to return to England to attend terms at Oxford University. He completed his degree in 1881, after eight years of sporadic study.

Although Rhodes' accumulation of a vast fortune may suggest that money was his overriding motivation, his own interpretation of his actions was that he served a higher purpose than commerce alone. At Oxford, he had been inspired by John Ruskin, a professor of art who advanced a mystical view of imperialism. Ruskin's inaugural lecture at the university in 1870 gives a flavor of the ideas that Rhodes took to heart: "Will you youths of England make your country again a royal throne of kings, a sceptred isle, for all the world a source of light, a centre of peace ... This is what England must either do or perish: she must found colonies as far and fast as she is able, formed of her most energetic and worthiest men".[3]

Rhodes wrote a number of wills during his life, and they give a further clue to the seriousness of his ambition. This is from Rhodes' "Last Will and Testament":

> I have considered the existence of God and decided there is an even chance that He exists. If He does exist, he must be working to a Plan. Therefore, if I am to serve God, I must find out the Plan, and do my best to assist him in its execution. How to discover the Plan? First, look for the *race* that God had chosen to be the divine instrument of future evolution.
> Unquestionably that is the *white* race ...
> I shall devote the rest of my life to God's purpose, and help Him to make the world English.[4]

Such racist attitudes, springing from a misreading of Darwin's theory of evolution and his notion of "survival of the fittest", were commonplace at the time. In fact, surprisingly for someone who wrote these words, Rhodes as a young man showed an interest in, and even some respect for, the indigenous way of life. In his travels in his first years in Africa, he would sleep in Africans' huts and share meals with them. He trusted his indigenous workers, and lent them money. Later in life, as will become all too clear, this relative open-mindedness would reveal itself only occasionally.

Rhodes' difficult personal life also may have intensified his ambitions, encouraging him to seek fulfillment in public life in place of private contentment. Some historians have argued Rhodes was homosexual, or perhaps a repressed homosexual,[5] as he formed his most emotional attachments with young men – and it goes without saying that homosexuality was considered unacceptable in Victorian society. The death of one young male friend – Neville Pickering – triggered in Rhodes first an intense bout of grief, followed by a particularly ruthless burst of activity in business and politics. Whatever his sexual orientation, it is clear that he had a strong emotional impact on others, inspiring deep feelings of both adulation and dislike. Olive Schreiner, a famous South African writer who was later to become his most damning critic, described him in 1890 as "the only great man and man of genius South Africa possesses".[6]

Stampede for diamonds and gold

Prior to his conquest of the Matabele and Shona, Rhodes had already notched up some dramatic victories. In the diamond business, he had started in the early 1870s as the owner of three small claims in the aptly-named "New Rush" mine, a giant, dust-choked operation in a distant part of the South African veldt, swarming with thousands of other diggers. By 1888, he controlled the entire South African diamond industry, which meant 90% of world production, through a company – De Beers – which still monopolizes the world diamond trade. This was a remarkable rate of growth without question. But in the context of this chapter, it is not the fact of Rhodes' commercial success that is intriguing, but rather the manner by which he achieved it. For his actions provide a foretaste of his energies and momentum which he was later to employ to such devastating effect in his forays in the lands of the Matabele and Shona.

For example, he manipulated the share prices of companies he wished to acquire, and – to strengthen his influence – bought the main English newspaper in South Africa ("the press rules the minds of men",[7] he believed). When necessity demanded, he had the drive, in 1887, to make a last-minute dash to London to win the financial backing of Nathaniel Rothschild, the influential European financier. To win over local politicians, Rhodes gave them shares in his companies, and he entered politics himself, first as a member of parliament for the British Cape Colony and later as the Colony's prime minister. To help secure a disciplined African workforce for his mines, he supported the Diamond Trade Act of 1882, which allowed for the strip searching of workers and the flogging of diamond thieves. African workers in De Beers mines were crowded into prison-like compounds, surrounded by guard towers and patrolled by company police and their dogs. By this stage in his career, it would appear that Rhodes had forgotten his earlier camaraderie with the Africans. His ambition was driving all before it.

What attracted Rhodes and other entrepreneurs to the lands of the Matabele and Shona in the 1880s was partly the rumors that it was rich in gold. There had been various small discoveries there, and some explorers speculated that it once contained the kingdom of Ophir, the site of King Solomon's fabled mines. However, it was not just competition between individuals, but also competition between the white colonies in South Africa and their supporting powers back in Europe that made the invasion of these tribal lands inevitable. They had yet to be claimed by colonizers, but they were facing pressures literally on all sides.

To the south were two main sets of colonies. The British ran the Cape Colony (which had originally begun as an outpost of the Dutch East India Company, and had been taken over by the British in 1806), and also Natal. Also to the south were the Boer republics of the Transvaal and the Orange Free State (the Boers, descendants of the original Dutch settlers, had fraught relations with the Cape Colony, in part because their brutal treatment of Africans concerned even the British, who themselves were hardly progressive on race relations). To the east, the Portuguese had their sphere of influence in what is now Mozambique. To the north, the Belgians were staking out the Congo.

What particularly concerned British imperialists was that in 1884 the Germans had declared a protectorate over the coast of South-West Africa (or modern-day Namibia). One fear was that the Germans in the west might link up with the Boers in the Transvaal, thus preventing the expansion of Britain's Cape Colony northwards. According to one British colonial official, "the ultimate aim of the German government is to possess a belt of country stretching from this coast [the west coast] to Zanzibar, so as to cut off our colonies from the interior".[8] If they were to keep ahead in the scramble for Africa, the British had to act quickly.

Rhodes, who himself had fantasized about British territory stretching from "the Cape to Cairo", was skilled at playing on these imperial ambitions. In a speech to the Cape Colony he argued:

> The question before us really is this: whether this colony is to be confined to its present borders, or whether it is to become the dominant state in South Africa – whether, in fact, it is to spread its civilisation over the interior ...[9]

Rhodes began to answer the question through his own actions. Partly as a result of his political maneuverings, Britain in 1885 extended its empire northwards to include Bechuanaland, the tribal land which lay between the Cape Colony and Matabele territory. Unbeknown to the resident tribes, Matabeleland was now set to become the next arena of competition between the white powers. The Germans and the Portuguese were already circling the territory, sending in emissaries to befriend Lobengula, the Matabele king. When Rhodes received news in 1887 that Lobengula had agreed to a treaty of friendship with the Transvaal Boers, he flew into action. He had no time to lose in securing the territory for Britain and his own corporate interests. The elephant charge was underway.

Two tribes

To understand the interactions between the British South Africa Company and the Matabele and Shona it will help first to draw a rough picture of these African societies. With few written sources available, their history is shrouded in fog, but what is known about them is enough to defy attempts to characterize them in any simple way. Neither lawless barbarians, nor Rousseau's "noble savages", the people of the region would have taken some time to understand, even for a well-intentioned, intelligent multinational manager. In the variability of their societies can be appreciated the difficulties for some modern companies in understanding the local context in which they operate. And – as will be seen later – Rhodes and his men made some foolishly incorrect assessments in this regard.

Unlike the Matabele, the Shona were indigenous to the region. By the 1890s they were living in dozens of separate kingdoms, some large, some small, and spoke a variety of dialects – Kalanga, Karanga, Zezuru, Korekore, Manyika and Ndau. Political relations between the various Shona kingdoms varied between friendship and war, and were evolving continually, as were the kingdoms themselves. The issue of succession often sparked internal conflict: typically the son of a ruler would fight one of the ruler's younger brothers over the right to assume power, sometimes with the result of splitting the kingdom in two. "Outsiders frequently find the internal politics of the Shona impossibly complicated", remarks David Beach, who has specialized in the study of these people.[10]

In the past, many of the separate Shona kingdoms had been united as part of indigenous empires – such as the Mutapas, and the Rozwi Mambos – all of which had since disintegrated. Like their European counterparts, these empires witnessed for a time the creation of considerable wealth and the flourishing of culture. For instance, it was predecessors of the Mutapas who built the vast stone structures of "Great Zimbabwe", a tourist attraction of modern Zimbabwe, which early white settlers refused to believe ever could have been constructed by Africans. And again like other empires, the Shona confederacies also depended in part on economic exploitation. According to research by one archaeologist:

> The Rozwi monarchs organised their production and managed their exports for their own personal profits as capably as the nineteenth-century Randlords [i.e. white imperial entrepreneurs]. One may venture to guess from the poor material culture of the mining villages and the frequency of traces of mining accidents, that the mine-girls of pre-history got no more share in their chief's profits than the modern mine-worker does today.[11]

As late as the 1890s, many of the separate Shona kingdoms retained political rituals and elaborate formal rules developed during the time of the Mutapas and Rozwis. For example, Shona rulers were supposed – at least in theory – to be physically perfect, and to commit suicide if they became flawed in some way; in some kingdoms, they were also supposed to commit incest with a sister or a daughter. In practice many of these regulations were disregarded: for example, "the only Teve ruler known to have been asked to commit suicide (because he had lost a tooth) refused on the grounds that this was a silly custom",[12] according to David Beach. Although seemingly "primitive", some of these customs had relatively sophisticated consequences. For example, the belief that a ruler should be ritually murdered if he lost a war or failed to prevent famine had the effect of constraining a ruler's power and behavior, making him more responsive to the needs of his people.

Matabele society in the 1890s was strikingly different from that of the Shona. The Matabele were relative newcomers to the region, arriving in the early nineteenth century. They had started out as a rebel faction of Nguni warriors from the south, and had incorporated many Sotho people, whose communities they plundered, before being driven northwards in clashes with the Boers. The territory they came to control in the land of the Shonas was in itself relatively small. However, unlike the Shona, the Matabele inhabited a single, highly centralized kingdom, and their culture was based upon military expansion and the spoils of war. The Matabele regularly raided neighboring Shona communities for cattle, which they accumulated in great number.

Lobengula, who was king of the Matabele at the time of Rhodes' growing interest in the territory, was an astute, physically imposing man, and his power struck fear into the hearts of many who met him. One of Rhodes' agents wrote that "he has great bulging, blood-shot eyes, and when he rolls them to look you up and down, in his lordly way, I tell you it's enough to scare a man off-hand".[13] But Lobengula's power was not absolute. He needed to secure the co-operation of the influential chiefs, or *indunas*, who commanded his regiments, and to satisfy the appetite of his warriors for cattle and other riches.

Political relations between the Matabele and Shona varied considerably. Some Shona kingdoms were over-run and subsumed within Matabele territory, others agreed to offer regular tribute to the warrior-state in return for protection from raids, while others were simply too far from the Matabele power-base to feel its effects. While many Shona kingdoms remained proudly independent, some Shona youths joined Matabele regiments, or set up raiding bands of their own to plunder nearby villages and kingdoms. A career in such a band, points out David Beach, "with its stress on distinctively clad and armed young men enjoying a life of raiding, increased access to young women and beef eating proved to be highly attractive to young men seeking relief from a life dominated by their elders".[14]

Finally, no less intricate than the internal and external political systems of the indigenous societies were their systems of belief. Like many Africans, the Shona and Matabele believed – and still believe – in the power of the spirits of their ancestors to protect them and their land, to form a bridge of communication with the forces of the divine. They consulted spirit mediums, people believed to be possessed by important ancestors. Elaborate cults sprang up around the use of these mediums. One such was the Mwari cult: "Mwari speaks through or inspires the utterances of the chief officer of the cult, the Mouth; he receives petitions from another high officer, the Ear, and information from a less important officer, the Eye".[15] In the past, these mediums had played a key role in advising Shona kings. They would prove influential again in shaping the native response to the arrival of the British South Africa Company.

Rhodes northwards

Whether by chance or design, one of the misinterpretations of the native culture by Rhodes and the British actually happened to serve their purpose. This error was the false assumption that the Matabele had conquered the entire Shona people. Lobengula "is undisputed ruler over Mashonaland and Matabeleland", according to the British colonial secretary.[16] What this meant was that Rhodes could claim that an agreement with Lobengula to allow white incursion on his territory was tantamount to a license to operate throughout the entire region.

As mentioned before, it was news that the Boers had made headway with Lobengula which had set Rhodes on the warpath. He sent a series of emissaries to the Matabele king's headquarters in Gubulawayo, a vast hill-top encampment of huts. Here they flattered the king, and offered bribes to him and his *indunas*, and – though they had been given no such mandate by London – they promised Lobengula the British government's military protection against the other imperial powers queuing up for a piece of his land. They stayed for weeks, and were often taunted and threatened by young Matabele warriors. "Our men behaved throughout with admirable coolness, and looked at the dancing savages with the most stolid indifference", insisted Sir Sidney Shippard, a local British imperial official who had also happened to turn up in Gubulawayo at the time.[17]

Lobengula was in a difficult position: eager to grant a concession to at least one band of whites so that they would help him fend off the others, but also concerned not to trigger a rebellion by his own *indunas*, some of whom wanted him simply to drive all the whites away. Eventually, in 1888, he decided to put his mark to an agreement with Rhodes' agents. Lobengula had been particularly impressed by Shippard's arrival on the scene – though no record was kept of the talks between Shippard and the king, the British official may well have recommended Rhodes, who was an old friend of his, even though this was not British government policy. The agreement granted Rhodes monopoly rights over all metals and minerals in his kingdom, in return for £100 a month, a thousand rifles, a hundred thousand cartridges, and a gunship on the Zambesi river. It also gave him the right to expel – with the king's help – all other claimants to the land. Rhodes had thus closed off the territory both for the Boers and for any other imperial fortune hunters.

Lobengula little understood what he was signing away: he probably expected just a few whites digging a few mines on his territory, leaving his power largely intact. Later, when it became clear that more was at stake, he tried to repudiate the agreement, sending two of his *indunas* to visit Queen Victoria in London. The British government was sympathetic, and distanced itself from the agreement. In a letter to the Matabele king, the British Colonial Office emphasized that Rhodes' agents were not themselves repre-sentatives of Queen Victoria. But Lobengula's pleas were to no avail, in part because Rhodes could control the flow of information on the ground. Another of his agents in Matabeleland at the time – Dr Leander Starr Jameson, a cavalier character who will crop up again later – simply tore up the official reply by the British government to Lobengula's complaints and unashamedly substituted a version he drafted himself. This gave Lobengula the impression that Rhodes had Queen Victoria's blessing.[18]

Rhodes meanwhile was busy consolidating his advantage. In a hectic trip to London he lobbied politicians to support his sudden territorial gain and, again demonstrating his understanding of media power, bought off liberal journalists, including W.T. Stead, editor of the influential *Pall Mall Gazette*. To lend an air of respectability to his new British South Africa Company, which was to oversee the new territory, he recruited various eminent aristocrats to join the board. Eventually he persuaded the government to award the company a Royal Charter. This granted the company the right – at least as far as the British government was concerned – to operate as an effective sovereign power in the region, just as the East India Company had been a proxy for the British empire in another part of the world.

This was a considerable leap from the award of mere mineral rights, which was all Lobengula thought he had offered. Even more pleasing for Rhodes was that the charter did not make explicit any northwards limit to the reach of his company. Like the self-respecting boss of any modern multinational, he was keeping in mind the big picture, which in this case was the continuing rush for territory by the white powers. Determined to stay ahead of his competitors – the Boers, the Germans, the Portuguese and the Belgians – he was already planning further conquests northwards.

With such grand strategies in mind, the actual implementation of his most recent acquisition would have to be delegated to a junior. Accordingly, he asked Frank Johnson, a former gold-prospector still in his early twenties, to put together a pioneer column of white settlers to proceed into the new territory. In 1890 the settlers set off for Mashonaland, the region the British insisted was controlled by the Matabele. Rhodes also delegated to the settlers the task of striking a deal with the chief of Manicaland, a patch of territory on the eastern edge of Mashonaland, for "the mineral and other rights" in his kingdom,[19] a task they duly performed. The Portuguese had in the past considered Manicaland part of their sphere of influence in Africa, but Rhodes' men fought a few brief and victorious skirmishes with local Portuguese soldiers, which put paid to that notion. Manicaland thus fell under the sway of Rhodes' company too.

Back in Shona territory, the corporate takeover was peaceful at first. The Shona initially offered little resistance, and were even hospitable, to the small band of pioneers who unexpectedly wandered into their territory. Embroiled in their own political concerns, they were unsuspecting to say the least. The whites appeared to offer them new trading opportunities, including a market for their crops. From the Shona's naïve perspective, the company pioneers also could be co-opted as allies in the frequent disputes which flared between and within the various kingdoms. Only at a late stage did the Shona understand the scale of the whites' ambitions (which of course was to divide among themselves all the land and the minerals under it). There were some portents of what was to come, however, had they been paying heed. In 1892, for example, a Shona headman called Ngomo and twenty-one of his followers were gunned down in their *kraal*, or village, by a British South Africa Company police officer. Ngomo had been accused by a white trader of stealing his goods. "I am sure a very wholesome lesson has been given to all the chiefs of the district", wrote the police officer.[20]

Imperial protestors

Back in London, activists were beginning to raise concerns about the behavior of Rhodes' company. But as with the home-grown "ethical" concerns which shaped the policies of the East India Company in its final decades, the outlook of the London campaigners – however enlightened they believed themselves to be – was skewed by western assumptions of the time and was focused on problems which appeared important from a western perspective. The key issues, in the campaigners' view, were combating slavery, preventing the spread of drunkenness among native people, and introducing Christianity. They shared the assumption that "civilization" needed to be brought to Africa – provided the "inferior" Africans were protected from any possible ill-effects. Among the most influential British groups was the Aborigines Protection Society; an 1896 entry from its journal, *The Aborigines' Friend*, gives a taste of its world-view:

It was the mission of the Anglo-Saxon race to penetrate into every part of the world, and to help in the great work of civilization. Wherever its representatives went, the national conscience should go also ... Native races were like children;

they must be protected against the superior brain power of the races which had reached maturity.[21]

The two *indunas* sent by Lobengula to meet Queen Victoria were fêted in London by various groups, including the Aborigines Protection Society, who hosted a gala breakfast for them. Demonstrating how little he grasped the situation on the ground, Sir Fowell Buxton, the Society's chairman, expressed the hope that "the day would soon come when the Ndebele [Matabele] and English would meet 'in the valleys of the Limpopo as happily as they did that day at Westminster'".[22] Other groups who complained about Rhodes and his company were concerned more about drawing lessons for the great domestic political issues of the day, such as the merits and demerits of capitalism or monopolies, rather than about native rights *per se*. *The Economist*, for example, campaigned against Rhodes and monopoly company rule, complaining that "sovereign companies ... want to make good dividends for themselves, not to see the ordinary emigrant flourishing".[23]

The fact that the concerns of London groups did not always coincide with the issues most relevant on the ground played into Rhodes' hands. It allowed him to adopt some of these home-grown "ethical" concerns as his own, thus fending off criticism of the company, without compromising his freedom of movement in Africa. In fact he could sometimes turn the "ethical" concerns to his commercial advantage. The British South Africa Company's charter, for example, committed the company to combat the slave trade, and to "prevent the sale of any spirits or other intoxicating liquor to the natives".[24] The latter commitment was certainly no problem for the company given that drunken Africans would be less productive as mine laborers. To win support from the British public, the Company also sent an official representative to a major anti-slavery conference in Brussels in 1889–90 where it supported tougher regulation not only on slavery, but also on traffic in spirits and arms.[25] In London in 1889, meanwhile, Rhodes tried to advance his claim over Nyasaland (present day Malawi), another territory over which he had ambitions, by offering to help clear Arab slave traders from the region.

Significantly, the London board members of the British South Africa Company appear to have been little more abreast of local details than the London campaign groups. In September 1893, shortly before Leander Starr Jameson launched the company's military attack on the Matabele, Albert Grey, one of the aristocratic board members, wrote to Rhodes:

> We are in the dark here, at least, I am, as to your plans but I have the fullest confidence in the wisdom of any move agreed on by you and Jameson ... and we will support you whatever the issue but keep us as fully informed as you can for our guidance with Government and the Public.[26]

The attack on the Matabele was not so much planned by Rhodes and Jameson; it was more the result of an organic, local process: the friction generated by the interaction of the political economy of the Matabele state with the ambitions of local company men (a phenomenon which parallels the embroilment of the East India Company employees in political disputes in Bengal). Lobengula needed to allow the raids against the neighboring Shona kingdoms to continue, not just to keep his rebellious *indunas* happy, but also because the Matabele economy depended upon the cattle and other wealth that these raids brought in. From the white settlers' perspective, meanwhile, excitement at the gold prospects of Mashonaland was turning to disappointment. Discoveries had been few and far between, and speculation was growing that in fact it was the Matabele, rather than the Shona, who were sitting on the fabled kingdom of Ophir. As the company began to view Matabeleland with increasingly covetous eyes, the Matabele raids were at the same time making it more difficult for the whites to recruit Shona laborers to work on their farms. On the London stockmarket, the shares in the company were doing badly.

For these reasons, it was only a matter of time before the conflict erupted. It was one of the periodic Matabele raids on a Shona clan that provided the company with an excuse to move. In July 1893, Matabele warriors slaughtered Shona laborers around the white settlement of Fort Victoria. In Jameson's words: "We have the excuse for a row over murdered women and children now and the [sic] getting Matabeleland open would give us a tremendous lift in shares, and everything else."[27] Rhodes bankrolled the attack with some of his own shares in the company, and volunteers in the white army were promised as a reward a 6,000 acre farm, and a share in the gold claims and looted cattle from Matabeleland. The contest was unequal, and hence over within weeks. The company's army had Maxim machine guns, while Lobengula's forces had just spears and some rifles which they had not been trained to use. The African warriors were quite simply mowed down. It was at this point that a British officer noted to a colleague: "I should like to lay out about 2,000 more Matabele as we have not killed enough of them".[28]

With defeat imminent, Lobengula and some of his followers fled his headquarters at Gubulawayo. The once-proud and powerful king died shortly after. The historical sources differ on the precise cause of his death, but it appears that he committed suicide by poisoning himself.[29] "The white men will never catch me", he had said to his remaining warriors shortly before his demise. According to Matabele custom, his body was wrapped in the skin of a black ox, and buried in sitting position in a nearby cave. "It is really very sad",[30] wrote Rhodes in 1893, in a passing moment of pity over the plight of the king. However, Rhodes was assuming that the war had extinguished both Matabele power, and – given that the Matabele were believed to have conquered the Shona – Shona power too. Several years later, he was to be proved very wrong.

A false calm

At this stage of the story – the period between 1893 and the rebellion of 1896–7 – it is important to distinguish more than ever between the company's perspective on events, and the viewpoint of the indigenous people. For the rebellion was the result not just of the company's ill-treatment of these people, but also of the failure of its managers to comprehend a perspective other than their own. Preoccupied with fast-moving, grand-scale events outside Matabeleland and Mashonaland, the company had little idea about the build-up of local resentments. Modern multinationals are not guilty of such brutality as the British South Africa Company; but when working with local cultures they encounter similar problems of differing focus, and mutual incomprehension.

For Rhodes in particular, the period between the crushing of Lobengula in 1893 and the outbreak of the rebellion, saw no let up in his preoccupation with grand schemes of expansion – but, by 1896, these were on the brink of disaster. Again, it was competition for the north and the securing of new mineral resources which drove him onwards. As prime minister of the British Cape Colony, his strategy at first had been to seek friendly relations with the Boers in the Transvaal and with the Dutch inhabitants of the Cape Colony itself. A South African federation uniting both British and Boers, after all, would be in a particularly strong position to undertake northwards expansion. To set the foundation for this reconciliation, Rhodes attempted to create common standards for the treatment of Africans (the Dutch, it may be recalled, were even less enlightened on the issue of native rights). So he pushed legislation in the Cape Colony such as the Glen Grey Act of 1894, a forerunner of twentieth-century *apartheid* policies, which designated a special land reserve for Africans, and forced them to pay a special tax if they did not sell their labor outside this area.

Rhodes soon became impatient with the strategy of negotiation with the Boers, who were proving unco-operative. He also worried that he was missing his big chance. The gold reserves of Matabeleland, like those of Mashonaland, were not as rich as had been hoped, whereas the reserves of the Transvaal were proving themselves to be vast. With his heart causing him increasing physical pain, it may be that Rhodes was also anxious that he had little time left ("the great fault in life is its shortness",[31] he once complained to a friend). So he decided to step up the pace. Together with Jameson and other accomplices, he hatched an audacious plan to trigger an armed rebellion and takeover of the Transvaal. It was a scheme that, like Rhodes' other grabs for power, required hectic behind-the-scenes diplomacy. This included persuading the board of the British South Africa Company to authorize the purchase of huge amounts of arms, without – so the directors later claimed – telling them to what use they would be put.

The plot ended in disaster. The supporters of the rebellion within the Transvaal wavered at the last moment, causing Rhodes to have second thoughts. But it was too late. His over-eager subordinate Jameson launched a raid into Boer territory nonetheless ("You may say what you like, but Clive would have done it",[32] Jameson said after the event, referring to the ambitious East India Company manager).

A number of Jameson's men were killed, and the rest of his force was captured. Rhodes – his underhand maneuverings now exposed – was facing humiliation. He was forced to resign as prime minister of the Cape. The British government, eager to distance itself from the affair, threatened to revoke the charter of his South Africa Company. How could Rhodes now rescue his reputation and his empire? The answer would have to wait, for it was at this point, early in 1896, that the rebellion in Matabeleland broke.

Seeds of rebellion

With the benefit of hindsight it is clear Matabele and Shona would want to rebel. Following the defeat of Lobengula in 1893, the company and the white settlers lost no time in carving up Matabele territory and taking tribal cattle for themselves. A pattern of land distribution was established, the legacy of which still fuels anger in modern-day Zimbabwe. The Matabele were allocated two meager reserves, while the whites took much of the farmable land. This redistribution allowed Jameson, the company's administrator in the new territory, to indulge his taste for snobbery. As a later British administrator complained, "Jameson has given nearly the whole country away to the Willoughbys, Whites and others of that class ... It is perfectly sickening to see the way in which the country has been run for the sake of hobnobbing with Lord this and the Honble that. I think Jameson must have been off his head for some time before the raid".[33]

The cattle herds of the Matabele were ravaged, first by the appropriations of the company and the settlers, then by an outbreak of rinderpest, a cattle plague. Both Matabele and Shona tribespeople were subject to the rough justice of the company's police. The ranks of the police were now swelled by units of co-opted Matabele warriors who were often just as brutal to their fellow Africans as the whites. The company administration also introduced a widely despised "hut tax", the idea being to create a financial obligation among Africans which would induce them to seek labor and wages on white farms and mines. As an alternative, some whites simply threatened violence to obtain labor (thus ignoring the commitment in the company's royal charter to combat slavery). As if to intensify the humiliations of the Matabele and Shona, the company re-christened their lands "Rhodesia" in 1895.

What blinded company managers to the growth of native resent-ment was not just their preoccupation with the dramatic events in the Transvaal, but also their own simplistic models of Matabele and Shona society. This was not helped by the fact that the white settlers numbered just 5,000 in 1895, and were therefore spread thinly across the vast territory. Their resources were stretched, and like the managers of modern multinationals, they had many concerns which took priority over spending time studying the local culture. With respect to the Matabele, company men reasoned to themselves that the bulk of the native population would be glad to be free of a regime which was as tyrannous as Lobengula's and in which their property could be confiscated at the king's whim. As apparent justification for this belief they looked to the fact that no native ruler had risen to replace Lobengula. As Rhodes told the company's shareholders in 1895:

> I visited the territory the other day and saw nearly all the chiefs of the Matabele and I may say that they were all pleased and naturally so. In the past they have always "walked delicately" because anyone who got to any position in the country and became rich was generally "smelt out" and lost his life. You can understand that life was not very pleasant under these conditions.[34]

This was perhaps a projection on Rhodes' part: from a businessman's perspective, what could be more unpleasant than a society which punished enrichment?

There was also an assumption that the Shona equally welcomed the arrival of the company as it had freed them from subjugation by the Matabele. In fact, from the company's viewpoint, the two tribes could be categorized neatly: "the Mashonas, dirty, cowardly lot; Matabele bloodthirsty devils but a fine type",[35] in the words of one Rhodesian. Or, according to the white magistrate of Salisbury, the Shona have been "cowed by a series of raids from Matabeleland into a condition of abject pusillanimity, and [are] incapable of planning any combined or pre-meditated action".[36]

Another spurious company belief about the Shona was that they had little notion of religion, and that the cults of the Shona and

Matabele were mere superstitions fostered by unscrupulous mediums. As for the reluctance of both Shona and Matabele to enter the cash economy as wage laborers, this could only be rationalized as laziness. As the company's annual report for 1897–8 states: "the vast majority of the natives in this country either do not work at all or do not work for more than one or two months in the year, the remaining period with occasional brief spells of work on their lands, being spent in absolute idleness".[37]

The company's assumptions about the natives bore little relationship to the reality. It was not just that, as has been seen, only some Shona kingdoms had been conquered by the Matabele, and hence only some Shona would have been delighted at the conquest of Lobengula. The Matabele were even less happy about Lobengula's defeat. The reason they had not yet rallied under a new king was not that they had surrendered their political system to the company, but rather that royal succession in Matabele society was traditionally a slow process; it would take time for different political factions to come to an agreement on a successor. Meanwhile, hidden to the whites, the Matabele military structure was in large part intact. In fact, by 1895, some *indunas*, or regimental chiefs, were holding meetings in the Matapos hills, a rugged terrain to the south of Gubulawayo, to plot their revenge against the company.

The spirit mediums, whether honest characters or not, continued to hold sway over the minds of both Matabele and Shona. The historian Terence Ranger has argued that the rebellion was actually co-ordinated by priests of the Mwari cult,[38] though this has been disputed by a later historian.[39] But whether or not they were the masterminds of the rebellion, the mediums certainly conveyed messages, apparently sent by proud ancestors, which stoked the desire for vengeance against the whites. And the tribes were listening.

Cattle was another issue of cultural blindness for the company. In taking cattle from the Matabele, the company was doing more than appropriating an economic resource; as in many African societies, cattle played a key role in upholding Matabele social order, providing a measure of status for their owners, and a medium of payment for wives. As for the apparent "idleness" of the Africans, the company might have better understood this as a rational decision on their part not to work for low wages when they could satisfy their needs by traditional methods such as growing their own food.

The blindness of the whites persisted until the last moment. "There was a rumour of a possible rising among some of the tribes in the Matappo Hills", one of the white settlers wrote to his mother in February 1896, "but that was of course all moon-shine ... The natives are happy, comfortable and prosperous and the future must be magnificent".[40] The terror began a month later. The Matabele *indunas* had been emboldened by news of Jameson's defeat in the Transvaal, and they took this as their cue. Warriors advanced on remote white farms and mines, slaughtering entire families, and sometimes mutilating their bodies. Within weeks, perhaps 200 whites were dead. One Matabele warrior subsequently explained, "We were going to kill all the white people because we had news that the Mlimo [the Matabele word for the high god] was going to help us". He described one attack in which his fellow warriors had approached an unsuspecting settler who was working in a field. "When they got to him, he greeted them and told them that as they had come they had better help him with the reaping. They walked near him and then they hit him once and Ngonye then chopped his neck with an axe".[41]

When the Shona rose three months later, the outbreak of violence was just as unexpected, and just as horrific. The ethnic group assumed by the company to be a grateful, "cowardly lot", within a week had hacked or bludgeoned to death all whites in an 80-mile radius of countryside surrounding the town of Salisbury.[42] Not all the Shona kingdoms united against the company, but many that did fought ferociously, and they were spurred on by fiery words from their spirit mediums.

Rage and redemption

So the rebellion erupted because the company, wrapped in its own concerns, had failed to understand the indigenous perspective. A modern multinational might have attempted to rectify the situation by examining, and trying to deal with, the root causes of local anger. But this being the imperial era, a less intellectually demanding solution was available: overwhelming force. The British South Africa Company's main strategy during 1896–7 was to use its superior military power, together with that of British government forces who were drafted in, simply to annihilate native resistance.

An interesting exception to this overall strategy was the behavior of Rhodes in the Matapos hills, where at a late stage in the fighting he sought a negotiated settlement with the Matabele. It is this sub-plot which reveals an aspect of enlightenment in Rhodes' otherwise unredeemed character. It also provides hope for modern multi-nationals that the clash between corporate and indigenous perspectives sometimes, and with effort, can be resolved peacefully.

At first Rhodes was as eager as anyone to crush the Matabele and Shona uprisings, and he welcomed a distraction from the problems which Jameson's raid on the Transvaal had caused him. Physically reckless, and wearing white-flannel trousers which marked him out to the enemy, he often led battle charges against the Matabele himself. He insisted that no mercy be shown to the survivors. "You should kill all you can; it serves as a lesson to them when they talk things over at night. They count up the killed, ... and they begin to fear you", Rhodes explained to an officer after one battle.[43]

The Africans had murdered defenseless white women and children, and hence – in the eyes of the British troops – they deserved everything they got. As an aside, it is interesting to note that when white women had the temerity to criticize the brutality of the company's response, the British men were simply baffled. One such woman was Olive Schreiner, the South African writer who had once idolized Rhodes. Over time she had become concerned about his methods and in 1897 she published an eloquent critique of the company in the form of a book illustrated with a photograph of African corpses hanging from a tree with whites standing by, smiling.[44]

One of the British officers fighting against the Matabele who could not comprehend such female ingratitude was Robert Baden-Powell. The man who would later found the Boy Scout movement wrote in his own account of the crushing of the rebellion:

> A man here does not mind carrying his own life in his hand
> – he likes it, and takes an attack on himself as a good bit of
> sport; but touch a woman or a child [and] he is in a blind fury
> in a moment – and then he is gently advised to be mild, and

to offer clemency to the poor benighted heathen ... And though woman is his first care, and can command his last drop of blood in her defence, woman is the first to assail him on his return, with venom-pointed pen, for his brutality![45]

With the British men in such a "blind fury", the Africans had little hope. The Matabele had learnt from the war of 1893 to take cover from the Maxim gun, but they were still no match for the well-resourced British troops. The Shona, meanwhile, were fighting under their separate rulers, and hence lacked an overall military strategy. Both sets of tribes were quickly beaten back – the Matabele sought refuge in the Matapos hills, and the Shona in the hills and caves of their region of Rhodesia. The Shona rebellion sputtered on for over a year, but all their rebels eventually either surrendered or were dynamited in their caves together with their families, a tactic the British found to be very effective.

The British also made a point of executing the spirit mediums, whom they now realized – too late – had been fomenting the rebellion. Baden-Powell, for example, captured a medium and rebel leader called Uwini:

> I was sorry for him – he was a fine old savage; but I signed his warrant directing that he should be shot at sundown ... I have great hopes that the moral effect of this will be particularly good among the rebels, as he was the head and centre of revolution in these parts, and had come to be looked upon by them as a god.[46]

Amid the rout of the rebel forces, why did Rhodes decide to seek a negotiated settlement with the Matabele? There were some good strategic and commercial reasons for this. The craggy Matapos hills, where the remaining Matabele regiments had taken refuge, provided ideal terrain for guerrilla attacks on British forces. Completing the destruction of the Matabele would require a long military campaign, largely at the company's expense. But something also appears to have stirred Rhodes on a personal level. Perhaps it was the battles which caused him to think further about his own mortality. Perhaps he was growing concerned about his reputation and legacy. Perhaps he had recalled his trusting relationships with

Africans when he was a young man. Whatever the reason, what emerged unexpectedly was a degree of sympathy for the Matabele, and a strange personal identification with their dead kings.

Rhodes himself led the first peace-mission into the Matapos hills. In his small party was Vere Stent, a journalist of the *Cape Times*, who documented this and the subsequent *indabas*, or negotiating sessions, between Rhodes and the Matabele chiefs. It was a sunlit winter's day, according to Stent, "the grasses, bronze and golden, swaying in the slight wind; the hills ahead of us blurred in the quivering mirage of early afternoon".[47] Once in the hills, Rhodes was surrounded by Matabele warriors, and met by a procession of chiefs. "This is very exciting", he said to one of his party, "This is one of the incidents in life that make it worth living." With Rhodes seated on an ant-heap, listening, one of the chiefs, Somabulana, started on a long rendition of the history of the Matabele nation. The speech culminated in the story of the humiliation of Lobengula by the chartered company, and the cruelties of the company's Native Police. Rhodes did not take offence; in fact he was in a mood for compromise. "There are no more Native Police; they will be done away with", he said.

There were several more such *indabas* over the next few months, and though the young Matabele warriors were at first keen to continue fighting, Rhodes continued talking, apparently relishing the process of negotiation. For the first time in years, he was no longer in a rush. He eventually sealed the peace with promises of more land for the Matabele and salaries for their chiefs. At the last *indaba*, Somabulana named Rhodes as "Umlamulanmkunzi", the bull who separates the two fighting bulls, or the peacemaker. Rhodes called the Matabele "my children".[48] The next year Rhodes held a 44th birthday party for himself and invited 1,200 Matabele to a new farm he had bought on the edge of the Matapos hills. He planned everything in detail himself, including the slaughter of 200 sheep, and gifts of blankets and tobacco for his guests.[49] He seemed to be entertaining in his mind a new self-image: that of an African chief.

Rhodes's brief transformation had other manifestations too. During his months negotiating in the Matapos hills, he would go on regular horse-rides, admiring the landscape. At one point, he visited the tomb of Mzilikazi, the former Matabele king and father of Lobengula. Like Lobengula, Mzilikazi had been buried according to

© Hulton Archive

Cecil Rhodes (centre), shortly after he had crushed the Matabele rebellion. This was the spot, in the Matapos hills, where he decided he would be buried – in the manner of an African king.

tradition sitting upright in a cave. The grave had been desecrated by British soldiers, and Rhodes ordered that it should be restored. Rhodes was particularly taken by a panorama from a nearby hill which he dubbed "View of the World". He later returned to the same place with a friend whom he told: "I admire the imagination of Umzilagazi [Mzilikazi]. There he lies, a conqueror alone, watching over the land that he had won. When I die, I mean to be buried here…"[50]

This is where the story of this chapter must end, with the Matabele co-opted by Rhodes and the Shona crushed by him, for these tribes had now been brought entirely under the company's control. In spite of Rhodes' moment of enlightenment, the basic facts of the story remain: like other multinationals examined in this book, his company had failed to comprehend the perspective – and predict the reaction – of the indigenous people. It had incorrectly assumed the Africans were accepting of its rule, and then had survived their anger largely because it had access to superior firepower.

Multinationals in the post-imperial era would not be able to call upon such force to defend their assets, which would make it all the more important from their perspective to maintain good relations with host societies. Whether they would succeed in this task – in spite of the inherent tensions highlighted by Rhodes' story between the fast-moving, large-scale processes of international business, and the intricate nature of many societies – is a subject for Parts 3 and 4 of the book.

The transformation of Rhodes was indeed brief, and the last years of his life saw a return to form. He continued to pursue schemes for northward expansion. He blustered his way through an official British inquiry into Jameson's raid on the Transvaal. Though he was criticized in its concluding report, he persuaded the government not to revoke the company's charter. In 1899, a new conflict broke out between Britain and the Boers, this one not directly fomented by Rhodes, but rather by an imperial official called Alfred Milner, who – like Rhodes – was keen to see the Transvaal brought under British influence. The Boer War, as it came to be known, would result in the deaths of some 60,000 whites, and an unknown number of Africans who had been roped in on both sides. Rhodes energetically helped defend Kimberley, the heart of his diamond empire, against Boer attack. Two years later he died; the heart problem which had always threatened to cut his life short finally did so.

One of Rhodes' best-known legacies in the west is the system of "Rhodes scholarships", which sponsors students from around the world to study at Oxford, and which remains a model of corporate philanthropy. In southern Africa, his legacies are less fondly remembered. The British South Africa Company continued to rule Southern Rhodesia (or present-day Zimbabwe) until 1923, when the white settlers took over, and though these local whites had become increasingly irritated by the company's administration of the region, they continued to occupy the land it had taken on their behalf from the Matabele and Shona. The company's rule over Northern Rhodesia (or present day Zambia) ended a year later in 1924, when the British Colonial Office assumed control; but the British government also failed significantly to reverse the company's neglect of African interests.

Over the subsequent decades indigenous resentments slowly mounted, then exploded in full-blown nationalist movements.

Zambia was granted independence in 1964, and Zimbabwe finally won hers in 1980. Interestingly, the Zimbabwean guerrillas who fought against minority white rule in the late 1970s sought inspiration from the 1896 rebellion against Rhodes' company. And like the Matabele and Shona warriors of that earlier war, they also sought support and guidance from spirit mediums.[51]

But all this, of course, is beyond the era dealt with in this chapter. Rhodes' funeral, on 11th April 1902, provides a fitting endnote for the story. The conqueror of the region was buried – as he had intended – in the Matapos hills, near the dead king Mzilikazi. Thousands of Matabele came to the funeral. Though Rhodes was their oppressor, he had also won their grudging respect. After a Christian ceremony, the Matabele chiefs and warriors paid their own tribute to Rhodes. They filed past the grave, and descended the hill in absolute silence. Then, according to a white account of the funeral, there arose:

> the most wonderful chattering as they made their way up the radiating valleys and gorges leading to their camps, their high pitched voices reaching the ears of the mourners lingering on the top of the mountain.[52]

The Africans may have lost their appetite for resistance for the time being. But they would not be silent for long.

Empires II

INTRODUCTION

The Mayan ruins of Quiriguá, in the sweltering tropics of eastern Guatemala, provide an intriguing glimpse into an ancient empire. But what visitors may not realize as they wander around the mysterious stone monoliths which dot the area like the giant stumps of fossilized trees, is that the ruins provide evidence of the activities of two old empires rather than one.

They will learn from their guidebooks that it was the Mayan ruler, King Cauac Sky, who in the eighth century commissioned masons to carve these monoliths as a testament to his own magnificence. Less well known is that United Fruit, an immensely powerful American banana multinational which is the subject of one of the chapters in this part of the book, was responsible in the 1910s for clearing away the thick jungle which used to cloak the site, and commissioning archaeologists to uncover its secrets. This was an act which may have been motivated as much by hubris as philanthropy, for the managers of United Fruit fancied themselves rather as modern Mayan kings, bringing their own brand of civilization to the jungle. Both empires were remarkable for their achievements, and for their ruthlessness, and both, at a later stage, would suffer catastrophic declines.

United Fruit still exists in some form: a modern American company called Chiquita, less politically powerful and more politically correct than its predecessor, runs many of its old plantations at the time of writing. But United Fruit's significance to the modern world is greater than the assets it has bequeathed. It helped create a pattern of international trade in bananas which still today recalls an imperial past. One of the most fractious and high-profile disputes at the World Trade Organization in recent years, for example, involved America and Europe promoting banana exports from their respective spheres of influence: America backed Latin banana exports – in which its multinationals, including Chiquita, continue to have a significant stake – while Europe sought in turn to protect the

banana industry of its former colonies in Africa, the Caribbean and
the Pacific. But United Fruit's legacy is even broader than that.
Among left-wing activists throughout Latin America, its name still
stands as a symbol of American imperialism, and its record is sure to
be recalled again if ever a modern multinational meddles, or is seen
to meddle, in a Latin country's internal affairs.

The other chapter in this part also covers a period in history
which resonates strongly with present events, as well as providing an
indication of how peaceful trading relationships can sour over the
long term. For the modern age is not the first time that China has
opened itself to a vast wave of foreign investment, nor the first time
that Japan's multinationals have expanded across Asia. Around the
turn of the nineteenth century, major Chinese cities such as
Shanghai were as buzzing with foreign cultural influences and were
as enticing a destination for foreign trading houses as they are today.
The Japanese multinational which is the particular focus of the
chapter – the South Manchurian Railway Company – was a principal
force behind Japan's penetration of north-east China in the 1910s,
20s, and 30s, a process which started by means of peaceful trade, and
– in the face of rising Chinese nationalism – culminated in an
outright invasion of the region.

Standards of corporate behavior have without doubt improved
since then, and no company these days would even entertain the idea
of invasion. Nonetheless, memories of the period – and the
resentments which it triggered – persist. While the South Manchurian Railway Company no longer exists, for example, a number
of other old Japanese firms have in recent years faced lawsuits from
Chinese litigants accusing them of profiting from their slave labor
during the war years.[1]

Current waves

But, as with "Empires I", this part of the book aims not just to trace the
effect of past events on current institutions and attitudes. It also pin-
points certain political problems and dynamics faced by these historic
multinationals which have relevance to some modern corporations.
Put to one side the violence surrounding the South Manchurian
Railway Company, for example, and its experience shows how an

economically successful company can become drawn into local political disputes, a process which it may find difficult to control, especially in an unstable developing country. A similar process of political suction, with its attendant dangers, was experienced by the East India Company. The chapter on United Fruit illustrates another unintended consequence which may spring from financial strength. Success in a company often goes hand in hand with a strong sense of pride and purpose among its employees, but such a strong internal culture also can blind a company to the effect of its actions on local societies – with possibly dangerous consequences, as United Fruit discovered.

The reason these two companies feature in "Empires II" is that both sprung from countries among the second wave of industrializing nations following Britain's lead in the eighteenth century. From the mid-nineteenth century onwards, America, and then Japan, were both convulsed by industrial revolutions of their own. Of course, there were other countries in this second wave: a number of continental European countries, including Germany and France, were also growing rapidly by around this time, and they too had empires, and imperial multinationals, to match.

The scramble for Africa in which Cecil Rhodes led the charge for Britain, for example, also involved the corporations of the other European powers. Until the 1920s, dozens of French concessionary companies directly ran, and pillaged, much of Equatorial Africa. The Deutsch Ost-Afrika Gesellschaft was for a short while a significant power in East Africa. Most notorious were Belgium's commercial interests in the Congo. Under the supervision of Belgium's King Leopold II, companies made fortunes tapping the region's rubber, a commodity increasingly in demand as sales of bicycles and motorcars grew in Europe and America. But the rubber was extracted largely by terrorizing local villages into providing sufficient quantities: according to one estimate, 5–8 million Congolese were killed during this period. Leopold's methods caused an international outcry, as well as inspiring Joseph Conrad to write *Heart of Darkness*.

So it is not for lack of choice of extraordinary enterprises that no European multinational is featured in this part of the book, but simply that United Fruit and the South Manchurian Railway Company stand out as examples of powerful multinationals of the era. The omission will be rectified by giving Europe its due weight in the third part, which covers the period of "backlash". For the remainder of this introduction, it will help to sketch briefly the broad historical processes at work in the countries and regions that are covered in this part. For, as before, the clashes between the companies and the local cultures which will be described are not random events, nor just the result of individuals' ambitions, but are driven by a set of powerful, underlying forces.

A divided hemisphere

As an American company investing in Central and Latin America, United Fruit straddled two continents moving at strikingly different speeds. Some historians and theorists have speculated that the reason why the economy of the United States raced ahead in the nineteenth and twentieth centuries, while that of Latin America languished, was due in part to the colonial legacies of the different regions. Whereas the Spanish and Portuguese imprinted a feudal, authoritarian political structure on their colonies, the British bequest of more democratic and more effective institutions may have helped create the conditions for broader-based development. A variety of other explanations for the United States' success compete for attention too; these include its rich natural resources, its use of standardized production, and also its highly motivated labor force, swelled by waves of immigrants.

Whatever the causes, the effects were dramatic: by the end of the nineteenth century, to cite just one indicator of America's industrial strength, its output of iron and steel had surpassed that of Britain. Energetic entrepreneurs such as John D. Rockefeller, Andrew Carnegie, and Cornelius Vanderbilt, accumulated unheard-of quantities of wealth. And economic crises, when they came, were equally titanic in scale. Such was America's importance in the global economy that a downswing in its business cycle in the late 1920s brought the Great Depression to the world.

Rapid industrialization also brought with it two phenomena which will be familiar from the British experience in the century before. One was a degree of popular disquiet with unfettered markets and big business at home. In America this expressed itself more in pressure to dismantle large monopolies or trusts, rather than in calls for Marxist revolution. Theodore Roosevelt and Woodrow Wilson, both presidents allied to the "Progressive" movement, for example, took aim at trusts in the oil, tobacco, railroad and various other industries. Among the most notorious trusts was John D. Rockefeller's Standard Oil Company, which in 1911 was ordered to divest itself of all its major holdings.

The second phenomenon was the emergence of an American overseas empire, smaller and less enthusiastically pursued than Britain's, but still profound in its effects for the colonized countries. A war with Spain in 1898 resulted in the sale of the Philippines to America for £20 million, though moves were soon made to prepare this territory for self-rule. But it was closer to home, in Central and Latin America, that the United States pursued its interests most vigorously. Encouraged by big business, and by the 1823 "Monroe doctrine", by which America had proclaimed its desire for a sphere of influence in the western hemisphere, a series of administrations took the opportunity to meddle as they saw fit. In 1903, for example, America helped engineer a revolution in Colombia to ensure that it could proceed with construction of the Panama canal. Even the "Progressive" Woodrow Wilson dabbled in foreign ventures: he imposed a puppet government on Haiti in 1915 and occupied the Dominican Republic the following year. And it should not be forgotten that vast swathes of America's own territory, including California, Arizona, Nevada and Utah, had been acquired in 1848 following a war with Mexico.

In theory, moral concerns about big business at home together with the growth of an empire, might have combined to produce a powerful domestic critique of big American businesses abroad. But this movement was for the time being more notable by its absence. It is true that there were various factions in America opposed to the growth of empire in general, but before the Second World War such anti-imperialism was motivated more by a concern to prevent America becoming embroiled in conflict with other great powers, than by a desire to protect the rights of indigenous people. In fact, some in the American anti-imperialist movement openly argued that such folk were in need of "civilizing". As one of their number chose to put it: "there is no human right to the status of barbarism".[2]

The Latin and Central American countries which emerged out of independence from the Spanish and Portuguese empires in the early nineteenth century certainly exhibited "barbarism" in one sense: most came to be ruled by a succession of *caudillos*, military strongmen whose main concern was the preservation of their own power. In place of an industrial revolution of its own, the region experienced instead stagnation, instability and corruption. With the independence movement driven by local Spanish elites, the indigenous population – including the Mayan Indians of Guatemala – fared miserably too.

Centuries before, during the colonial period, a few Catholic priests, such as Bartolomé de Las Casas, had become concerned for the welfare of Indians, but this had failed to translate into significant material gains for them (and even Bartolomé de Las Casas had a blind spot when it came to Africans: he himself owned some as slaves). Admittedly intermarriage between Europeans and native Indians over time had helped blur the racial boundaries to a degree. Nonetheless most post-independence Latin countries inherited a form of apartheid from their colonial past which they did little to dismantle; people of European descent continued to dominate the urban and political elite, while the predominantly poor Indians worked the white-owned plantations and the mines.

There were some hopeful signs. Parts of the region were rich in resources, and many countries began to attract large amounts of foreign investment in the nineteenth century – first from the British, then the Germans, and then the Americans. Some countries even flourished briefly. The invention of refrigerator ships in the 1880s, for example, boosted Argentina's exports of meat, especially to Britain, and for a short period the former Spanish colony joined the ranks of wealthy nations. But most countries continued to languish economically, the benefits from foreign investment failing to penetrate much beyond the urban, fairer-skinned elites (who naturally supported the phenomenon most vigorously). Large corporations had helped power North America to economic greatness, but further south they were operating in a very different social and political environment, with unpredictable consequences. As will be seen, this was the situation, complex and fraught, which confronted United Fruit in Guatemala.

A tale of two giants

The cultures brought into collision by the South Manchurian Railway Company were in some ways less divergent. For Japan and China not only shared various ancient Asian cultural bonds such as Confucianism and Buddhism, but both were faced by the mid-nineteenth centuries with growing incursion from the west. In fact, one of the reasons the Japanese established the South Manchurian Railway Company was to resist western encroachment in the region. The reason the company features in a book about "western" corporations is simply that it fits the basic pattern of a large and powerful multinational operating in a region less economically developed than its home country.

What thrust Japan onto the world stage as an economic power was partly an internally driven process of industrialization. Several centuries of political stability, and cultural and economic isolation, during the Tokugawa era had enabled the growth of agricultural production and also some early capitalist institutions. For much of this period the only European traders allowed in Japan were the Dutch – and even they were restricted to a trading outpost on a small island in Nagasaki harbor. In this period, too, indigenous merchants and trading firms began to thrive. These were the seeds of the *zaibatsu*, Japanese conglomerates which eventually would become as powerful as America's trusts. Foremost among them was Mitsui, a family firm of bankers and retailers dating from the seventeenth century (and which exists to this day).

Industrialization accelerated dramatically once Japan opted for a course of interaction with the west. This was partly forced upon the country when the American naval officer Commodore Perry sailed the first foreign squadron into Japanese waters in 1853. But the "Meiji Restoration" of 1868, a domestic revolution which brought the emperor back to power, also heralded a conscious rethink by Japan of its approach to the outside world. Henceforth Japan's national pride would be upheld not by keeping out the foreigners, as before, but by emulating, and bettering, their methods. Hundreds of Japanese officials and students were dispatched to Europe and America to learn assiduously about western technology and production techniques; the country's feudal political structures were replaced with western-style institutions; universal public education – and military conscription – was introduced.

It was a remarkable transformation that is still studied by poor countries hoping to engineer their own catch-up with the west. Across the country there sprouted cotton mills, coal mines, electricity generation plants, and the like. As the economy powered ahead, millions of industrial workers (including women, whose average wage-rate was about half that of men[3]) labored for long hours in hazardous conditions. Some of the coal mines were so dangerous that, in the words of one economic historian, they "made the infamous British pits of an earlier time look like a promenade".[4]

As with Britain and America before it, industrial success in Japan also began to express itself in an imperial appetite. Among the first areas to fall under Japanese sway was Korea. This was wrested from China's sphere of influence after Japan fought a war with its giant, but militarily weaker, Asian neighbor in 1894–95, and it was then fully annexed in 1910. From Japan's perspective, Korea – a territory geographically on its doorstep – provided an ideal buffer against any western powers with their own designs in Asia. But for insecure Japanese nationalists this was not protection enough. They also enviously eyed Manchuria, one of the next regions outwards. This territory, however, was not only part of China, comprising as it did three large provinces of the country's north east; it was also on imperial Russia's wish-list of acquisitions.

This was the geo-political pressure cooker in which the South Manchurian Railway Company had its birth. Japan had already tried to secure possession of a strategically important part of south Manchuria – the Liaotung Peninsula (see map on page 88) – as part of its peace terms with China in 1895. But Russia, with France and Germany's support, forced Japan to back down on this claim; Russia then went further, and through a combination of threat and bribery, persuaded China to grant it a 25-year lease on the peninsula, plus the rights to build railway lines northwards from the local ports of Dairen and Port Arthur (or Lushun).

It was then only a matter of time before Japan and Russia came directly to blows: a bloody conflict erupted between the two countries in 1904. Japan's victory in this war resulted in the lease on the Liaotong Peninsula falling into its hands, as it had originally desired.

For the time being, meanwhile, the Japanese agreed to respect Chinese sovereignty over the rest of Manchuria. Japan also inherited the newly built local railway lines from Russia, and it established the South Manchurian Railway Company to manage these. As will be seen, however, running trains would be only a part of this corporation's myriad activities.

China's political and military weakness in this period and the related inrush of western, as well as Japanese, investment in the country, will be explored more fully later. But a basic point of context which it will help to note here is the unprecedented nature of the transformation China was experiencing. For thousands of years, the country had proved to be relatively immune to foreign influences, and had developed a culture as self-absorbed and proud (in many ways justifiably) as those of western imperial nations. The contrast with the Indians of Latin America, whose cultures had been crushed by a first wave of imperialism long before the arrival of the western multinationals, could not be greater.

It is not that China had not been invaded at various points (the Mongols, for example, overran the territory in the thirteenth century), but rather that the invaders had tended to assimilate its culture, and become Chinese, rather than foreign, rulers (thus the Mongol ruler, Kubilai Khan, established his capital at Peking). Chinese dynasties rose and fell over the centuries, their decline often hastened by peasant rebellions (the vast rural population remained mired in poverty). Nonetheless important constants remained: a large bureaucracy built on Confucian learning, an emperor worshipped as a God-like "Son of Heaven", and a sense of superiority over foreigners.

For centuries, the Chinese had shown little interest in western goods, agreeing only to buy silver and also some European clocks and toys, which they found amusing. Theirs, after all, was a culture which had invented such marvels as gunpowder, printing, and the magnetic compass, long before the west (though when it came to gunpowder, they were less adept than the Europeans at making the guns which would channel it to such fatal effect – which would prove crucial). When an emissary from the British government arrived to try to do business with China in 1793, the Chinese emperor rebuffed him, though happily noted King George III's "submissive loyalty" to his great empire. "My Ancestors' merit and virtue must have reached their distant shores", the emperor congratulated himself in a poem. "Though their tribute is commonplace, my heart approves sincerely."[5]

When the Ch'ing, the last of the Chinese dynasties, began to totter in the nineteenth century, what was different from previous dynastic collapses was that this time an even more powerful set of cultures was waiting in the wings. For by now the westerners were not only well-armed with their guns, but were competing with each other for the spoils of empire, and were driven on by the confidence, and thirst for new markets, brought by industrialization at home. In short, unlike previous invaders, the westerners would not allow themselves to be assimilated or absorbed by China.[6]

The British were the first to force their way into the Chinese economy. Britain's victory in the Opium War in 1842 allowed this western power to secure a set of trading concessions even more generous than legalized drug-pushing (the war had been sparked when China tried to prevent sales of the drug to its citizens, a trade that the British East India Company had helped to pioneer). Many other western entrepreneurs followed into the ancient Asian nation. And now among the westerners' ranks – even if not "western" as such – were the newly powerful and wealthy Japanese, whose South Manchurian Railway Company was to be the spearhead of their country's penetration of China. With this context in mind, the events of the next chapter can now begin to unfold – and because this fits the tone of the era so well, the story can begin with an explosion.

THREE

Violent acquisitions
The South Manchurian Railway Company

By developing the region for the benefit of China and Japan and all of its industries to their fullest measure, the economic ties between both countries will be tightly forged.

Yamamoto Jōtarō, president of the South Manchurian Railway Company, 1927–1929.[1]

Are we in for real trouble!

Japanese army officers plotting the invasion of Manchuria behind the backs of their commanders, 1931.[2]

Chang Tso-lin, the Chinese warlord of Manchuria, boarded the train at 1.15a.m. on 4th June 1928. As the locomotive rolled out of Peking towards Mukden, an ancient city within his territory, he was little aware that its progress was being followed carefully – and that soon it would be brought to a shocking halt – by local Japanese military units. The problem was that, like the indigenous potentates encountered in previous chapters – like Siraj-ud-daula, the Mughal ruler of Bengal, and like Lobengula, the Matabele king – Chang had been obstructing the interests of an imperial multinational. And even if this one was Japanese rather than British, he was still going to have to pay the price.

Illiterate, and timid in appearance, Chang did not look the part of a warlord. In 1922, his biographer described him as "a thin, yellow-faced little man, five feet two in height. Despite his fame, he is meek-looking and there is nothing distinctive about him. At a glance he is a complete rustic [...] completely ordinary".[3] Little is known about Chang's personal life, except that he had five wives, and enjoyed smoking opium and playing mah-jongg. But appearances were deceptive, and the ambition and audacity of this diminutive warlord was obvious to anyone who had stood in his path.

The son of a vagabond and gambler, he had gained early experience in political leadership as the boss of a local gang of bandits, whose activities, though not known for sure, are likely to have involved raids on other gangs, and robbing and kidnapping wealthy people (such banditry was relatively common in the unstable north-east of China at the time).[4] Following the collapse of China's Ch'ing dynasty in 1911, Chang gained full control of Manchuria and his regime was then for a time supported by Japan. In return for this support Chang provided a relatively conducive climate for Japanese investment which helped its multinational, the South Manchurian Railway Company, to dominate the economic infrastructure of the region. But this peaceful coexistence could not last.

Part of the problem was that Chang's ambitions were insatiable. He was intent not just on ruling Manchuria, but on becoming the emperor of the whole of China, and as he sought to turn this ambition into a reality, the Japanese had become increasingly annoyed about his incessant warmongering to the south of Manchuria with Chinese nationalist, or Kuomintang, forces. One Japanese fear was that Chang's military expeditions might at some point provoke a nationalist incursion in Manchuria itself. Indeed it was after a major battle with the nationalists in the southwest, which had proved a disaster for Chang, that he was returning from Peking to Mukden on 4th June. This time the Japanese would not let the matter rest. The plot against Chang was not official Japanese policy. But such was the frustration of the government in Tokyo at the warlord's activities that a number of radical Japanese army officers in Manchuria, including a certain Lieutenant-Colonel Kōmoto, decided to take the matter into their own hands.

Kōmoto and his colleagues had used their military training to plan the incident carefully. Cement bags had been packed with explosives and placed by the railtracks near Mukden, just by a bridge under which Chang Tso-Lin's train was due to pass. Japanese observers had been stationed at key points along the line between Peking and Mukden and, in order to create the impression that the plot was actually the work of Chinese nationalists rather than the Japanese, three Chinese beggars had been seized by Kōmoto's men, and planted with evidence suggesting they were Kuomintang agents. Two of these unfortunate down-and-outs had then been bayoneted by Japanese soldiers near the railway tracks, although the third managed to escape.

It was past five in the morning by the time Chang Tso-lin's train approached the fateful point. Chang was in the eighth carriage along, a special "palace" car. He had just finished playing a game of mah-jongg with some of his military advisers when a thunderous explosion ripped across the tracks. Carriages seven, eight and nine were blown into the air. According to one account, Chang was struck in the nose by a lump of steel before he was able to take cover under the mah-jongg table; according to another, it was a chest wound which floored him. Either way, within hours the troublesome warlord had been pronounced dead at a Mukden hospital.[5]

This, as it turned out, was far from the end of the conflict between Chinese leaders and the Japanese and their giant corporation. As will be seen later, the death of Chang did not lead – at least not at first – to Japanese supremacy in Manchuria. For Chang was replaced as local ruler by his son, Chang Hsüeh-liang, who would prove even more troublesome to the Japanese, in spite of their hopes to the contrary. Indeed the warlord's son had set his mind against compromise from the very start; for soon after his father's assassination, the third Chinese beggar, the one who had escaped bayoneting, had let him know that it was the Japanese who were responsible for the plot, and not the Chinese nationalists. So the scene was set for a further confrontation – this time between an angry, grieving son and a Japanese imperial force determined, more than ever, to assert its authority.

Signal failure

The South Manchurian Railway Company, though little heard of in the west, was among the most powerful companies Asia has ever seen. Likened by some of its supporters at the time to the English

Like father, like son: Chang Tso-lin (left), the diminutive warlord of Manchuria,
and his son Chang Hsüeh-liang. Both would provoke the wrath of Japanese
imperialists.

East India Company, it was intended by the Japanese to be the
principal tool of their country's influence in Manchuria, this region
of north-east China roughly the size of France and Germany
combined. Far more than a railway company, it ran collieries,
ironworks, schools, hospitals, parks, libraries, and indeed entire
cities. Mantetsu – as the company was known to the Japanese
themselves (and, for the sake of brevity, as it will be referred to in the
rest of this chapter) – played a pivotal role in the expansion of the
Japanese empire, a process which culminated in a full-scale war with
China in 1937, and ultimately in the Second World War itself.

The most fascinating aspects of Mantetsu from the perspective of
this book lie not so much in its indirect contribution to the
breakdown of relations between states in the 1930s, but rather in
what it reveals directly about the patterns of interaction between
multinational corporations and host societies. The story of Mantetsu
in this chapter illustrates in particular two related themes. The first
is pertinent to the hundreds of western multinationals which have
invested in China in recent years. China's entry into the World Trade

Organization in 2001, together with the prospect of over 1.2 billion consumers eager for western standards of living, understandably excited the appetites of modern multinationals. History should not necessarily deter the foreign investors, but they would do well to understand the degree of resentment evoked by the last significant wave of foreign investment in China. Mantetsu was the most prominent foreign multinational in China in the period leading up to the Second World War, though a host of European, American, and other Japanese firms were also involved, and these will be mentioned briefly in this chapter. Resentment against such foreign actors was one factor which underlay the rise of the Nationalists in China before the war, and – after the Japanese had been beaten – the triumph of the Communists in 1949. As a result of these epic revolutionary movements, the country kept itself largely isolated from the global economy for decades. For all modern China's appetite for foreign investment (and this phenomenon will be re-examined in the last part of this book), it can be reasonably assumed that history has deposited layers of suspicion in the national psyche which are unlikely to wash away overnight.

The second theme will be familiar from the chapter on the East India Company. The political difficulties encountered by Mantetsu in operating in Manchuria provide another piece of evidence that large multinationals, by dint of their size and economic influence, cannot avoid becoming embroiled in local political disputes. The story also indicates that the manner in which they deal with these disputes, or allow them to be resolved, can be surprisingly lacking in co-ordination. The focus of this chapter is on the company's history until the early 1930s – rather than until its demise in 1945 – as this period illustrates the often haphazard processes by which Japan's economic influence in the region metamorphosed into political control.

Between 1906, when the company was founded, and Chang Tso-lin's assassination in 1928, the company managed to conduct its business by relatively peaceful means. But pressures had been mounting for a while, and – as will be seen – would culminate in a full-blown, and violent, Japanese takeover of Manchuria starting in 1931. This invasion was not planned by the company but was rather undertaken by over-enthusiastic Japanese soldiers, many of whom

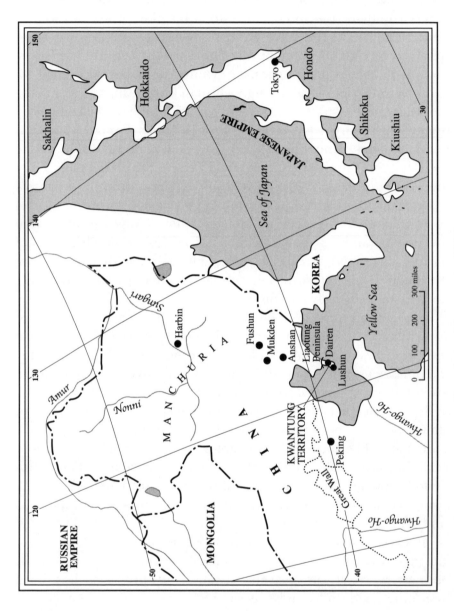

REGION OF MANCHURIA 1920S

had originally been stationed in Manchuria to guard the company's assets and who – like Chang Tso-lin's assassins – decided to take matters into their own hands. While these local military men were state soldiers rather than company servants (unlike, for example, Clive of India), and hence the blame for failing to rein them in rests largely with the Japanese government, the company also appears to have exerted little influence or restraint over a development which would have an enormous impact on its future. Interestingly, the company devoted considerable resources to long-term social and economic planning for Manchuria both before and after the invasion, and it also conducted detailed studies of local Chinese culture. But such efforts, however enlightened, manifestly failed to protect the company from local political turbulence, or from warmongering local soldiers.

Of course the timeless elements of Mantetsu's story should not be over-emphasized. For this multinational, like others in this book, was partly a creation of its era. It was established by the Japanese state with the explicit purpose of extending Japan's political influence in Manchuria. Its bosses never actually made a commitment to trade by peaceful means alone, as had the directors of the East India Company. And the political takeover of Manchuria was partly the result of the emergence of aggressive military ideologies in Japan at the time. Even so, underlying the particular historical circumstances of the story can be traced some of the timeless dynamics of multinational rule – and in particular the tensions inherent in the relations between any large foreign firm and its host society. It is such broader phenomena which will be teased out in the following narrative.

Fragile China

Before resuming the story of Mantetsu itself, in which the assassination of Chang Tso-lin presages an even bloodier climax, it will help to sketch briefly the situation in China as a whole. The background has already been given in the introduction. Now some further context is needed. For various factors – the collapse of a dynasty which had tried and failed to control the influence of all sorts of foreigners, and not just the Japanese, and also the insensitive behavior of the foreigners themselves – set the turbulent conditions under which Mantetsu tried to pursue its goals in Manchuria.

The fall of the Ch'ing dynasty in 1911 had parallels with the decline in the Mughal empire in India in that it was replaced by a complex patchwork of states run by competing warlords. But, unlike India in the eighteenth century, China at this later period possessed a modern nationalist movement – the Kuomintang – eager to reunite the country. What helped bring about the Ch'ing dynasty's decline, as mentioned before, was its weakness in the face of foreign intrusion. Since the first Opium War, the Chinese had been attempting to limit demands from the Europeans, Americans and Japanese for trade concessions by playing off one set of foreigners against the other – or in the words of Chinese officials, "using barbarians to control barbarians".[6] The success of this strategy, however, was hampered by the barbarians' superior military technology. Well-armed westerners, for example, were only temporarily inconvenienced by the Boxer Rebellion of 1900. This was a Chinese peasant movement which aimed to drive all foreigners out of China and which was driven by the peasants' belief that their mystical boxing skills provided them with magical protection against bullets.

China's territory was not carved up between the western powers in the manner of their scramble for Africa. Instead, a tacit agreement emerged between the westerners to limit direct territorial competition in the country, which would have proved risky and costly, in place of a system of "treaty ports" from which each foreign power was able to trade freely. Chinese sovereignty was compromised nonetheless, for the threat of foreign gunboats and troops obliged the Ch'ing rulers to agree to treaties governing these ports which would be considered unconscionable by any twenty-first-century state. In dozens of cities and ports including Shanghai and Canton, foreign powers were not just exempted from many Chinese customs duties and taxes, but were awarded territorial enclaves under the jurisdiction of the consuls of their home governments. Thus parts of some of the most significant trading nodes in the country became, in effect, foreign territory, governed by foreign laws.

Admittedly, western investment in China was never that large in absolute terms: even near its peak in the 1930s, net private foreign investment comprised only around 1% of China's GNP.[7] Farming, which comprised most of national output, remained isolated from external influence. But foreign firms loomed large as symbols of western power. Until the rise of Mantetsu, British firms were the largest foreign investors; principal among them was Jardine, Matheson and Company, headquartered in Hong Kong and with branches in every major port. Jardine's tentacles extended in many directions, including general trade, banking, insurance, and cotton milling, and it controlled a large fleet of steamships plying the coast and the Yangtze river.

Other nationalities had their flagship firms too. Japanese foreign investors included not just Mantetsu, but some of the large *zaibatsu*, the longer-established, family-controlled conglomerates. Early on, for example, Mitsui built up a network of offices in China and it operated its own steamer line and spinning mills in the country. Among the large German trading houses, was Carlowitz and Company, which had started business in China in 1840. From its giant offices in Shanghai it co-ordinated exports from China of wool, straw braids, egg products and bristle, while importing rather different products: heavy machinery and weapons. And America's Standard Oil established a large network of sales agents to sell its kerosene across the country.[8]

In theory, trade offered many opportunities for cultural inter-mingling between Chinese and foreigners which might have aided mutual understanding (a phenomenon which was observed in the early stages of the East India Company's development). It is certainly true that most foreign firms, unlike Standard Oil, relied on Chinese merchants and agents to conduct trade on their behalf outside the main ports and cities and to navigate the Chinese bureaucracy. But such interactions were largely limited to the sphere of business. And while the treaty ports contained a fascinating mix of cultures, in practice many foreigners isolated themselves in their enclaves, adopting an attitude of haughtiness to the surrounding society, which rivaled the Chinese own sense of superiority to the "barbarians".

Life in the foreign concessions of the treaty ports was modeled to a remarkable degree on the culture back home. In the international settlement in Shanghai, for example, the westerners – who were predominantly British – socialized with each other at a specially built racecourse, cricket field, and tennis courts. For their leisure, they would promenade along boulevards lined by plush expatriates houses, and take tea on each others' lawns. They sent their children to European schools, one for the English, one for the French, and one for the Germans. Even the cuisine was European. One American employee at British-American Tobacco Company, which had large operations in China, described a typical meal at the company's local canteen in 1911 thus: "a thin consommé, breaded veal cutlet, rice, a boiled vegetable, and a sticky pastry. English cooking – the flavor cooked out – with the inevitable Lea and Perrins sauce".[9]

Foreign diplomats might have been expected to exhibit a greater degree of cultural sensitivity. But many did not even speak Chinese. A curious indication of this was noted by the Italian minister to the Diplomatic Body in Peking, a group of ambassadors from 15 countries. Sitting in the courtyard outside the room where this high-level international group often met, observed Signor Varè, was a parrot which, while loquacious, "only spoke Chinese, so that his remarks were unintelligible to most of the assembled diplomats".[10]

An aspect of the foreign diplomatic presence more explicitly annoying to the Chinese was the fact that, under the treaty port system, westerners were subject to the laws and regulations of their own consular courts. Thus, for example, Europeans accused of crimes or other infractions by Chinese would be judged in European courts, and according to European laws. Perceptions naturally arose that the western powers tended to favor their own. In fact, an American diplomat admitted in 1906 that, given the pressure of public opinion back home, the American minister to China "is bound to assume that in all cases his countrymen are in the right and the Chinese are in the wrong".[11]

Popular irritation at such biases mounted, and, in the first few decades of the twentieth century, helped trigger a string of Chinese boycotts of foreign goods, and also strikes by Chinese workers in foreign firms. These included a strike in the early 1920s at the British and Belgian-owned Kailan coal mines. "The English are more concerned with an injury to their donkeys than they are with the casualties we may suffer", complained one Chinese worker at these facilities.[12] Such angry episodes aside, however, no European or

American firm faced pressures quite as conflicting or turbulent as those which confronted Mantetsu.

Eastern ideologies

The Japanese company's political problems would reach a crisis point in the late 1920s and early 1930s. But it is important also to examine the first few decades of its existence, when it conducted its business amid a relatively peaceful local environment. For although the company achieved considerable financial success during this period, and although it made concerted efforts to promote general economic development in Manchuria – and also to understand the region's culture – in all these apparently positive aspects of the company's record can be detected ambiguities and the seeds of future conflict.

As previously noted, the company was itself founded as a result of Japan's victory in one of its first imperial wars: the 1904–5 conflict with Russia. This resulted in the transfer to Japan of Russia's leases on the South Manchurian Railway, and also the Kwantung territory (see map on page 88), which was on the tip of Manchuria's Liaotung Peninsula, leases which Russia had itself obtained from China several years earlier. Nearly 100,000 Japanese soldiers had died in the war with Russia, and the acquisition of the railway was etched in the consciousness of many ordinary Japanese. In the words of one of the most popular military songs in Japan at the time:

> Here in far-off Manchuria
> Hundreds of leagues from the homeland,
> Our comrades lie beneath the rocky plain
> Lit by the red setting sun.[13]

The creation of a profit-making corporation, Mantetsu, to run the railways, was one half of a structure put in place by the Japanese government with the explicit aim of protecting and furthering Japanese influence across Manchuria. The government not only took a 50% stake in the company (which, with the Imperial Household's 1% stake, gave the state a majority holding), but also appointed its top managers.[14] Although many army leaders feared that Russia would soon launch a fresh assault on Japanese interests, a full, pre-

emptive invasion of Manchuria was not considered a possibility for
the time being, in part because such a move would incur the wrath
of the other western powers. Manchuria was also still a part of China,
although of course the Ch'ing dynasty's collapse and the rise in its
place of local warlords – and in particular of Chang Tso-lin in
Manchuria – soon would make it easier for the Japanese to assert
more political influence locally. The other half of the Japanese
structure in the region, which would be the source of much violence
in the future, was a local administration for the Kwantung territory.
A key part of this administration was the Kwantung Army, a specially
formed military unit of the Imperial Japanese Army. Ominously, one
of the main tasks given to this band of soldiers was to police
Mantetsu's railways.

Mantetsu's ambitious, energetic first boss – Gotō Shinpei –
perhaps best encapsulates the complex vision which drove the
company. Trained as a medical doctor in Germany, where he
developed a faith in "rational", "scientific" solutions to social and
economic problems, Gotō had served as civil governor of Taiwan,
another of Japan's early imperial footholds, before he moved on to
Manchuria. In Taiwan, he had rebuilt Tapei, the capital, in a grand
imperial style, with impressive public buildings, parks and broad
boulevards. Also in Taiwan, he had commissioned detailed studies
into the local culture, resurrecting a traditional Chinese system of
collective responsibility for maintaining law and order in villages –
known as *pao chia* – so as to help uphold Japanese rule in rural areas.[15]

Gotō's ambitions for Mantetsu were equally broad in scope. He
wanted the company not just to bring in profits, but to assist in the
economic and social development of the region, and to facilitate mass
migration of Japanese citizens to the vast, fertile, plains of
Manchuria. A degree of respect for Chinese culture was another
aspect of Gotō's vision. As he once instructed Mantetsu's railway
officials: "passengers should be treated with kindness and cordiality,
and special attention should be given to Chinese passengers lest
mutual ignorance of speech should cause impoliteness on the part of
the officials and consequent bad feelings on the part of the passengers."[16] But as with Gotō's use of ancient Chinese traditions in
Taiwan, this sensitive approach appears to have been as much a
means to an imperial end – that is, to persuade the locals quietly to

accept Japanese rule – as for the sake of cultural harmony *per se*. Describing his philosophy, Gotō once argued that the aims of Japanese colonial policy should be "military preparedness in civil garb". "Certain scholars have said that the secret of administration lies in taking advantage of the people's weaknesses",[17] he noted with approval.

This ambiguous outlook was paralleled by Japan's complex attitude to the various peoples, including the Chinese, who were subjugated by its empire.[18] One strand in Japanese thinking drew from western notions of social Darwinism: the fact that Japan had achieved a more advanced level of industrialization than other Asian countries led some Japanese to infer that they were racially superior, although to some this also implied an obligation to help "less civilized" people. Coexisting with this idea, however, was the popular notion that Japan should act as a sort of "anti-colonialist" protection force, using its superior fire power to help other Asian nations to resist the tide of western encroachment. This strand in Japanese thinking grouped Asian countries together in opposition to the west. It suggested that China deserved respect, not least because Japan's own civilization shared a Confucian heritage with its culturally (though not economically) rich larger neighbor.

Even though this was a compliment of sorts, however, it was not always returned by the Chinese. They in turn often viewed Japan's economic advances as a demeaning mimicry of western behavior. Initial Japanese requests for special trading rights in the 1870s in China, for example, had been rebuffed in no uncertain terms. "We cannot do anything about the Western nations, but we should not allow any such treatment from Japan", explained one Chinese statesman at the time. "The Japanese are poor, greedy and untrustworthy."[19]

Track record

The sheer energy with which Mantetsu undertook its mission, however, sufficed at first to push such Chinese sentiments into the background. For like one of its own modern locomotives, the company advanced swiftly and powerfully across the economic and social landscape of Manchuria. The company's assets grew from 163 million yen to over a billion yen by 1930, with annual rates of return on these assets rarely falling below 20–30%.[20] Mantetsu's most profitable activity was the operation of the railroads, and principally the transport of soybeans – the region's main export commodity – which were taken to the port of Dairen in the Kwantung territory, from where they were shipped to Japan, Europe, and other markets. But the trains also carried passengers, and visitors often remarked on the punctuality and efficiency of the service compared with the other railways in the region. It helped that Mantetsu had invested in the latest, most advanced rolling stock from America.

Mantetsu's rail network grew fast in size and value, soon linking over 100 towns and cities across the region. Japan's aggressive diplomacy helped here. In 1915, for example, Japan took advantage of the western powers' preoccupation with war in Europe to press on China what became known as the "Twenty-One Demands", which included a request – eventually granted – to extend the original railway lease from 25 to 99 years. With such heavyweight government support, Mantetsu became not only Japan's largest company, but the biggest foreign investment in China.

Mantetsu's employees, who numbered some 38,000 by 1924 (compared with 14,000 in 1908), comprised a variety of nationalities, including Chinese, Koreans, Mongolians, and even Russians. But the management cadre was overwhelmingly Japanese. Recruited from Japan's best universities, and generously paid, these managers were treated well, even by the standards of modern multinationals. They received housing and medical benefits, and education for their children. Promotion often brought short periods of company-sponsored travel or study leave.[21]

Gotō's plans for mass Japanese migration to Manchuria proved over-optimistic, but conversely many Chinese flocked to Manchuria during Mantetsu's first decades, and – in spite of the undercurrents of nationalism – thousands sought work with the company, or in the numerous Japanese businesses which sprang up to provide services to it. At the Dairen wharves, one observer noted "swarms of dark-skinned [Chinese] men, clothed in ragged blue cotton trousers and blouses, streaming in procession from the ships, carrying sacks, bales, packages of merchandise on their shoulders."[22] Japanese immigrants could not be persuaded to undertake such back-breaking work, at least not at the low wages which the company paid for unskilled labor. As Mantetsu's new boss noted in 1915, the "strong points" of Chinese workers "lie in their willingness to accept the lowest standards of living and to tolerate the extremes of the climate".[23]

As well as Mantetsu's railways and wharves, the company ran a vast coalmine at Fushun and an iron and steel works at Anshan. Its research laboratories pioneered techniques such as obtaining oil from coal shale and the processing of soybeans, which aimed to help industrialize a backward economy. Equally important was the role Mantetsu played as a facilitator of development, co-ordinating the activities of the smaller Japanese firms, and channeling finance to them.

Mantetsu also acted as an effective municipal authority in the dozens of cities which lay near its tracks and formed part of its leases, and thus operated hotels, schools, hospitals and other social services. It even permitted a degree of local democracy: Japanese and Chinese residents were allowed to elect representatives to advise the company's authorities on town governance. And just as Gotō had made Tapei a showcase of imperial town planning, Dairen too became a symbol of modernity with grand buildings, an electricity grid, and "a network of broad, perfect roads, equipped with grand systems of water and drainage works".[24]

Planners, Marxists, and poets

The most unusual aspect of Mantetsu's behavior, given that it was a profit-making organization, was its devotion to academic-style research. This was one of Gotō's passions, and, in theory at least, it ought to have helped the company better understand the political and economic environment in which it operated. Soon after the company was founded, Gotō set up its Research Department, and appointed as its head Professor Okamatsu Santarō, an expert in Chinese law from Kyoto University.[25] Okamatsu had previously undertaken the research on ancient customs in Taiwan which Gotō had used to his advantage in that other colony. From a handful of researchers in 1907, the department grew to over 2,300 in 1940. Over its lifetime it produced more than 6,000 survey reports, covering everything from inflation and coal mining to Korean and Manchurian history.

Many of the research department's works have stood the test of time. In the recent words of an American expert on East Asia, the "investigations of the department were of such high quality that its findings have become an indispensable source for scholars in the post-World War II era to achieve a deeper understanding of Chinese society and economy".[26] But an even more unusual feature of Mantetsu's research department was that it provided a home for a number of Japan's leading left-wing intellectuals, including various Marxists and opponents of Japanese imperialism. Itō Takeo, one of the company's officials, who was left-leaning himself, described in his memoirs how "men who had experienced the intellectual trends of Taishō democracy and believed in liberalism entered the research organs [of the company]. Anticolonialists may be ill-suited to a colonial company. However, a liberal tradition of sorts was preserved within the Research Department until the Pacific War began [...] ."[27]

Thus, for example, many of the studies on Chinese society and economics conducted by the department were based on a Marxist theoretical framework. Senior researchers included Ōgami Suehiro, a Marxist from Kyoto University, and Nakanishi Tsutomu, a covert operative of the Japan Communist Party. There were even informal study groups on Marx's *Capital*, and one researcher described how, at his leaving party, his colleagues sent him off with a rendition of the "Internationale", the socialist's anthem. In spite of the unorthodox, anti-imperial nature of such activities, the Japanese military authorities, as will be seen at the end of this chapter, only came round to purging the radical researchers from Mantetsu's ranks in the early 1940s, by which time the company was in the final years of its life.[28]

How was it that left-wingers could operate in such a colonial setting? From the company's perspective, it made sense to recruit researchers solely on the basis of intellectual merit, irrespective of their political beliefs. As for the researchers, they no doubt felt that working for the company – in spite of the compromises involved – presented opportunities for implementing their ideas in practice. In any case, as the Pacific War approached, socialist and Communist intellectuals were having trouble finding jobs back in Japan.

A more difficult question, however, is whether the work of the research department actually assisted the company in understanding and shaping political developments which affected its operations. Certainly, it provided no clear solutions to the company's problems in this respect, for local resistance to the Japanese was mounting. And the left-wing researchers, for all their empathy with the common man, were not necessarily best placed to engender good relations with the local people. For, rather like the home-based critics of multinationals encountered in previous chapters, they were an unintentional part of the imperialist apparatus. The critics of the East India Company and Cecil Rhodes admittedly did not go so far as working for their respective multinationals but what they share with Mantetsu's radical researchers is an ideological outlook shaped by their own particular concerns, and a top-down approach of applying pressure to the multinational. In all three cases, the critics or researchers did not always genuinely represent the interests of the people on the ground, whether these happened to be Mughal subjects, Matabele tribespeople, or Chinese peasants.

A hint of the same pattern is apparent in criticisms of Mantetsu by Japanese from outside the company. Another of Japan's left-wing opponents of colonialism, for example, was the poet Kitagawa Fuyuhiko, whose father worked for Mantetsu as an engineer. His poem "Railway of Annihilation" was clearly aimed at the company:

> The military state's railway progressed through the frozen desert planting numberless teeth, numberless teeth that sprouted spikes.

> Suddenly, one clod of streets appears. In this frozen ash-colored desert, where not one bush grows, not one bird flies. Around the caterpillar-like railway construction cars, the constituent elements of a town gather one by one. [...]

> [...] The railway will only be completed with pain to human beings.[29]

But even such explicit condemnation of Mantetsu seems to have been distorted by common assumptions in Japan at the time. One recent commentator on Kitagawa's writing has pointed to his repeated use of the term "desert" to describe Manchuria. "This points to a disturbing collusion between Kitagawa's poetic vision and the myth, current in Japan, of an unpopulated Manchuria. This myth helped conceal the forceful displacement of Chinese farmers [...]". Put another way, the poet's pre-war writing "articulated a rare challenge to Japanese militarism and colonialism, and yet could not avoid reproducing the very colonial structure it would critique".[30]

Military complexes

As noted before, the plot to assassinate Chang Tso-Lin and the subsequent military takeover of Manchuria, cannot be attributed solely to the inherent difficulties of operating a multinational in a poor country. Attention needs to be paid as well to the unique, and uniquely aggressive, ideological currents in Japan at the time. To summarize a complex situation briefly, Japanese foreign policy in the first decades of the twentieth century oscillated between two competing approaches. One supported assertive diplomacy and trade as the means to establish Japan's position in a rapidly changing international order, while the other argued for more explicitly forceful tactics. It was the growth of factions supporting the strong-arm approach in the 1920s which accelerated the confrontation in Manchuria.

The moderate line was favored by the majority of Mantetsu's directors, by Japan's civilian bureaucrats and its foreign ministry – and especially by Shidehara Kijuro, a career diplomat who had married into the family which owned Mitsubishi, and who was Japan's foreign minister in 1924–7 and 1929–31. Admittedly, people in this camp were moderate only by the standards of the time; they enthusiastically supported Japan's right to a sphere of influence in East Asia, for example. But in the eyes of Shidehara such an aim was best achieved through "economic diplomacy".[31] This meant vigorously pursuing trade in China while respecting the country's sovereignty and avoiding interfering in its numerous internal conflicts. It also meant striking agreements – such as the 1922 Nine Power Treaty – to respect other countries' interests in the region. Such pacts were in any case increasingly being urged upon Japan by America and Britain.

To those who supported the second approach, and who were found in increasing numbers in the Japanese military – and especially the Kwantung Army in Manchuria – such tactics smacked of humiliating subservience to the west. Leaders such as Tanaka Giichi, a general who was also prime minister at the time of Chang Tso-Lin's assassination, argued that Manchuria should serve as an imperial buffer state for Japan, providing it with protection from invasion and with a secure source of raw materials. To this end, they also believed that Japan should be ready to use force to isolate and protect Manchuria from external influence, both from the tides of nationalism and Communism sweeping China, and also – after the Russian Revolution – from the threat of Soviet Bolshevism. Theirs was an aggressive, and insecure, world-view.

Interestingly, this second approach also incorporated a degree of hostility to big business, though again from a uniquely Japanese perspective. To many young, modestly-paid, army officers, the wealthy *zaibatsu*, and the corruption associated with them, symbolized western-style capitalism which – in the view of those officers – had tainted Japanese culture. This outlook had clear implications for other large companies such as Mantetsu. Though the railway giant would survive the army's takeover of Manchuria, in the subsequent period, as will be seen, it came to resemble even less an independent capitalist enterprise, and even more a subservient tool of imperial planning.

It is important to note, too, that this second approach itself comprised a variety of factions, and even Tanaka Giichi was considered insufficiently assertive by younger, more extreme army officers. Many of these extremists belonged to "patriotic" groups such as the Kokuryukai, or Black Dragon Society, and one of their leading ideologues was Ishiwara Kanji, a brilliant military strategist who was predicting a final, Armageddon-like war between Japan and the superpower of the capitalist world, America, in which the conquest of Manchuria was a necessary first step towards Japanese victory.[32] It is of little surprise that Ishiwara was an enthusiastic supporter of the plot to assassinate Chang Tso-lin.

Inherent tensions

Such extremists would not have been able to achieve their goals, however, were it not for the instability of Mantetsu's political base in China, which provided them with fertile ground for their plotting. It

is in the fraught dynamics between Mantetsu and Chang Tso-lin and
his son, and the concurrent rise of nationalism in China, that can be
discerned an example of the tensions inherent in the relationship
between any large multinational and its host society.

The fact that it was originally Chang Tso-lin who, in the early
1920s, suggested that the Japanese should support his regime,
rather than the company which made the first approach, shows how
easily economic influence can draw a corporation into local politics.
The former bandit saw co-operation with the Japanese giant as a
means of protecting his power base against other warlords, and as a
springboard to further conquests. For the Japanese, the approach
was not unwelcome, as support for Chang's regime could facilitate
the company's expansion, they hoped, and also insulate Manchuria
from the political turbulence in the rest of the country. "For our part,
we must treat Chang well if we want to develop our position in the
Three Eastern Provinces [Manchuria]. As a matter of happenstance,
the interests of both sides are in harmony at this point", wrote prime
minister Hara Takashi in 1920.[33]

For a time, there was a degree of harmony. Mantetsu secured
promises of contracts to build new railway lines from Chang as well as
other profitable concessions. In turn the Japanese provided him with
money and arms, and the mere fact of Japanese support helped deter
enemies who would challenge his rule. But, precisely because Chang's
ultimate goals were not identical to those of the company, problems
soon arose. As mentioned at the start of the chapter, his ambitions to
rule the entire country led him into wars with other warlords and
with the nationalists and Communists outside Manchuria, and these
increased the risk of an invasion of Manchuria itself. To help fund his
wars, and also to prove to nationalists within Manchuria that he was
not a Japanese puppet, Chang began in the last years of his life to
promote businesses which competed with Mantetsu. These included
Chinese-owned railway lines, ports, mills, and a soybean trading
organization. By the mid-1920s, Japanese attitudes to Chang had
shifted dramatically: "The malignant cancer today of Japan's
Manchuria and Mongolia policy is Chang Tso-lin", proclaimed one
restless Kwantung Army officer at a speech at a hotel in Dairen.[34]

With Chang failing to provide the insulation the company
sought, the Japanese could not ignore popular movements growing

across China, and at a grassroots level in Manchuria itself. In fact, one of the first upsurges in Chinese nationalism was triggered by international negotiations following the First World War at which former German rights in China's Shantung province were demanded by Japan (who, this time, had supported the winning side). Angry Chinese students held demonstrations across the country. The whole basis of foreign incursion in China, including the "treaty port" system, began to be called into question.

Anti-imperialist boycotts and strikes were held against British and other foreign firms too. But, unlike the Japanese, and in contrast to their own response to the Indian rebellion of 1857, the British eventually chose to accommodate these new forces rather than fight them (trade with China was "not so important as to warrant incurring vital risks for its protection", explained a British minister[35]). While Britain thus began to surrender some of its concessions in the late 1920s, Japan felt the need to reinforce its grip on Manchuria.

Both the Kuomintang, the Nationalist party, and the newly formed Chinese Communist party, drew strength from growing anti-imperial sentiments, and for a time these two forces united in a campaign to fight or co-opt the numerous warlords, and to reunify China. In their "northern expedition" launched in 1926, both factions were led to a temporary victory by Chiang Kai-shek, the Kuomintang boss. Yet soon after the unification of part of the country, Kuomintang and Communist forces began fighting each other. The Communists, under Mao Tse-tung, retreated into the hills of the southeast. Their time was yet to come.

In Manchuria, in spite of Chang Tso-lin's assurances of support, Mantetsu found the population increasingly restive. Local Chinese newspapers were demanding the return of the company's leases. Chinese students at the company's medical college walked out of their classes, carrying banners and protesting at the "slave-like status" of Chinese workers. By 1927, tensions were running even higher. On 10th September in Mukden, for example, a Japanese car driver was mobbed by crowds and Japanese police who tried to restore order were hit by a barrage of stones. The following day, Japanese police tried to arrest a Chinese person who had scrawled "Down with Imperialism" on the back door of a Japanese shop, and were again attacked by an angry mob.[36]

The protests were also increasingly sophisticated, using methods which will be familiar to modern anti-multinational campaigners. Merchants' associations in Mukden, for example, ordered their members to boycott Japanese goods. Even international financiers came under pressure to withdraw support from the Japanese. When Mantetsu tried to secure a $30 million loan from the Morgan banking firm in America in 1927, a group of prominent Chinese businessmen and diplomats sent cables to Washington condemning the Japanese company as "imperialist" and an "instrument of alien domination over a large and rich portion of Chinese territory". Apparently as a result of this pressure, the American bankers withdrew from the deal.[37]

For the extremists in the Kwantung Army, such political volatility suggested only one solution: protecting Japanese interests in Manchuria by force of arms. Their hope was that by assassinating Chang Tso-lin, they could bring about a full Japanese takeover of the territory. Their political bosses in Tokyo, even military men like Tanaka Giichi, would not sanction such an audacious plan, and nor had their actions been authorized by Mantetsu. But for the likes of Colonel Kōmoto, the local officer who conceived the details of the plot, this just reinforced the need to present the politicians in Tokyo and the corporation with a *fait accompli*. And so it was that on 4th June 1928, when Chang Tso-lin, the mah-jongg-playing warlord was returning by train to Manchuria from his latest clash with the nationalists, his carriage was blown sky-high.

The plotting resumes

For a time after the assassination, however, the Kwantung Army extremists failed to achieve their goals. For the moderates in Tokyo, men such as Shidehara Kijuro, were still a significant force. They not only refused to consider any form of takeover of Manchuria following Chang Tso-lin's death, but pressed for the prosecution of the conspirators. Tanaka, on hearing news of the assassination is reported to have sighed, "What fools! They [the Kwantung Army] behave like children. They have no idea what the parent has to go through".[38] Several years later, however, with Mantetsu under even greater pressure in Manchuria, and with the moderates in Tokyo in retreat, Tanaka's unruly children – that is, the officers on the ground – would have their way.

At first the moderate Japanese held hopes that Chang Tso-lin's son, Chang Hsüeh-liang, who they allowed to succeed his father, would be more understanding of the needs of Mantetsu and other Japanese interests in the territory. But this was a serious misjudgment. The problem was not just that the younger Chang was aware that the Japanese were responsible for the explosion on the tracks, he was also as much a risk-taker and ruthless tactician as his father. Educated by an American tutor, and with a taste for fast cars and high-stakes poker, he had been given charge of one of his father's armies at the age of 24. At a later stage in his life, the dashing general is reputed to have ended a discussion with two of his commanders, whose advice he disagreed with, by shooting them dead.[39] In short, he was hardly a malleable character.

Though the young Chang wanted to avoid provoking a Japanese attempt on his own life, he began to sail close to the wind. He stepped up the building of a network of Chinese railways in Manchuria which would compete with Mantetsu's lines. He encouraged the growth of all sorts of indigenous industries, including mining, forestry, and milling. At an anti-Japanese demonstration in Mukden in November 1928 (and such protests were becoming even more frequent), he proclaimed to a crowd of students, "I shall uphold Chinese suzerainty in the face of all difficulties and will give my word that I shall not sell my country".[40] Most provocative of all, he struck an alliance with Chiang Kai-shek, the Nationalist leader, and began to refer all diplomatic issues to the Kuomintang government in Nanking. In 1931, the Kuomintang issued a foreign policy demanding the eventual return of all foreign-owned leases and railway rights in China, including those in Manchuria.

With Chang Hsüeh-liang providing even less protection from nationalist currents than his father, the Japanese on the ground in Manchuria began to fear they would be swept away. Their insecurity was compounded by the Great Depression which started in 1929, and which seriously dented Mantetsu's profits the following year. Mantetsu employees looked for support to societies such as the Manchurian Youth League, led by the head of the company's medical section, which pushed for greater protection of Japanese rights in the territory. They helped circulate long lists of Japanese grievances against the local Chinese, including attacks on Mantetsu's property, anti-Japanese propaganda in schools, and apparently excessive taxation. "If each irritation in itself has been only a pinprick, it was still the case where a thousand pinpricks equaled a slash of the saber", in the words of one angry Japanese activist.[41]

In Tokyo, meanwhile, moderate politicians were increasingly under attack, sometimes literally. The world-wide depression began to hit small businessmen and farmers across Japan. Unemployment and bankruptcies bred resentment against the powerful *zaibatsu* and the politicians who appeared to protect their interests. In 1930, the prime minister, Hamaguchi Yuko, was shot by a young man linked with one of the "patriotic" societies. The following year an even more audacious far-right plot was uncovered. Involving the deceptively peaceful sounding "Cherry Society", the plan, fortunately foiled, had been to eliminate the entire cabinet by air attack.[42]

It was in such a charged atmosphere, much more receptive to their goals, that the extremists in the Kwantung Army plotted their second attempt to secure Manchuria. Among their ranks now was Ishiwara Kanji, the ideologue who was predicting a final apocalyptic war with America, the western capitalist superpower. And Chang Hsüeh-liang, like his father, would be powerless to stop them.

Derailment

At this point in the story, the narrative can be accelerated. Although the history of Japan's takeover of Manchuria, and its subsequent construction of a puppet state there – called Manchukuo – holds many fascinations, and though the inherent tensions of multinational management created the conditions for these events, the story is now entering a period less relevant to the themes of this book.

Admittedly Mantetsu survived as an entity until Japan's military defeat in 1945, but from the early 1930s onwards, it was reduced to a component of a larger military machine and was operating in a territory now effectively controlled by the Japanese state. The East India Company had undergone a similar process, beginning as an independent multinational enterprise in a territory ruled by foreigners and ending up as an arm of Britain's imperial bureau-cracy. Manchuria in the 1930s, like India after 1857, is thus a subject more for historians of state-led imperialism, and international relations, rather than those interested in the dynamics of multi-national rule.

The historical significance of the "Manchurian Incident", as the start of the army takeover of Manchuria in 1931 came to be known, lies principally in the challenge it posed to international relations at the time – for it exposed the Japanese state's inability to rein in its own military. But it is worth restating the basic observation that it was the company, and not just the government in Tokyo, which failed to restrain the soldiers – even though their actions would fundamentally alter the political environment in which it conducted its business.

The plotting for the incident was undertaken not just by Ishiwara Kanji, but by dozens of Japanese officers in Manchuria, Korea and Tokyo. The government admittedly did make a flimsy attempt to stall them. When the cabinet in Tokyo heard rumors of their plans a messenger was sent to Manchuria to order the officers to desist, but the messenger chosen, a General Tatekawa, turned out to be a party to the plot himself. He contrived to arrive in Mukden after the first explosion had occurred and allowed himself to be plied with sake at a local inn until he passed out. Later excusing himself for failing to stop the plot, he explained, "I didn't make it in time".[43] As for Mantetsu's response to the plot, at the last moment one company director did try to warn the Kwantung Army against undertaking any rash moves – but his pleas fell on deaf ears;[44] and many of the company's managers appear to have been simply taken by surprise by the actions of the local soldiers.

The first explosion was a bomb planted on Mantetsu's tracks by Kwantung Army officers on 18th September 1931. In contrast to the bomb which killed Chang Tso-lin, this was a device so small that it merely left a tiny gap in the rails, and an express train was able to pass safely over them half an hour later.[45] But, as a fabricated act of Chinese aggression, it was sufficient – in the eyes of the Kwantung Army – to justify what followed. By the following morning, Japanese soldiers were in control of Mukden. Various staged incidents elsewhere in the territory helped escalate the situation in subsequent months, and the army moved from a takeover of the railway zone to a stage-by-stage invasion of the whole of Manchuria. This was largely complete by the following year. Chang Hsüeh-liang's army offered little resistance, though he himself survived. He concentrated what remained of his forces across the south-western border of Manchuria, from where they were reduced to launching guerrilla-style attacks on the Japanese.

The government in Tokyo did send reproving messages to the Kwantung Army, but these were mostly ignored. In the face of such defiance from their military representatives on the ground, both the cabinet and the army high command were persuaded to accept the invasion as a *fait accompli*. The directors of Mantetsu found themselves taking a similar position. One concession to the moderates in Tokyo and in the company was that, rather than formally annex the territory, the Kwantung Army established the puppet state of Manchukuo. This was nominally ruled by Pu Yi, a Chinese emperor deposed in 1912 who had been brought out of retirement by the Japanese. The Kwantung Army, however, pulled all the strings in his regime. Meanwhile, international criticism of Japan began to mount, and the League of Nations commissioned a report into its actions in Manchuria. At this point – in 1933 – Japan simply withdrew from the League.

With the Kwantung Army in control of Manchuria, it asserted its authority over Mantetsu too. This chimed with the anti-business sentiment of many officers. "In view of the evils of an uncontrolled capitalist economy, we will use whatever state power is necessary to control that economy", in the words of an official economic plan for Manchuria in 1932.[46] Admittedly Mantetsu's rail network expanded dramatically as a result of the invasion, but the military cut the company down to size in other ways. From 1937, for example, many of its subsidiaries, including its industrial holdings, were transferred to a new entity, the Manshū Heavy Industries Development Company, which became the prime engine of industrialization in the region. Even Mantetsu's remaining business – the railways – became much less profitable over time. With the war effort accelerating (a full-scale war with China broke out in 1937), the company was increasingly forced to transport troops and build new lines according to the needs of the military rather than commercial requirements.

One of the few parts of Mantetsu which the military allowed to flourish during the 1930s, and indeed depended upon heavily, was its research department. Though the Kwantung Army was an invading force, and often brutal in its methods, its intentions with regard to Manchuria were as utopian in some respects as Gotō Shinpei's vision for Mantetsu, and included rapid development of the region and a massive influx of Japanese immigrants. Such grand ambitions created fresh demands for research. This may help explain why the numerous left-wingers and Communist intellectuals in the department were allowed to continue working until a surprisingly late stage. But by 1942 and 1943, the military began to imprison them. One of those arrested was Nakanishi Tsutomu, the covert Communist operative. He had recently helped complete a detailed study, commissioned by the army, on the "Resistance Capacity of the Chinese" which argued that Japan would be unable to defeat China. These were conclusions that the military evidently preferred not to hear.[47]

Unsurprisingly, Mantetsu's collapse coincided with that of the army, in 1945, and its railway lines were taken over by the Soviets and the Chinese. A company that emerged out of the ashes of one war had burnt itself out in another. And Manchuria, the region whose colonization it had pioneered, was soon part of Chinese territory again, though – like other parts of China in the immediate post-war years – it became at first a battle-zone between Communists and Nationalists.

Current changes

Disentangling the historical and timeless elements of Mantetsu's story has not been easy – and few modern multinationals have been so embroiled in violence and war as was this Japanese giant. Even so, in the unavoidable political tensions faced by the company in its earlier peaceful period (which all its efforts at social research and economic development failed to prevent), and in its general difficulties in predicting and influencing local actions and events, can be discerned phenomena which will recur regularly in subsequent chapters.

It is difficult, too, to disentangle the imprint left by Mantetsu on attitudes to foreign investment in Asia in the post-war period from

the impact of other companies, including the *zaibatsu*, and from
hostility to Japan as a result of the war. The role of the *zaibatsu* in
Japan's descent into war is a complex and controversial subject in
itself – in spite of the anti-business sentiments of some in the army,
these giant conglomerates often profited from territorial expansion
and from the forced labor of Chinese and other Asians;[48] in fact,
shortly after the war, General MacArthur, the allied commander in
charge of the occupation of Japan, took steps to dismantle them.
What can be said for sure, however, is that local memories of
Mantetsu mingled with those of the *zaibatsu* and of western firms
create an underlying sense of suspicion towards foreign investors.

It is a fitting quirk of history that the Communists' post-war
victory in China, which led to that country's decades-long isolation
from the global economy, was indirectly due to the actions of Chang
Hsüeh-liang, the Manchurian warlord's son. His contribution to the
Communists' success actually occurred roughly a decade before, in
1936. At this stage, Chang, having been expelled from Manchuria,
had leant heavily on the Chinese Nationalist leader, Chiang Kai-shek,
to stop fighting the Communists and instead to unite with them in a
common front against the Japanese. This resulted in a second period
of alliance between the Kuomintang and the Communists and
although this did not succeed in holding back Japanese advances, it
did help the Communists to escape defeat and live to fight another
day. In other words it was Chang Hsüeh-liang's desire to fight the
imperial power that had killed his father which assisted the
Communists at an important juncture.

Chang Hsüeh-liang may not have intended the eventual victory
of Mao Tse-tung's forces over the Nationalists in 1949, but the
Communists considered his intervention crucial and, for them, he
became a national hero. The defeated Nationalists, however, were
none too happy with him: they took the warlord's son with them
when they fled to Taiwan, and kept him their effective prisoner until
1990. Confined in his house in Taipei, the once-dashing former ruler
of Manchuria kept himself occupied studying Chinese history as he
grew old. Chang Hsüeh-liang died in October 2001, at his home in
Hawaii, where he had settled after his release. He had reached 101.
On news of his death, the Chinese president Jiang Zemin hailed him
as a "great patriot".[49]

The last word, however, goes to Itō Takeo, one of Mantetsu's researchers imprisoned in the early 1940s. Like a number of his colleagues, Itō became involved in leftist politics in post-war Japan. He visited Manchuria in May 1961. With his sense of idealism, and perhaps naivety, undiminished in spite of his age, he marveled at Communist China's efforts to industrialize the region, and at what he described as their "splendid" city planning. He also visited Mantetsu's old railway lines, now efficiently run by the Chinese, which he found moving. He wrote in his memoirs:

> The morning sun glistened on the roadbed, and the sense of cleanliness at the station was stunning. I felt this sense of cleanliness again when I saw the Rail West Factory Area and when I visited a suburban commune. I had a strange feeling of self-reproach and a deep impression that this was a reborn visage of the "Chinamen" whom Japanese had ridiculed as "filthy".[50]

What Itō was witnessing was the Chinese trying to build an industrial empire of their own out of the rubble of Mantetsu. And they had no intention – for the time being at least – of allowing the patronizing foreigners back in.

FOUR

Jungle culture
The United Fruit Company

When the trumpet sounded, it was
all prepared on the earth,
and Jehovah parceled out the earth
to Coca-Cola, Inc., Anaconda,
Ford Motors, and other entities:
The Fruit Company, Inc.
reserved for itself the most succulent,
the central coast of my own land,
the delicate waist of America.
It re-christened its territories
as the "Banana Republics" [...]

Pablo Neruda, Chilean poet, on the United Fruit Company.[1]

Bananas may seem to be an improbable focus for a story about international power politics, intrigue and corruption. But United Fruit, the American banana multinational, was involved in exploits as extraordinary as the fruit is innocent-looking. More than any other company (with the possible exception of ITT, whose controversial maneuvers in Chile are described briefly in the next part of the book), United Fruit's name has been seared on the consciousness of Latin Americans as a symbol of American economic imperialism. Its actions have been reviled by a generation of indigenous writers, including Pablo Neruda and Gabriel Garcia Marquez.

United Fruit operated in a variety of countries throughout the region, particularly in Central America, but the episode for which it has been most fiercely attacked took place in one country,

CENTRAL AMERICA 1950s

MEXICO

GUATEMALA
Guatemala
City

BRITISH
HONDURAS
Belize

Usumacinta
Motagua

EL SALVADOR
San
Salvador

HONDURAS
Tegucigalpa

NICARAGUA
Managua

COSTA RICA
San José

PANAMA
CANAL ZONE

PANAMA
Panama
City

COLOMBIA

Ciénaga

Caribbean Sea

JAMAICA

HAITI

Pacific Ocean

0   200   400   600 miles

75

80

85

90

5

10

15

Guatemala, in 1954. For there, as will be seen, the company had a hand in toppling a democratically elected government, one of the first experienced by the country after many decades of dictatorship. Following this coup of 1954, Guatemala once again entered into a period of authoritarian rule, and out of that emerged a civil war which tore the country apart for 36 years. Were it not for the company's actions, its critics say, this terrible historical trajectory might have been avoided.

This particular episode, the coup of 1954, will provide the focus for this chapter. For it allows a crucial question to be posed: what sort of mind-set leads a multinational company to support a coup against a democratic government? The period in history is important to bear in mind. In the days of the East India Company and the British South Africa Company, the toppling of native governments was – one might say – a standard business technique. But this was the 1950s: a world war had recently been fought to uphold the principles of democracy and freedom, and to bring an end to the aggressive imperialism of countries such as Japan – whose South Manchurian Railway Company also had been closely associated with such violent business methods.

So what made United Fruit act as it did: was it a case of managers coolly calculating the risks posed by the new government, and then consciously disregarding their ethical principles by deciding to support its downfall? Or was this more of an unthinking reaction – not necessarily more justifiable – but a case of the company's internal culture, its own set of principles, blinding it to what lay in its own interests, as well as to the rights and wrongs of the situation?

An outline of the plot

Before delving into the psyche of the company and its bosses, it will help first to understand some of the basic facts. Guatemala was one of a number of small, poverty-stricken Central American nations in which United Fruit had large plantations. Every year, the company sold tens of millions of bunches of bananas from its plantations to markets in America, Europe and elsewhere. This was a steadily, if unspectacularly, profitable business – since it was founded in 1899 United Fruit had made an average return of around 13% on its net assets.[2]

The company was gigantic by the standards of Central American economies – locals nicknamed it "El Pulpo", or the octopus, because its tentacles of power seemed to reach everywhere. But it was in turn dwarfed in size by many other American firms, including a number of the chain-stores to which it sold the fruit, so perceptions of its size depended on the perspective taken.

The right-wing dictators who had long ruled Guatemala had mostly inclined to the company's point of view. They granted it concessions on favorable terms, often in exchange for bribes, and they allowed a company with which it had close links, the International Railways of Central America, to monopolize the building and management of the country's railways. But in 1944, this lucrative situation for "El Pulpo" began to come under threat. A popular uprising of students, middle-class professionals, and young military officers brought to power a series of more left-wing governments. The first of these was run by a former university lecturer and philosopher called Juan José Arévalo, who believed in what he called "spiritual socialism". He was succeeded in 1951 by Jacobo Arbenz Guzmán, a young, intelligent, good-looking army officer.

It was President Arbenz who was to provoke the octopus into its response. Admittedly he may not have been above criticism himself. He had won power through democratic elections, but a year before that his chief political rival was mysteriously gunned down on a bridge outside the Guatemalan capital. Some said that Arbenz had given the order for the killing. But whatever suspicions surrounded Arbenz's past, he was not – as United Fruit argued – a rabid Communist, and nor was he receiving support from the Soviets to turn Guatemala into an arm of their Communist empire, as some in the American government feared at the time. Subsequent research has indicated that the Russians were, in fact, little interested in this small Central American country, focused as they were on events in Europe and Asia. At one point Guatemalan Communist politicians did persuade Czechoslovakia to sell them some weapons but the support such local reds received directly from Moscow, it transpires, extended little further than being sent some free copies of *Pravda*.[3]

Similarly, rather than being evidence for an international Communist conspiracy, the reforms Arbenz promoted once in power were a moderate attempt to create a broader basis for development

Guatemalan president Jacobo Arbenz (right) shares an apparently friendly toast
with America's ambassador, Rudolf S. Schoenfeld, in 1952. Two years later
Arbenz's government would be toppled by an American-backed coup.

– for the structure of the Guatemalan economy remained semi-
feudal, dominated as it was by a small number of families (in 1950,
for example, just 2% of the population owned three-quarters of its
arable land). Although Arbenz counted among his allies a number of
Communist politicians in Guatemala, he was equally influenced by
his intelligent, ambitious wife, Maria, a socially concerned daughter
of one of El Salvador's wealthiest coffee families. In his inaugural
speech, Arbenz talked of turning Guatemala into a "modern
capitalist state" and insisted that:

> foreign capital will always be welcome as long as it adjusts to
> local conditions, remains always subordinate to Guatemalan
> laws, cooperates with the economic development of the
> country, and strictly abstains from intervening in the nation's
> social and political life ...[4]

This was left-leaning, but hardly revolutionary, talk. However, one aspect of Arbenz's policies in particular made it difficult for United Fruit's bosses to restrain themselves: his land reform program. This involved expropriating and redistributing uncultivated land held by the country's largest property owners. United Fruit was one such landowner. Interestingly, the United States itself had sponsored similar moderate land redistribution schemes in Japan and Formosa (Taiwan), and even the CIA sometimes supported such programs as a way of taking the wind out of the sails of real Communist revolution. But, with its interests directly threatened, United Fruit was disinclined to compromise.

Samuel Zemurray, United Fruit's boss, laid the foundations for the dramatic events of 1954. "Sam-the-banana-man", as he was nicknamed, had a colorful history, which will be explored later in the chapter. In the early 1950s, towards the end of his career, he instructed the firm's public-relations consultant to launch a campaign to alert the American public to the threat posed by President Arbenz. Dozens of influential journalists were flown to Guatemala on lavish trips paid for – and carefully stage managed – by the company. They returned, and wrote impassioned articles about the specter of Communism in Guatemala. "There can be no battle more decisive than the Battle for the Western Hemisphere", proclaimed one journalist.[5] The American public had few reasons to doubt these stories – Guatemala was a small Central American country of which most people had heard little before.

The company was also making full use at the time of its impressive list of political contacts in Washington, pressing on them the need for firm action. On United Fruit's payroll as a consultant was Thomas G. Corcoran, a well-connected lawyer described by *Fortune* magazine as a "purveyor of concentrated influence".[6] One of his friends was Walter Bedell Smith, a former CIA director and senior State Department official who later was appointed to United Fruit's board. The Secretary of State himself, John Foster Dulles, had represented United Fruit in his early days as a lawyer, as had his brother, Allen Dulles, the head of the CIA.[7] These were powerful contacts, so the company's concerns could not fail to be heard in America.

Smoking guns

United Fruit did not actually pull the trigger in 1954. As will be seen, the main actor behind the actual coup was the CIA, which was motivated by its own exaggerated views about the threat of Communism, as well as by the concerns expressed by the company. Even so, United Fruit's support for the events of the period went beyond lobbying American journalists and politicians.

It appears to have had a direct hand, for example, in an earlier attempted coup against Arbenz in 1953 when some disgruntled Guatemalan army officers and several hundred of their supporters captured and held for 17 hours the provincial town of Salamá. This revolt – unlike the one that was to follow – was quickly crushed by government forces. But according to the rebels who were arrested, they had received US$64,000 in cash from United Fruit to undertake the little experiment.[8]

The company's actions remain shrouded in a degree of mystery. However, a particularly useful and revealing source for this chapter – because it provides an inside perspective – is the memoirs of Thomas P. McCann. McCann joined United Fruit in 1952, as an eager young recruit, and rose to a senior public-relations role within the company. His attitude towards the giant corporation which nurtured him for several decades was a mix of admiration and suspicion. According to his frank memoirs, written after he had left the company in the early 1970s, United Fruit was "involved at every level" of the coup in Guatemala. He had been told by his colleagues, for example, that the CIA "shipped down the weapons by Fruit Company boats", and the coup's leader was "provided food and housing on Fruit Company property".[9]

Indeed, one prerequisite for the coup had been to find a suitably sympathetic Guatemalan military figure to lead it. Some CIA agents together with a former United Fruit manager began by approaching Miguel Ydígoras Fuentes, a general then living in exile in El Salvador.[10] As a henchman of a former Guatemalan dictator, Ydígoras was suitably right-wing. However, even he blanched at some of the conditions which the Americans demanded for their support. These included "to promise to favor the United Fruit Company and the International Railways of Central America" and "to destroy the railroad workers labor union", as Ydígoras later noted in his autobiography *My War with Communism*.[11] So instead the CIA settled on another exiled army officer to lead the coup, Castillo Armas, a neat-looking, mustachioed man whom the Americans found working as a furniture salesman in Honduras.[12] He accepted the deal on offer.

With a frontman procured, the military preparations proceeded. A ragtag army of mercenaries and Guatemalan exiles was assembled in Honduras. "The voice of liberation", a propaganda radio station, broadcast denunciations of Arbenz across the airwaves of Central America. The CIA funded purchases of American weapons and planes through a dummy company and American fighter pilots, many of them retired from the air force, were secretly recruited in preparation for an aerial bombardment. And so the stage was set. One of Guatemala's first democratically elected governments was about to be toppled. The story of the actual coup and its aftermath will be returned to later. With the basic facts in place, the crucial question now can be examined more closely: what sort of mind-set leads a multinational company to act in this way?

It would be wrong to assume that the company's managers consciously surrendered their principles to protect the company's profits, or that their actions were part of a carefully conceived political strategy. The point of this chapter is not to defend United Fruit, which would be a difficult task. It is rather to suggest a more true-to-life explanation for what occurred: that United Fruit's support for the coup was a knee-jerk response partly brought about by the insularity of the company's internal culture, and its failure to evolve with the times. Put briefly, the company had become imbued from its early days with an audacious, proud and inward-looking ethos, an approach to business which had underpinned its commercial success through the decades. Yet this internal culture was also what helped blind United Fruit's managers to the external ramifications and perceptions of their actions, so that – in their eyes – support for the coup in Guatemala was a natural and justifiable response to the political situation at hand.

As it turned out, this response was not only unethical. As will become apparent from the dramatic events following 1954, it also would damage the company's long-term interests. For by this point in history the political environment in Central and Latin America was changing in a way United Fruit's managers, wrapped up in the company's out-dated view of the world, had failed to anticipate. In this way, and as with the companies examined in previous chapters, United Fruit's story illustrates a challenge facing many modern multinationals – even those with admirable intentions. For multinationals past and present, a strong corporate culture is crucial for success: it unites employees, and brings a sense of direction to what are often vast and disparate organizations. But it also holds risks – for if it becomes too strong and enveloping, companies can become dangerously insulated from the outside world. As with United Fruit, they may become blind to the external impacts of the decisions they take, and to broad political shifts which can threaten their future.

Conquerors of the tropics

The various strands that made up United Fruit's culture will be teased out in the following pages. But for their origin it is as well to start with some stories of the company's founders, wild and determined men, who were said to have brought civilization to the jungle. For these stories, not dissimilar to the creation myths which unite many tribes, undoubtedly would have been recycled and retold repeatedly within the company, thereby instilling in new recruits a sense of identity and pride. They are reproduced in a number of the early accounts of the company.[13]

One of the mythologized founders was Minor Cooper Keith. The nephew of a well-known American entrepreneur – Henry Meiggs – who had built railroads in Chile and Peru, Keith's principal ambition was to criss-cross Central America with railtracks. The degree of his determination was clear as early as 1870, when he and his uncle were contracted to build a railroad in Costa Rica from a port on the Caribbean to the country's capital. The route traversed dense jungle, where tropical diseases such as dysentery and malaria were rife. The first 25 miles of railroad alone cost the lives of some 4,000 workers. Among other casualties during the construction of the line were three of Keith's brothers. Nonetheless Keith, at the time still in his early 20s, continued the project undaunted.[14] In spite of – or perhaps because of – his unshakable nature, Keith was able to earn the res-

Samuel's battles

The legends of the swashbuckling endeavors of United Fruit's founders did not begin and end with Minor Cooper Keith. Another of the company's legendary managers was Sam-the-banana-man: Samuel Zemurray. His significance to the story is not just that, as mentioned before, he helped prepare the ground for the 1954 coup, but that his complex character also helped shape the very culture of the company. (Also, later in the company's history, in the 1960s and 1970s, there arose another colorful senior manager with curious similarities to Zemurray – but that is a tale for the end of the chapter.)

Zemurray had arrived in America in 1892, a Jewish immigrant from Bessarabia, Russia. From poor beginnings as an independent banana trader in Alabama, he built a multinational banana empire of his own – the Cuyamel Fruit Company – which was taken over by United Fruit in 1929. As with Keith, his employees spoke fondly of his down-to-earth charm, lack of ostentation, and interest in individuals – "a trait that caused him, for example, to shun a bankers' banquet in New Orleans while talking trade and home problems with nondescript tung-nut gatherers".[22] Then there was Zemurray's charity, which will be explored in more detail below.

Yet it was the same individual who – in a foretaste of the events of the 1950s – engineered the downfall of a government in Honduras in 1911. This was an episode, in itself, of great, and intricate, intrigue. To summarize briefly: Zemurray was worried that the Honduran government would be unable to grant him the concessions he desired for his banana business, which included relief from import duty. This was because the government of the small country was also under pressure from another set of foreign capitalists: American banking interests were demanding control of the country's customs collection to help them finance the large debts which the government owed. If this were to happen, Zemurray knew, the American bankers would be unlikely to grant him the concessions he desired.

Sam-the-banana-man's solution to this political Gordian knot was to shoot his way through it. He made a deal with Manuel Bonilla, a former Honduran leader living in exile in America. Bonilla bought a surplus navy ship with Zemurray's money, and hired a small army of tough mercenaries led by "General" Lee Christmas (a man who "would fight anybody at the drop of a coin"[23]) and Guy "Machine

Gun" Malony. Early one morning the conspirators set sail from New Orleans to Honduras. Fittingly, they had hidden for the night in a brothel in order to give the slip to American secret service agents who were watching their every move: "Well, compadre, this is the first time I've ever heard of anyone going from a whorehouse to a White House. Let's be on our way!", bellowed Christmas to one of his colleagues.[24] Honduras proved an easy country to invade, and the government was soon toppled. Bonilla was set up as the new president and, with the American bankers' plan now dead in the water, Zemurray was granted the concessions he desired.

The integration of Zemurray's business within the larger United Fruit empire was also a turbulent process, and the battles between Sam-the-banana-man and United Fruit's management at the time provide a further key to the corporate culture, and the internal tensions which drove the company onwards. In fact, long before United Fruit's acquisition of Zemurray's firm Cuyamel in 1929, the two companies had engaged in bitter competition, motivated at least in part by personal factors. Zemurray had once mentioned how he enjoyed "poking the giant's knees with his little shovel".[25] This was an understatement. Competition between the two firms at various points came close to provoking war between Guatemala and Honduras on account of the fact that both companies were developing banana land in the region of the Motagua valley, an area along the border between Guatemala and Honduras which was claimed by each country. With Cuyamel allied with Honduras, and United with Guatemala, both governments sent troops to the area, and various skirmishes erupted between 1915 and 1929. But however much Zemurray enjoyed "poking the giant's knees", when the time came he was also willing to enter into a peace agreement with the giant – he received $31.5 million in United Fruit stock for the sale of his company in 1929, making him the largest single shareholder in the banana giant. He also, for the time at least, went into retirement.

Personality clash

The tensions surrounding the company, however, did not end there. By the 1920s and 30s, United Fruit had begun to grow apart from its roots: its most senior managers were no longer men in the mold of Minor Cooper Keith, tough men with an appetite for a dangerous life in Central America. Rather they were members of America's east-coast establishment who preferred to manage the company from its Boston headquarters. The company's board, for example, included various powerful Bostonian bankers and lawyers, and some descendants of American presidents.

By contrast, Zemurray not only retained his appetite for the rough and tumble of life in the banana-growing regions, he also was excluded from the society of such folk. As a Jew, he was unable to join Boston's establishment clubs, nor live in Boston's most socially exclusive suburbs (at the time anti-semitism had little of the stigma now attached to it in America).[26] "Over the years I have heard many stories about how this treatment galled Zemurray, but [...] Zemurray was too big a man to care", argued Thomas McCann in his memoirs (the former public relations manager was himself an admirer of Sam-the-banana-man).[27]

While Zemurray may have disregarded such slights, however, just a few years after he had sold Cuyamel, his relations with United Fruit's board hit a crisis point. The trigger was the Great Depression, which had caused a slump in profits. With his own wealth tied up in the company's stock, Zemurray demanded an audience with the board in 1933, and lashed out at what he saw as their incompetence. "You gentlemen have been fucking up this business long enough. I'm going to straighten it out", he roared.[28] However much the company's directors might have disdained Zemurray, they could not ignore such a major shareholder. Zemurray demanded – and was granted – the position of managing director. Such was his no-nonsense reputation in the financial markets that United Fruit's stock soared on his reappointment.

Sam-the-banana-man remained at the helm of the company for almost two decades. He overhauled its operations, and devolved power to the company's managers in Central America, the local men whose judgment he trusted most. Though it took more than a decade for profits to reach pre-Depression levels, the company slowly recovered under Zemurray's leadership. His style remained tough, uncompromising, and – when the circumstances demanded – audacious. In short, he imprinted his personality on the culture of the company, just as Keith had done before him.

With such stories in mind, the company's behavior in the 1950s is starting to look more like the application of a trusted old formula by the managers, an instinctive response rather than anything they themselves would have viewed as a moral compromise. But before returning to the dramatic events of 1954, it is necessary to look more closely at how interactions between United Fruit and the Guatemalan political system had evolved over time – for that holds another clue to the company's response at the time of the coup.

Compromising politicians

Amid the intricacies of United Fruit's dealings in Guatemala, two basic points are clear. First the company came to depend over the decades on the continuation of a certain sort of right-wing, authoritarian regime in Guatemala known – in the political terminology of Central America – as a "liberal dictatorship". Such a pattern is not universal. The relationships between companies and governments can take a variety of forms, some of which are described elsewhere in this book, and many are more benign than this. But in the case of United Fruit and the Guatemalan dictators, such was the degree of co-dependency in the relationship that any threat to this historic pattern – as occurred with the emergence of left-wing regimes in the 1940s and 1950s – could only trigger a fierce response from the company.

The second point is that over time these "liberal dictatorships" had helped to insulate United Fruit from popular pressure, thereby discouraging it from developing a broader understanding of Guatemalan society. For had it done so, it certainly would have viewed the reforms of the 1950s in a more pragmatic light. In previous chapters it was seen how indigenous resentments against a foreign multinational often can prove explosive. The absence of such a backlash against United Fruit until the 1950s is not because such resentments were not rife, but because the political system – itself a legacy of an earlier wave of colonialism – had put a tight lid on dissent.

The liberal dictators of the late nineteenth and early twentieth century – men such as Justo Rufino Barrios, Manuel Estrada Cabrera, and Jorge Ubico Castaneda – tended to believe that exports and foreign investment offered one of the best hopes for Guatemala's backward economy (which was perhaps not unreasonable); but they also usually convinced themselves that Guatemala needed a period of authoritarian, military-backed, rule. Some of the dictators were positively paranoid about dissent. "I have no friends, only domesticated enemies", Jorge Ubico, who ruled from 1931 to 1944, once told *Time* magazine.[29] Ubico had a habit of executing his political opponents, and kept a network of spies and informants across Guatemala. (He also believed he bore a physical resemblance to Napoleon, and surrounded himself with portraits of the emperor.[30])

Across Central America the liberal regimes of the period followed a basic pattern. Ralph Lee Woodward Jr, a historian of the region, has characterized them thus:

> They built roads, ports, and bridges, and they expanded agricultural production and exports. Yet they failed to promote the general prosperity. One landed oligarchy dedicated to traditional values simply gave way to another which, in concert with foreign investors, reserved the advantages of modern civilization for itself.[31]

An indication of the attitude of the Guatemalan dictators towards foreign investors can be seen in the public festivities which were sometimes arranged to celebrate deals with them. Following the signing of a railway contract in 1900, for example, "fireworks were set off, the President was serenaded and universal joy was shown", according to an American diplomat at the time.[32]

While negotiations between the dictators and United Fruit and its associated companies were not without their tensions, they resulted in a series of generous concessions for the Americans. A few details from a concession negotiated between Minor Cooper Keith and Estrada Cabrera in 1904 will suffice to illustrate the point. This gave Keith the job of completing the main railway line in the north of country – which was admittedly a significant task – but in return it assigned him and his associates not just ownership of the entire railway for 99 years, but also 168,000 acres of prime banana land, and exemption for all bananas from export duties or local taxes for 35 years. It also guaranteed the company an annual income of 5% on its investment for 15 years.

This was the sort of deal that might have provoked howls of outrage from an independent parliament, had such an institution existed in Guatemala. At a later stage it was revealed that Keith had given Estrada Cabrera 500 shares in the railroad company – though this was a minor payment compared with the bribery which was allegedly involved in other concessions. "I am particularly pleased at the fair and liberal manner in which the terms of our contract have been carried out by the government of Guatemala", noted one of Keith's delighted business partners in the 1904 deal.[33]

To summarize the *quid pro quo* which developed between the company and Guatemala's elite: the latter received bribes and kick-backs,[34] tax revenues (or at least whatever tax the company paid after allowing for the exemptions it was granted), and of course the company's investment in projects such as railways deemed to be important to Guatemala's development. By providing a safe haven for United Fruit's investments, Guatemalan dictators also could help ensure US government support for their regimes, which was an important deterrent to would-be coup-plotters.

What United Fruit got in return was not just lucrative concessions, but also the state's enthusiastic and occasionally brutal protection of its interests. Crimes against foreigners were often punished with particular severity, which was comforting for Americans anxious about the dangers of operating in the region. Also Guatemalan soldiers and police were made available to crack down on workers who threatened to strike. In fact, the most bloody example of such state support occurred not in Guatemala, but in Colombia where in 1929 the military gunned down striking United Fruit workers, killing as many as 400, according to one estimate[35] (the Colombian novelist, Gabriel Garcia Marquez, provides a vivid account of this particular episode in his novel *One Hundred Years of Solitude*).

Hidden dissent

United Fruit might have developed a better understanding of the need for reform were it not for the fact that, as mentioned before, the political structure of many countries in the region still reflected a colonial system that effectively stifled popular pressure. And even at home in America, criticisms of the company were rare. Within Guatemala, the imbalance in power extended beyond the office of the dictator: a minority of the population of European descent controlled most economic resources, while native Indians (and to a lesser extent the offspring of intermarriages between these two groups, who were growing in number) languished in poverty. It is not that United Fruit faced no criticism within Guatemala, nor that the company simply ignored political developments. But the loudest complaints the company heard came from sections of the country's elite – such as, for example, the independent coffee and banana planters who often were annoyed about the rates the company charged them for transporting their produce.

As for the Indians, the liberal dictators tended to view them in much the same way as Cecil Rhodes's men had regarded the natives of Africa – as a backward, often lazy, group of people who needed to be compelled to work in the plantations and industries of fairer-skinned families. Any suggestions that the natives deserved stronger representation in national affairs were often quickly dismissed. "It is not yet time for the Indians to consciously poison themselves with politics", as Jorge Ubico once explained.[36] Even Miguel Angel Asturias, the Guatemalan novelist who was a fierce critic of United Fruit, described Indians in 1923 as "dirty, slow, barbaric and cruel",[37] and called for the immigration of more Europeans to Guatemala to help solve the problem.

Under the liberal dictators, as in colonial times, Indians continued to be dispossessed of their communal lands. Vagrancy laws and systems of bondage (whereby they were encouraged to incur unpayable debts) helped push them into the wage labor market. United Fruit benefited from these policies, though its labor force included not just native Indians, but many ethnic groups – including Jamaicans and African Americans – who sought work with the company voluntarily.

Another mechanism which might have encouraged United Fruit to ponder the long-term stability of Guatemala's feudal system would have been pressure from politically influential groups in America. But, in spite of the longstanding current of concern about the behavior of large domestic firms, such as Rockefeller's Standard Oil, American criticisms of United Fruit were more notable by their absence, at least in the first half of the twentieth century.

An analysis of press coverage of the company in the *New York Times* in the 1930s, for example, shows a preponderance of positive stories about, among other issues, the company's financial performance, and the pleasures of taking a cruise on one of its ships (the "Great White Fleet" made space for American holiday-makers as well as bananas).[38] And one of the few occasions that the American government took major issue with United Fruit prior to the 1950s was over the level of railroad rates charged to American exporters to transport their produce in Guatemala. In other words, it was concern over domestic economic interests, rather than the welfare of Guatemalan peasants, which prodded the home government into action.

Admittedly Samuel Zemurray had an American critic, in the form of Huey Long, a populist, anti-big-business governor of Louisiana, who had made a name for himself attacking the Standard Oil Company of Louisiana. But, in a now familiar pattern, it appears to have been domestic issues which really angered Long – in this case, his suspicion that Sam-the-banana-man was bankrolling his political opponents in Louisiana. And while Long complained about Zemurray's habit of provoking coups in Central America to protect his assets, his argument focused on the loss of American lives. "Time after time, except for the blood of the soldiers of this country, his [Zemurray's] 'concessions' would have gone up in smoke", railed one of Long's political tracts.[39]

There is one interesting exception to this pattern of American ambivalence about the impact of United Fruit on native societies: a critique of the company published in 1935 entitled *Banana Empire*. Written jointly by an academic from Columbia University and a former United Fruit manager, some of its criticisms were sharp, and strangely prescient:

> [...] this powerful company has throttled competitors, domi-nated governments, manacled railroads, ruined planters [...] Such usage of power by a corporation of a strongly indus-trialized nation in relatively weak foreign countries con-stitutes a variety of economic imperialism [...] Its very domination of so many different interest groups may prove its downfall, since competitors, planters, workers, politicians and the proverbial "man in the street" find common cause in opposing its dictatorship.[40]

More exposure to these sort of ideas might have led the company to expect, and to work with, the democratic, left-ward shift in

Guatemalan politics which began in 1944. But before returning to the story of the coup, one last detour is needed, one last journey back into the minds of United Fruit's managers. For it was not just stories about the audacious founders of the company, nor the insulation provided by Guatemala's political system, but the manager's very understanding of the outside world, which helps explain why it supported the toppling of one of the country's first democratic governments.

Through the octopus's eyes

For a start, the direct experiences of managers in Guatemala are likely to have upheld a sense of pride and belief in the moral rectitude of the company. Many of United Fruit's plantations were enclaves, distinct from established population centers in the country. Out of the jungle, as mentioned before, the company had built entire towns with housing for workers, roads, electricity grids, and schools. Although workers were not paid much by American standards, their wages were far above the average in Guatemala.

In spite of United Fruit's dominant influence in these enclaves, a visiting manager would not necessarily have encountered a local populace cowed by United Fruit or one deferential to American values. An academic, Catherine LeGrand, has recently studied a former United Fruit banana zone – this one in Colombia – and found a complex melting pot of races and cultural influences, of which the company was just one. As one local inhabitant recalled:

> We are open, but not submissive. It's impossible to dominate us. [...] The United Fruit Company had no concerted program of cultural change. They lived over there in their chicken coops. We didn't mix with them; we (pardon my saying this) never found their white women attractive; ours, yes, but not theirs.[41]

As well as the healthy skepticism of some of the local people, there were two other aspects of the company's presence which many managers would have witnessed with their own eyes. The first was its impact on public health. To protect its workforce from the diseases that wiped out thousands of Minor Keith's men, United Fruit invested in programs to eradicate malaria, yellow fever, hookworm and other tropical ailments. It set up clinics and inoculation programs, drained swamps and installed sanitation systems, and these efforts benefited not just workers and their families but entire communities. The results were often significant: the incidence of malaria among the company's workers on the Atlantic side of Guatemala, for example, fell from 22% in 1929 to 0.3% by 1955.[42]

The second was the company's philanthropy. Under Samuel Zemurray, United Fruit established a tropical agriculture school in Honduras, which provided free education to poor farm-workers from across Central America. Sam-the-banana-man also funded a botanical garden in Honduras, and a center for the study of Mayan art and Middle American research at Tulane University in the United States. The company's research into agricultural technology and the control of plant diseases was another activity which benefited the region as a whole.

The company's size, power, and apparent benevolence, also provided many managers with a sense of security – as though they were working for a sort of corporate welfare state. "I used to think that there was no catastrophe so big that the company couldn't protect everyone, including myself, under its umbrella", wrote McCann, United Fruit's public relations man – though the downside, he argued, was that "no country or ideology, or system of government on earth had more power over you."[43]

As for the company's past misdeeds, these could be brushed off as one-off events, or the fault of indigenous governments, and quite distinct from present conditions. As early as 1927, one senior manager was arguing that "all past troubles involving diplomacy have been caused by small, irresponsible companies and individuals [...] or by the entrance of foreigners into countries where governments were unstable and revolutions frequent. Fortunately these conditions do not exist today."[44]

The company's self-justifying ideology thus became like a shield of armor, insulating it further from popular sentiment. The dangers of this should have been apparent. In the 1950s, for example, United Fruit sponsored a series of adverts in Latin America that, while aimed at improving its reputation in the region, were unintentionally counterproductive. The adverts showed a map of the Americas on which was superimposed a circle symbolizing an apparently benevolent cycle of trade, with basic produce, such as bananas, exported from Latin America to the North, while sophisticated manufactured goods, such as cars and TV sets, moved in the opposite direction. Yet what was intended as a representation of the benefits of economic integration, was viewed by many as a crude symbol of imperial exploitation. In the words of McCann:

> The company was so isolated from the impact of its actions and attitudes that the ads continued for almost five years in the tropics, inflaming Latins and working against any conceivable company interest.[45]

One set of ideas, crucially, did penetrate the corporate mind-set: the anti-Communist fervor which was sweeping America after the Second World War. Although this certainly fueled the company's opposition to Jacobo Arbenz in Guatemala, it is unlikely that its adoption of these ideas was merely a cynical ploy to protect its assets. It is important to remember that America's eventual victory in the Cold War was far from assured at the time. For all the excesses of Senator McCarthy's paranoid trials, the fears across America about the "red menace" were sincere.

It may now seem laughable, for example, that in 1954 United Fruit produced a short propaganda film called "Why the Kremlin Hates Bananas", but McCann says of the manager who oversaw production of the film that "the movie had been [his] pride and joy, and he believed in it".[46] Another fervent anti-Communist, Spruille Braden, a former American ambassador to Chile, was hired as a consultant to United Fruit in the early 1950s. Like many advisors to the company, he was concerned that "if Arbenz and the Communists won out the malignancy would spread throughout Central America".[47]

State of emergency

If United Fruit's involvement in the coup of 1954 now seems more understandable (though still not excusable), if it can be recognized as the predictable outcome of a proud, blind culture, and as an instinctive reaction, based on a blinkered view of the external political environment, it may come as less of a surprise that it was not just ordinary Guatemalans who suffered in the wake of the coup, but United Fruit itself. For the world outside had now begun to change in ways the company's managers had not envisaged. The corporate culture had become outdated; it was now more a liability than a strength.

As mentioned at the start of the chapter, this encapsulates a dilemma for modern multinationals, and one which will be observed again later in the book. Strong cultures are important for corporate success, but they can also lead to insularity and inertia in the face of fast-moving external events. The most stark manifestation of this problem for United Fruit was the demise of Eli Black, the company's boss from the late 1960s until 3rd February 1975 – and thus it is with his death that the chapter will conclude.

It is not that the 1954 coup, in terms of its initial effects, was not a success from United Fruit's perspective. Jacobo Arbenz was deposed, and Castillo Armas – the exiled general turned furniture salesman – was installed in office as planned. A few details of the coup – as revealed in an internal CIA account, which has recently been declassified – will give some idea of how its aims were ingloriously achieved. (As explained before, while United Fruit had laid some of the groundwork for the coup, planning for the military action itself was undertaken by the CIA.)

The key elements were in place by the start of June 1954. An invasion force under Castillo Armas had been assembled in Honduras, American fighter pilots had been recruited and were ready to fly their missions, and a US-backed propaganda radio station was pumping out denunciations of Arbenz. But what drove Arbenz from office so quickly was not any demonstration of military prowess by Armas's CIA-backed force. The crucial development was instead a behind-the-scenes decision by Guatemalan army generals no longer to support the president. The mere fact that America was showing a willingness to topple Arbenz was enough to persuade these generals to switch sides.

In fact, Armas's invasion quickly "degenerated from an ambitious plan to tragicomedy", according to the CIA account.[48] Supported by occasional bombing raids, his small, ragtag army advanced into Guatemala at a meager pace, and his soldiers sometimes seemed more eager to surrender or flee than fight. One subdivision which planned to cross into Guatemala from El Salvador, for example, was stopped well before the border by curious Salvadoran police, who promptly threw all the soldiers in jail. Another column of 122 soldiers made it into Guatemala but was overwhelmed by a garrison of 30 men still loyal to Arbenz. Arbenz, meanwhile, delivered a radio broadcast – which the CIA tried to jam – claiming that "the United Fruit Company, in collaboration with the governing circles of the United States, is responsible for what is happening to us."[49]

Arbenz's hopes of defiance were swiftly dashed when Guatemala's senior generals made known to him their decision to switch sides. Arbenz had little option but to resign, which he did on 27th June. The coup was by then almost complete. All that was left to do was to maneuver into positions of power a set of military officers who would be positively receptive to a regime led by Armas. This was a task enthusiastically undertaken by the America's gung-ho ambassador in Guatemala at the time, John Peurifoy (Peurifoy's wife later commemorated her husband's achievement in an embarrassing poem which was printed in *Time* magazine: "[...] And pistol-packing Peurifoy looks mighty optimistic/For the land of Guatemala is no longer Communistic!").[50]

The strong men return

Once installed, Armas quickly made his political tendencies apparent. He imprisoned many of his opponents and recruited the former secret police chief of General Ubico (Guatemala's dictator until 1944). He also cancelled the land reform process which had threatened United Fruit's interests, and took the vote away from illiterate people (which meant some two-thirds of the electorate). Arbenz wisely fled to Mexico. For the rest of his life the defeated and often-depressed former president lived in exile in various countries, including Uruguay and Cuba. In 1971, at the age of 58, he died in his bathtub, apparently due to natural causes.[51]

For Guatemala, the long-term effects of the 1954 coup were even more miserable. It would be disingenuous to blame United Fruit and the CIA for all subsequent events in the country, but without doubt the coup cut short Guatemala's first major experiment in democracy.

By resurrecting a pattern of military-backed dictatorships, it may have helped create the conditions for the violent conflict of the next several decades.

To summarize a long period of history briefly, a succession of inflexible regimes from 1954 onwards (Armas was assassinated in 1957 but another right-wing strong man took his place) blocked hopes of moderate reform. A polarization of Guatemala's political landscape ensued. From the 1960s, left-wing guerrilla groups drawing support from poor Indians fought right-wing paramilitary organizations supported by the state and – at times – by America (which continued to be concerned about the spread of Communism). This civil war lasted for 36 years, killing more than 100,000 Guatemalans, and forcing many more – and particularly Indians – to flee their homes. Since 1996, a peace has settled on the country, and democracy appears to have become more firmly entrenched. Even so, the army remains powerful, and criminal violence is rife. Land distribution, too, remains highly unequal, as it has been since colonial times.[52]

The aftershocks of the coup were felt across Latin America. For a generation of left-wing activists, as mentioned before, it came to symbolize what they saw as the malevolence of American influence and investment in the region. The overthrow of Arbenz itself was condemned by crowds that gathered in cities across the region, from Buenos Aires to Havana. American flags and effigies of President Eisenhower were burned.

Interestingly, one activist in Guatemala at the time of the coup was a young Argentine doctor: Che Guevara. According to Guevara's first wife, "It was Guatemala which finally convinced him of the necessity for armed struggle, and for taking the initiative against imperialism".[53]

Bruised bananas

What is most relevant here, however, is the effect of the coup on United Fruit itself, and though the company's problems after 1954 cannot be compared with the bloodshed which ensued in Guatemala, they were intractable nonetheless. Armas's cancellation of the land reform program was among the only upsides of the coup for the company. For a start, relations with the American government became more fraught. The Eisenhower administration – stung by international criticism over its interference in Guatemalan affairs – was keen to distance itself from the company. Five days after Arbenz resigned, the Justice Department sued United Fruit in the federal courts alleging violation of US anti-trust laws. After several years of legal action, the company was forced to surrender its holdings in the International Railways of Central America and also some of its land in Guatemala. In the post-coup world, it was becoming clear, United Fruit could no longer rely on the American government to support its business methods overseas, at least not unconditionally.

Central and Latin America was also becoming a less friendly region to do business in the post-1954 era, and United Fruit was now viewed with more suspicion by nationalist local governments. Strikes were growing and a number of governments – including Costa Rica's – began passing legislation strengthening workers' rights. In 1958, Fidel Castro, together with his friend Che Guevara, seized power in Cuba and quickly began to expropriate United Fruit land. In Ecuador, meanwhile, a fast-growing banana industry, controlled by domestic rather than foreign firms, was eating into United Fruit's profits. United Fruit managers complained that these Ecuadorian planters were able to undercut their produce because they paid workers less, and also did not build houses, schools, hospitals, and roads to go along with their investments.

United Fruit made some attempts to adapt to these strange new circumstances. In an effort to reduce its political risks, it voluntarily sold off much of its land in the region, and began to buy more bananas from local producers, even from planters in Ecuador. It asked growers to switch to a new, more productive strain of the fruit, and also began to diversify out of tropical agriculture. Yet these efforts were only partly successful. According to calculations by Marcelo Bucheli of Stanford University, the return on United Fruit's equity, and also on its assets, fell substantially between 1950 and 1970.[54] American financial analysts were rapidly losing their enthusiasm for the company's stock. As Moody's Investor Service put it bluntly in 1959: "United Fruit has been hurt by political troubles in several Latin American countries [...] we would switch into U.S. Rubber for better prospects".[55]

United Fruit's support of the coup, in short, did little to rescue the company from its political problems – and in some respects, by fueling popular resentment against it, it had made matters worse. These were reactionary times in the developing world and a political maneuver in the style of the company's earlier exploits had inevitably backfired in such circumstances.

Blackening clouds

The story is now straying into the period of "backlash", which is the subject of the next part. But in the tragic fate of Eli Black lies a fitting epilogue – for he was a man whose style suited the company's imperial past better than the new world in which it was having to operate. In a number of respects, Black was a boss in the mold of Samuel Zemurray. It is not just that both men were Jewish immigrants to America (and according to McCann, Black encountered anti-semitism within the company, just like Sam-the-banana-man).[56] Black was also audacious in his business dealings, combined charity with ruthlessness, and – again like Zemurray – enjoyed hob-nobbing with Central American rulers.

Originally arriving in America from Poland, Black had first trained as a rabbi (he came from a long line of religious scholars), but his ambitions led him into investment banking, and thence into taking over, and running, various food companies. It was in 1968, as the hotshot, wheeler-dealing, boss of the conglomerate AMK, that Black shocked United Fruit's management by buying 733,000 of its shares in a single day, the third largest transaction Wall Street had yet witnessed[57] (indeed, the expressions around the boardroom table must have been as stunned as when Zemurray demanded control of the company in 1932). This was a prelude to a full-blown takeover. The new combined United Fruit-AMK entity was renamed United Brands.

In spite of his wealth, Black's tastes were unostentatious (according to McCann, "he gave the impression of a man whose pleasures were mainly of the mind"). Nonetheless he collected modern art, and was a particular fan of the abstract canvasses painted by his wife, Shirley (indeed a number of United Fruit managers, knowing how to please their boss, also bought her work).[58] As head of the company, Black also took the opportunity to cultivate friendships with prominent Central American politicians, including the flamboyant José "Don Pepe" Figueres, the then president of Costa Rica. But Black was operating in a different era from Sam-the-banana-man, and whereas Zemurray's skills helped revive the company's fortunes, Black's reign over the old United Fruit empire proved financially disastrous. United Brands' annual losses began to mount, and by 1974 reached $70 million.

Not all of these losses can be attributed to the fact that Black was a man out of his time. Some of the problems were due to sheer bad management which would have had an impact in any era (Black's personal style was often abrasive, for example, which alienated many of his lieutenants, including McCann). Bad luck played a part too: a hurricane destroyed most of the company's plantations in Honduras in 1974. Nonetheless, the old rules of doing business in the developing world were changing fast, and governments that were once easy to co-opt were trying to wrest more power from the company. In 1974 – inspired by the Middle Eastern oil nations – seven Central and South American banana producers, including Honduras and Guatemala, formed a cartel and demanded higher export taxes from United Brands and other firms.

In Black's eyes, the company's problems, and his involvement in them, were looking insurmountable. On the morning of Monday 3rd February 1975, he left his New York apartment for work, having said goodbye to his wife and daughter. As usual, he took the elevator to his office on the 44th floor of the Pan Am building. But on this particular morning, he used his briefcase to smash through the glass of the office window, and leapt to his death on the pavement below.

Shortly after Black's suicide it emerged that America's Securities and Exchange Commission, the regulatory agency, was investigating a $1.25 million bribe allegedly offered by United Brands to Honduran government officials in return for reducing the country's export tax on bananas. This may have been on Black's mind before he jumped. The bribery investigation caused a scandal not just in America; the Honduran president was swiftly removed from office, his government having been tainted by its apparent willingness to be bought by a foreign multinational. In the old days allegations of such behavior would have hardly raised an eyebrow.

As a last note, it is worth mentioning another event from this period, less dramatic, but significant in its own way. Thomas McCann, the public relations manager who had spent decades under United Fruit's "umbrella", and who used to defend its actions with pride, decided to stop working for the company shortly before Black's suicide. It was not only Black's abrasive style which caused McCann to leave, nor just his own desire for a new career challenge, but also his growing unease with the company's behavior. On encountering a prominent critic of United Fruit in 1973, for example, McCann describes how he found himself uncharacteristically shying away from a confrontation:

> Probably [the critic in the question] would have argued that the company's reaction to every public relations phantom in its history was equally wrong, starting with Lee Christmas and "Machine Gun" Guy Molony, through the invasions of Guatemala [...] And he probably would have said the machismo, the self-sufficiency, the piety, the oppression, the sleight of hand, the self-serving patriotism were all wrong as well.
>
> In my first fifteen years with United Fruit, I could have given [him] a terrific argument. But after five years with Eli Black, I no longer could. I knew better.[59]

Both McCann's resignation and Black's suicide in their own ways represent the final, belated, disintegration of an old corporate culture. The company's managers were once proud; now they were plagued by doubts. The hostile winds now blowing in the outside world had breached their and the company's defenses.

Backlash

INTRODUCTION

Several months before the attack on 11th September 2001 in which Islamic extremists, most of them Saudi nationals, brought crashing to the ground the twin towers of the World Trade Center, there occurred another event, less remarked, but related, and with a significance of its own. In May of that year, the government of Saudi Arabia unveiled a foreign investment program in the country's energy sector, announcing the names of eight firms, including ExxonMobil, the American energy giant, and Royal Dutch/Shell, the European oil firm, which it was planned would carry out a set of natural gas projects worth up to $40 billion.[1]

These may appear disparate events, one a symbol of terror and global discord, and the other an example of international economic co-operation. But together they illustrate the contradictory reactions of Saudi society to western economic and political power – the tension between those within the country who support outright rejection and those who seek integration with the west. Interestingly, both sentiments have many of their historical roots in another mammoth foreign investment project, known as Aramco, which is the subject of one of the two chapters in this part.

Owned by four American multinationals, Aramco oversaw the exploitation of Saudi Arabia's oil from the 1930s to the 1970s. The largest foreign oil concession in the whole of the Middle East, it helped bring not only lavish wealth to Saudi Arabia, but also rapid changes to the desert kingdom's traditional Islamic society. Combined with other perceived provocations – such as America's support for Israel – these changes fueled a deep dislike of western influences among sectors of the Saudi population, including the young Osama bin Laden.

Aramco was nationalized by the Saudi government in the mid-1970s, and foreign energy firms were excluded from the country for the next few decades. But the attractions of foreign investment have not been entirely lost on the regime, as the government's announcement in 2001 indicates. For the moment, the Saudis have only been offering western multinationals access to projects involving natural gas (opening up the more lucrative oil sector would still be too sensitive a step politically); and, at the time of writing, the government has yet to agree the financial terms of the deals with the companies concerned. But it is an indication of the overall hydrocarbon wealth still under the kingdom's surface, that the multinationals (which include some of the original American partners in Aramco) have even contemplated tying up billions of dollars of their capital to renew their relationship with the regime, in spite of the evident – and potentially explosive – political risks.

The other chapter in this part, which examines the role of two European multinationals – a Belgian corporate empire in the Congo and an Italian firm with investments in Iran – also provides a context for understanding current events. Iran, like Saudi Arabia, for example, has begun to re-open its energy sector to foreign investment, following a recent history of fierce opposition to western involvement. As in Saudi Arabia, this reopening involves considerable risks for western companies, for among both the conservative Muslim clerics and modernizing reformers jostling for power in Tehran in recent years, there are many who still regard the country's past oil nationalizations – in 1951 and 1979 – as moments of national triumph.[2]

Interestingly, the Italian firm which features in the chapter has been among the western companies that are taking a lead in striking deals in modern-day Iran. "This is a great day to remember," proclaimed the chief executive of Ente Nazionale Idrocarburi, or ENI, on signing a large gas contract with Iran in July 2000, "A day that evokes memories of a special relationship of co-operation between ENI and the Iranian people [...]".[3] But ENI's boss chose not to dwell on the fact that – as will be seen – the original period of co-operation between his company and Iran, which began in 1957, ended a few decades later in nationalization.

There has been little interest in recent years from western firms in returning to the Congo, for since the fall of its dictator, Mobutu Sese Seko, in 1997, the country – which covers an area more than four times the size of France – has been plagued for much of the time by political turmoil, civil war and ethnic conflict. But, even in this part of the world, modern events bear the imprint of history, including the past activities of Union Minière, the Belgian mining multinational.

Shortly after the country's independence from Belgium in 1960, for example, Union Minière supported a secessionist movement in the Katanga, one of the Congo's provinces. This helped to trigger a period of civil war and ethnic fighting which engulfed the country for several years, a situation which parallels the more recent chaos. And in 2002, the Belgian government issued an apology for its role in the murder in 1961 of Patrice Lumumba, a young, charismatic Congolese politician who was the country's first prime minister on independence. Through his death, Lumumba became a martyr and hero for nationalists across Africa. His assassination was a murky affair, the details of which are still unclear. Union Minière itself did not mastermind the plot, but equally the company's actions did help set the stage for the collapse of the young prime minister's government.

Morals of the story

As with previous parts of the book, these chapters aim to do more than set some historical context for modern events. Both chapters highlight patterns of interaction between western multinationals and developing countries which have timeless elements, and which may well find repetition in the future. At first sight the political processes described may seem specific to their time. This is the era of "backlash", the period stretching from the mid-1940s to the late 1970s, when developing countries – many of them recently granted independence – were eager to assert their economic as well as political independence from the former imperial powers. In practical terms, this meant an increased threat of expropriation of western-owned assets, and general suspicion towards new foreign investments. The modern period, which is covered in the book's last part, "Resurgence", is remarkable for the swift reversal of this opposition towards foreign firms.

The processes which will be described in "Backlash", however, may not be dead, just dormant, or even now at work on a less dramatic scale. In the case of ENI and Union Minière, for example, it will be seen how the initial tactics adopted by these multinationals

to cope with moderate nationalist sentiment in developing countries
were at a later stage overwhelmed by stronger nationalist tides. There
is a note of warning here for modern-day multinationals: the more
fragile and insecure the national identity of a developing country, or
the greater its internal tensions, the more tempting it may be for its
rulers to turn on foreign firms as a means of reinforcing their own
power.

The story of Aramco, the consortium of American firms in Saudi
Arabia, illustrates various timeless phenomena, too. In particular, it
shows how large-scale investments can so fundamentally alter the
social and economic structure of a developing country, or at least the
particular area in which they are located, that they may sow the seeds
of their own downfall. This general phenomenon is perhaps most
pertinent to oil and mining investments. In the modern era, these
typically involve large amounts of capital spending – often billions of
dollars – concentrated heavily in regions where mineral reserves
happen to be discovered, which heightens their local impact. Such
investments may also generate massive surges in revenue for local
and national governments, causing further instability.

A sudden injection of cash might appear to be an unambiguously
positive development. But particularly when the region in question
is a part of a developing country populated by indigenous societies
which have little experience of modern capitalism – as is often the
case – the influx of money may strain a social fabric that is likely to
have evolved over centuries, disrupting traditions and fueling
competition for revenues between different local groups, and also
between local and federal governments. Such tensions in turn can
rebound on the company. But the social changes triggered by
Aramco, it will be seen, were on an even larger scale than those
brought by most modern resource multinationals, spreading as they
did across an entire nation.

In previous chapters, it was observed how large companies of the
imperial era often struggled to understand, let alone manage, the
changes unfolding in the societies in which they operated. Aramco
was far more interested in, and enlightened towards, the native
culture than was, say, the East India Company, or Cecil Rhodes's
corporation, but it, too, eventually faced a concerted attempt by the
indigenous people to evict the company from their lands.

The failures of all three companies examined in this part should not be exaggerated. Aramco, for example, enjoyed decades of profitability in Saudi Arabia before being overwhelmed by such nationalist tides; and in Union Minière's case, even the actual nationalization of its assets was not a financial disaster, for the company secured compensation from the Congo for its losses. Even so, it is the political strategies of multinationals, rather than their financial performance, which is the focus of this book. And in terms of the avowed political goal of all three companies – to keep on good terms with their respective host societies and governments – all, in the long run, failed in the countries examined.

The three multinationals have been selected for inclusion because of the scale of their power (even if they wielded it clumsily) and also the degree of international interest their activities provoked; but the choice has been far from easy given the varied, and controversial, strategies for coping with nationalism followed by some other firms. In the 1970s, for example, the British mining firm called Lonrho became famous for developing close relationships with leaders of newly independent African states. French oil firms, such as Elf-Aquitaine, adopted a variety of techniques, some more successful than others, to protect their investments in former French colonies such as West Africa and Algeria.

Nor was the experience of "backlash" limited to oil and mining companies, even though foreign control over natural resources was often what enraged nationalist leaders the most. For example, there was the controversy in the 1970s over alleged plans by ITT, the International Telephone & Telegraph Corporation, an American conglomerate, to subvert the political process in Chile. This episode is worth describing briefly here, for it illustrates the growing dangers in this period for all sorts of multinationals of meddling, or even just being seen to meddle, in a host country's politics.

ITT's boss, Harold Geneen, a fiercely driven man and an accountant by training, had been worried that Salvador Allende, a Marxist, might win Chile's 1970 elections. ITT had substantial assets in the country, including a majority stake in the national telephone company and two major hotels. According to the testimony of a former ITT board member, Geneen offered the CIA $1 million in ITT funds to help secure the election of a right-wing candidate. ITT managers also apparently discussed with the CIA a plan to create "economic collapse" by temporarily freezing American business contacts with the country.[4]

The plan, however, remained on the drawing board. A liberal-minded Chilean general was assassinated, possibly with CIA support, but that did not prevent Allende becoming president – indeed he was the first freely elected Marxist chief of state anywhere in the world. Once in power, Allende's government took over ITT's assets at a fraction of their market value, and at the UN General Assembly, he denounced the company as an agent of "economic imperialism" and accused it of "attempting to bring about civil war in my country".[5] For ITT, the episode turned out to be more than a financial failure. In Washington, the Senate launched a special investigation into its activities, while Geneen – once lauded as a great tycoon – became reviled by many Americans as a symbol of corporate abuse of power.

Tracing the undercurrents

Before launching into the individual stories of Union Minière, ENI and Aramco, it will help to expand a little further on some of the political and economic trends during this period of "backlash". For underlying the particular interactions between these multinationals and the local societies concerned was a set of broad forces, of which the new-found spirit of defiance in the developing world was just one element.

Increasing prosperity in the west in the decades following the Second World War, for example, had created growing demand for such raw materials as oil and copper. This was what made such resource-rich countries as Saudi Arabia, Iran and the Congo a still-tempting investment destination for multinationals, in spite of the growing political risks involved. The motor behind the post-war global economic recovery was America, and American firms led the way in foreign investment (although most of this went to other industrialized countries); meanwhile war-battered western Europe, aided by the Marshall plan, was relatively soon on its feet, and a number of European multinationals – including Italy's ENI – began to expand their foreign operations.

Another underlying factor in the west was the growth of social movements such as environmentalism which were causing people to question more assertively the behavior of multinationals. Such western suspicions will be most apparent in the chapter on Aramco. However, anti-multinational sentiment was far from uniform; ENI's foreign endeavors, as will be seen, became a symbol of national pride in Italy.

What gave political momentum to some of the increasing criticism of multinationals' behavior abroad was that, for many westerners, it resonated with their own domestic concerns. In the 1960s, for example, many in the west had begun to feel that material prosperity – the acquisition of cars, televisions, and the like – had failed to translate into spiritual contentment. New worries were beginning to circulate, meanwhile, about the apparent costs of such materialism, such as pollution and the over-exploitation of natural resources. Throughout Europe and America, protest groups began to emerge, eager to challenge the institutions of established authority in their countries, which naturally included the large companies, over a range of issues.

The changes experienced by developing countries in the decades after the Second World War were just as seismic. Most notable of these, as already mentioned, was the end of colonial rule. A form of indirect colonialism persisted during this period, with both America and the Soviet Union supporting friendly regimes and toppling unfriendly ones in their respective spheres of influence. Nonetheless, the direct empires of the old European powers were surrendered at a remarkably rapid pace. The British, for example, left India in 1948, and the Dutch gave up Indonesia a year later, both territories having been won centuries earlier by their respective East India Companies.

Africa experienced a wave of decolonization in the 1950s and 1960s, with Britain and France – the main imperial powers in the region – staging a mostly voluntary retreat (one exception being Algeria where France fought a bitter and ultimately unsuccessful war to retain this former colony). Meanwhile, the Middle East, where the French and British had long before replaced the Ottomans as the dominant colonialists, was mostly free of direct imperial control by the 1950s (although the creation of a small new state – Israel – was viewed by many Arabs as a colonial-style imposition on their lands by the west).

Driving this retreat by the European powers was their reluctance to bear the continuing economic costs of maintaining their empires. There was also a genuine, if belated, recognition on their part of the merits of decolonization. Ironically many indigenous independence movements had been fostered by imperialism. Africans, Arabs, and Asians sent to study in British, French and other European universities had eagerly imbibed western ideologies of nationalism and self-determination and they sought to apply these ideas once they were back home.

However, the rapid retreat of the Europeans also created problems for their former colonies. Indigenous institutions of government were often given little time to take root. And the borders of many new countries, fixed in decades and centuries past as a result of competition and bargaining between the colonial powers, brought together ethnic groups with no common sense of nationhood.

The reason developing countries began to turn against western multinationals that were investing within their borders was not just that they were testing the limits of their political independence. A number of economic theories, fashionable in the decades up to and including the 1970s, held that rapid growth could be achieved by excluding foreign firms and promoting indigenous ones, and by relying on state bureaucracies to guide the development process.

Theories of "import substituting industrialization", for example, argued that cheap foreign imports should be kept out in order to give domestic firms a chance to build up a country's industrial base. "Dependency theory" – which suggested that western capitalism and foreign investment had actually perpetuated the poverty of developing countries – for a time became popular in Latin America. And in many African universities, "How Europe Underdeveloped Africa", a tract by a left-wing academic which argued that "African development is possible only on the basis of a radical break with the international capitalist system", became required reading for a generation of angry students.[6]

Developing countries could call on an armory of weapons to assert their economic authority. Among the available tools was tougher state control of private firms, outright nationalization, and the establishment of agreements with other countries to control the price of export commodities, such as rubber, tin and oil (and it was OPEC, the oil cartel, which achieved the greatest success and which will be examined in the chapter on Aramco). Between 1960 and 1976, the UN recorded 1,369 instances of nationalization, and – by the end of this period – the existence of 19 such producer associations.[7]

In the three developing countries that are the focus of the following chapters, these broad forces would mingle with local and historical factors to create situations of often dizzying complexity for the western multinationals concerned. In the Congo, for example, such was the speed of retreat by Belgium from its former colony, and such was its failure to prepare the country for independence, that Union Minière, the Belgian company, was left to contend with a political system barely able to contain a series of ethnic and regional conflicts.

In Iran, the colonial era in which imperial Russia and Britain vied for influence in the country – part of a broader regional competition which became known as the "Great Game" – was long over by the time ENI's story begins. However, the regime of the Shah, the country's moderate nationalist leader, with whom ENI had struck an alliance, was by the 1970s struggling to cope with the social and political effects of an OPEC-inspired oil boom. Instability was compounded further by the growing distrust of the powerful Islamic clerics who accused the Shah of pandering to western influences.

In Saudi Arabia, meanwhile, the very creation of the nation out of a set of warring factions by King Ibn Saud in 1932 had been achieved with the support of fundamentalist Islamic warriors. This political compromise at the heart of the Saudi regime would create endless, and eventually insurmountable, problems for Aramco, the American oil consortium.

How did the companies attempt to deal with such threats? Could they have done anything to prevent them? It is to the details of these political traumas, and the companies' coping strategies, that attention can now be turned.

FIVE

Post-imperial managers
Belgian strongmen and Italian charmers

[...] as long as he was alive he represented the stubborn rejection of the
neocolonialist solution. This solution consists basically of buying the new masters,
the bourgeois of the new countries, as classic colonialism bought tribal chiefs, emirs
and witch doctors.

Jean-Paul Sartre, French philosopher, on the assassination of Patrice
Lumumba, the first prime minister of the independent Congo.[1]

The people of Islam are wary of being exploited by foreigners. The big oil
companies must offer them more for their oil than they are getting.

Enrico Mattei, Italian oil boss, pitches for business in the Middle East.[2]

In the first few decades after the Second World War, when western governments had lost the will and the means to hold on to their colonies, how did western multinationals defend their own empires? What methods did they use to deal with the fiery indigenous leaders of nations that had suddenly asserted their independence?

Companies experimented with a range of tactics. But few followed paths as extreme, or as dramatically contrasting, as the Belgian mining giant Union Minière du Haut Katanga (or Union Minière for short) and the Italian firm Ente Nazionale Idrocarburi (or ENI). This chapter examines briefly both the attempt by Union Minière to hold on to its empire in the Congo and also the attempt by ENI to establish a new empire of its own in the Middle East. An initial taste of the story can be gathered from the differing experiences of Patrice

Lumumba, the young prime minister of the newly independent Congo – a figure who was to become an icon not just for African nationalists, but also for European intellectuals such as Jean-Paul Sartre – and those of the Shah of Iran.

As noted previously, Patrice Lumumba was assassinated in mysterious circumstances in 1961. Union Minière employees themselves did not undertake the killing. But the company certainly helped set the stage for the collapse of Lumumba's regime, for rather than paying its taxes – which amounted to around half the colonial state's revenue – to the independent central government of the Congo, it paid them instead to the breakaway province of Katanga, the region in which its mining operations were based, and where it had close links with the local political leadership. It was police officers serving the rulers of this secessionist province who, the evidence suggests, actually killed Lumumba, while the Belgians turned a blind eye. To hide evidence of the murder, the conspirators dissolved Lumumba's body in acid which – according to some accounts – came from Union Minière's stocks.[3]

The Shah of Iran's treatment at the hands of ENI in the late 1950s, meanwhile, could not have been in greater contrast. He was courted and flattered by Enrico Mattei, ENI's swashbuckling and charming boss. Mattei's goal was to win an oil concession for ENI which might elevate the company into the ranks of the world's giant energy companies; and to achieve this he offered the Shah what appeared to be radically more generous terms than those typically granted by the American and British oil firms that dominated the industry. Mattei also made a point of publicly denouncing western "imperialism", and at one stage even offered to procure an Italian princess for marriage with the Shah.[4] This was certainly more pleasurable treatment than the bath of acid provided for Lumumba.

The contrasting stories of Union Minière in the Congo and ENI in the Middle East are told here not to draw any moral conclusions, but rather because they raise an interesting question regarding the *realpolitik* of foreign investment. For a multinational, which is the more effective political technique for helping to protect or expand its assets during a period of intense nationalism in developing countries: trying to keep control over the forces of independence – as Union Minière appears to have done – or taking sides with, and wooing, the nationalists – which was ENI's tactic? This is a question which modern multinationals will have to consider if political opinion turns against them again in the countries in which they operate and they are unwilling simply to surrender their investments.

To answer the question it is necessary to look beyond the immediate impacts and interpretations of Union Minière's and ENI's actions. Put to one side the fact that, for example, the behavior of Union Minière in the 1960s was perceived by many as a symbol of corporate aggression in the developing world, or that, for many Italians, conversely, the exploits of ENI's Enrico Mattei elevated him to the status of a national hero. The crux of the matter is: did the contrasting political approaches adopted by these two companies actually succeed in their own terms over the long run?

Ultimately, it will be seen, neither approach, neither repression nor charm, proved to be very effective. The reason was that the initial successes of both these companies were submerged by further nationalist tides. It is here that their stories provide further evidence for a pattern discerned in previous chapters, that multinationals, for all their undoubted might, often struggle to predict, let alone manage, the political pressures they encounter.

Union of forces

The story of Union Minière is told first because, like United Fruit's machinations in Guatemala in the 1950s, it represents a hold-over from the past, an attempt to employ imperial-style tactics in a post-imperial era (whereas ENI's tactics were distinctly new-fangled). As with United Fruit, Union Minière's adoption of this approach was partly a result of its history and proud internal culture, although its actions understandably appalled many people outside the company.

By 1960, the date of Congo's independence from Belgian rule, Union Minière had come a long way from its origins in 1906 as one of the numerous organizations set up to aid the Belgian King Leopold II's exploitation of the region. King Leopold's ruthless methods – and the moral outrage they inspired in Britain and elsewhere in the west – have been mentioned previously in the book. But when the Belgian government asserted control over the Congo

Congo 1960–63

in 1908, transforming what was Leopold's private domain into an official colony, Union Minière's period of expansion, and moral evolution, had only just begun.

Union Minière was financed largely by Société Générale de Belgique, an influential Belgian holding company, though it also had a number of other financial backers, including at an early stage, a certain Sir Robert Williams, who was one of Cecil Rhodes's lieutenants (Rhodes, it may be remembered, was always eager to extend the tentacles of his empires northwards). The company devoted itself to mining the rich resources of the Katanga province, an arid, sparsely populated region in the south-east of the Belgian colony. It grew dramatically in size during the first half of the twentieth century, in the process transforming the Katanga into the industrial powerhouse of the entire Congo.

Union Minière mined not just copper (and by the early 1960s, it was producing 8% of the world's supply of the metal), but also cobalt (its share of world production here was over 60%),[5] uranium, and a variety of other commodities. Its strategic significance was underlined during the Second World War when the Americans depended upon uranium from Union Minière mines to produce their atom bombs (a senior manager of the company, Jules Cousin, was awarded America's Medal of Freedom in 1946). As well as its mines, the company built processing plants, smelters, railway lines, dams, grain mills, and power stations. Almost all economic activity in the region, excluding traditional farming and trade between villages, came to depend on the giant Belgian corporation. The company's workforce grew to over 20,000, but due to a scarcity of labor in Katanga itself in the early years, African workers were brought in from elsewhere – from the neighboring Kasai province of the Congo, from Northern Rhodesia, and from Ruanda-Urundi.

The company also built Elizabethville, the capital of the Katanga province, laying out a pleasant town of wide streets and parks. A visitor in the late 1940s noted that this was an untypically sophisticated mining town with its "trim cottages of dark-red, burnt brick, embowered in crimson and purple bougainvillea [...], its veranda'd hotels, its cool and well-stocked bars and restaurants, and its proud native traffic policeman waving the cars through the Place de l'Etoile in red fez, blue uniform, brass buttons, and bare feet".

The source of all this wealth, however, was never far from sight: "From the gay terrace of the Lido Club, with its outdoor swimming pool, one can see, a half-mile beyond the parasols and the diving towers, a gigantic brick chimney alongside a great black cone of slag. All day and night a yellow, sulphurous cloud floats off the giant stack [...]"[6]

Union Minière's "ethical" values and its approach to the development of the Katanga mirrored the Belgian style of colonial rule in the Congo as a whole. The Belgian imperial infrastructure was dominated by three institutions – the colonial administration, the Catholic Church, and the large companies – all working in close co-operation, and with a vision which, while more enlightened than that of King Leopold II, was deeply paternalistic and authoritarian. It was as though the members of the "Aborigines Protection Society", the British group which criticized Cecil Rhodes's activities in the 1890s (see Chapter 2), were now putting their patronizing ideals into practice. The following excerpt is from a Union Minière memorandum in 1946 on the company's social policy:

> The colonizer must never lose sight of the fact that the Negroes have the souls of children, souls which mold themselves to the methods of the educator; they watch, listen, feel, and imitate. The European must, in all circumstances, show himself a chief without weakness, good-willed without familiarity, active in method and especially just in the punishment of misbehavior, as in the reward of good deeds. [... the European camp head] must interest himself constantly in the life of the natives, in their well-being.[7]

Benefits provided by Union Minière for its African workers came to rival the welfare services supplied by United Fruit. By the time of independence, the company was running some 70 schools, and had built more than 20,000 homes for its African employees (though these were kept separate from the white housing). Its five general hospitals, five maternity hospitals, and scores of dispensaries had led to significant improvements in local health (between 1950 and 1955, for example, the infant mortality rate in Elizabethville fell from 20% to 6%). To provide spiritual and moral uplift for workers, the company had also enlisted the support of eighty-two nuns, chaplains and social workers.[8] Union Minière was also eager to encourage family life (though not, it would appear, the emancipation of women). The company sometimes would loan its male employees money to buy a wife, the payment of such a "bride price" being a common African practice.[9]

What drove these corporate efforts was partly enlightened self-interest. It was more cost effective in the long run to draw from a healthy, motivated, local workforce, rather than importing labor from far-flung regions, as in the company's early days. At the same time – however ironic and twisted this may appear given the subsequent events in Katanga – it may be that Union Minière's actions were also driven by a sense among managers that they were building a modern industrial utopia. Such an outlook certainly rubbed off on a number of visitors to the company's facilities, as it did with an American writer who visited the Congo in the early 1940s and who marveled how:

> Bantu workers, equipped with water-spray drills (to insure them against silicosis) work a thousand feet under an earth which once filled them with such superstitious awe that they sacrificed animals and fellow-tribesmen to it during the unpropitious seasons. The examples could be quoted at great length, but always with the same principle involved: that a careful handling of the primitive mentality [...] has resulted in mutual benefit. The level of the Congo population is constantly rising, and the economic returns have justified the patience and industry of the Belgians. Here is idealism with a practical basis.[10]

This then was the context behind the company's attempt to defend itself against the forces of nationalism in the early 1960s. It helps to explain the company's subsequent behavior, though not to justify it. Such was the edifice, physical and ideological, which Union Minière managers had constructed, such was their confidence in their own superiority, that they viewed Congolese independence with deep suspicion, fearing that the "civilization" which they had brought to the region would be ripped apart. A UN official who served in the Congo in this period, for example, records a heated exchange with a Union

Minière manager in Elizabethville who was worrying about "the dangers of a native revolt". "I can still see his bulging eyes," the official wrote, "the veins standing out on his forehead, the upper lip slightly flecked with foam as he thrust his face into mine and shouted: 'You have never seen the native city when it breaks loose!' (*Vous n'avez jamais vu la cité indigène déchainée!*)".[11]

Troubled provinces

Why exactly did Union Minière support the secession of the Katanga province in the early 1960s? And what form did this support take? (Later the crucial question can be considered: did the company's tactics actually achieve their desired effect?) The company's support for the secession was a defensive move, an attempt to insulate itself from the uncertain, and potentially damaging, political forces sweeping the Congo in the wake of independence (although, ironically, its actions gave momentum to the most destructive of these forces: the fragmentation of the country). The anxieties of Union Minière managers about political instability were certainly merited, but this was in part because Belgium had done little to prepare the Congo for independence in the period prior to 1960. The paternalism of the colonial state had stifled the development of indigenous institutions (the Belgians, for example, had waited until the 1950s before permitting even a degree of popular participation in municipal government; and as late as 1960, they had allowed only three Congolese into the ranks of the 4,645 senior positions in the colonial bureaucracy).[12] Their patronizing attitude had also retarded the emergence of a coherent sense of Congolese nationhood, leaving in its place a complex set of tribal and regional loyalties.

The Belgian's original plan in the 1950s had been to withdraw slowly, over the space of several decades. But in the event, their granting of independence was a rushed process and they were swept along by unexpectedly strong nationalist tides. In January 1959, for example, angry Congolese mobs rioted for several days, attacking colonial buildings and Catholic missions in Congo's capital Léopoldville (the fact that the Belgians continued to call the city after their rapacious former king arguably was justification enough for an indigenous riot). Shocked, the Belgians decided to accelerate the independence process, hoping that by swiftly surrendering their political power they might preserve their informal, economic influence in the country. By June of 1960, the Congo had been set free, and Patrice Lumumba, the energetic 36-year-old African – a man who worked variously as a postal clerk, beer salesman, and an accountant under Belgian rule – was appointed prime minister following the country's first national elections.

What set Lumumba apart from many of his fellow nationalist politicians was not just his youth and charisma, but his belief that the independent Congo should be a centralized state, rather than a federation of regions based around tribal allegiances. This contrasted with the views of men such as Joseph Kasavubu who, as the country's first president, for a time shared power with Lumumba. Kasavubu was a member of the Bakongo tribe, one of the largest groups in the country. Lumumba, by contrast, came from a small tribe, the Batetela. It was a testament to the young prime minister's forceful vision and eloquence that he was able for a time to unite the disparate Congolese peoples.

What particularly worried the Belgians about Lumumba, however, was that, while often proclaiming his desire for friendship with Brussels, anti-colonial fervor occasionally got the better of him. At the independence ceremony in 1960, for example, in front of King Baudouin of Belgium, Lumumba railed:

> The wounds that are the evidence of the fate we endured for eighty years under a colonialist regime are still too fresh and painful for us to be able to erase them from our memory [...] We have been the victims of ironic taunts, of insults, of blows that we were forced to endure morning, noon, and night because we were blacks.

The Congolese crowd cheered these words, while Baudouin squirmed.[13]

In comparison with Lumumba, Moise Kapenda Tshombe, the president of the Katanga province – who proclaimed its secession only a few weeks after independence – was an altogether more comforting figure for the Belgians (and Sartre may have had him in mind, when he talked of the "neocolonialist solution".) The genial son of a wealthy businessman, and a former president of Elizabethville's African Chamber of Commerce, Tshombe kept on good terms with local Union Minière managers. Typically attired in a smart suit, an American button-down shirt and a homburg hat, he was an astute politician. However, unlike Lumumba, his political vision was more tribal than ideological, and this again made him easier to deal with. He was a member of the locally powerful Lunda tribe, and the principal policy of his political party, called CONAKAT, was the "repatriation" of 160,000 Balubas, another tribe, back to the neighboring Kasai province from where they had come (it was the fact that many Balubas had taken up well-paid jobs with Union Minière which was partly what irritated the Lunda).[14] Another aim of Tshombe was to wrest control of Union Minière's substantial tax revenues from the central government in Léopoldville.

Union Minière did not actually mastermind Tshombe's Katangan secession, even though many African nationalists outside the Congo assumed this was the case. That would be to ascribe too much political foresight and expertise in covert operations to a company whose senior management was dominated by engineers.[15] One respected historian of the Congo has argued that "the most reasonable interpretation of the behavior of colonial corporations is that they were simply bewildered by the pace of events, [and] had had little experience in other countries to provide perspective in survival techniques for periods of political effervescence".[16] Certainly there were divisions within both Union Minière, and the Belgian government, as to the correct course of action.

Although Tshombe proclaimed the secession in order to advance his own political goals, Union Minière managers had little hesitation in supporting the move once it had occurred, for it appeared to them to be an ideal means by which they could insulate the company from uncertain political developments. Tshombe was not only friendly to the company's interests; in severing the region in which it operated from the rest of the country, he was now providing it with an apparently safe haven from potentially hostile, nationalist currents elsewhere in the Congo. From Tshombe's perspective, in turn, the company's support provided important sustenance for his new kingdom.

The most powerful form of support was financial. As Tshombe had hoped, rather than paying its taxes and duties to Léopoldville, the company channeled them to the Katangan government (thus making a payment of over 1.2 billion Belgian Francs after the secession was announced).[17] According to a recent Belgian parliamentary inquiry into the circumstances surrounding Lumumba's death, Union Minière meddled in other ways, too; it provided funding for a Katangan diplomatic mission in Brussels,[18] and it also made some attempts to provide military support to the secessionists.[19] Observers on the ground in Katanga had little doubt that local Belgians, if not the company itself, were lending a hand to Tshombe's gendarmerie, or police force. Meanwhile Union Minière bosses insisted to the outside world that the company was not interfering in "political" matters.

Lumumba, naturally, was incensed by the secession, which had left a gaping hole in his government's finances, and which was encouraging other provinces to demand their autonomy. He had asked the United Nations to send troops to restore the Congo's territorial integrity. UN forces arrived, but at first failed to suppress the Katangan revolt, at which point Lumumba appealed to the Soviet Union for help. Not long after, on 17th January 1961, he was assassinated.

The Belgian multinational appears to have done little to prevent the assassination – and Lumumba's death certainly removed an initial threat to the secession. The young prime minister's downfall, however, was due to a combination of forces including political meddling in the Congo by foreign governments (including both Belgium and America, which was concerned about potential Soviet intervention), as well as to the various shifts in internal Congolese politics in the unstable post-independence atmosphere. In particular, by late 1960, Lumumba had fallen out with Congo's president, Joseph Kasavubu, who together with his ambitious defense chief – a certain Joseph Désiré Mobutu, who will reappear later – began plotting against him. In December 1960, Lumumba was captured and imprisoned by Mobutu's forces. He was then taken to Katanga, where his murder actually took place. This was at the hands of Tshombe's gendarmes. However, according to the recent Belgian parliamentary inquiry, the assassination took place in the presence of Belgian officers. A number of senior government figures in Brussels, it appears, were happy to see Lumumba removed, and even King Baudouin appears to have known in advance of the plot to kill the Congolese prime minister. The inquiry found no evidence of direct

Patrice Lumumba, Congo's independence leader and nationalist hero, shortly
after his arrest by Mobutu's army in December 1960. He would be executed the
following month.

Union Minière involvement. But it concluded that Belgium bore a
"moral responsibility" for the events leading to the assassination.[20]

Shortly before his death Lumumba had sent a letter from his cell
to his wife Pauline. His defiant words would resound with Africans
long after his body had been dissolved in acid. "My beloved
companion," he began:

> I write you these words not knowing whether you will receive
> them, when you will receive them, and whether I will still be
> alive when you read them.
>
> [...] History will one day have its say; it will not be the history
> taught in the United Nations, Washington, Paris, or Brussels,
> however, but the history taught in the countries that have rid
> themselves of colonialism and its puppets. Africa will write its
> own history, and both north and south of the Sahara it will be
> a history full of glory and dignity.
>
> Do not weep for me, my companion, I know that my
> country, now suffering so much, will be able to defend its
> independence and freedom.[21]

Rumbled in the jungle

Suspicions over the extent of Union Minière's role in the tragic events of the early 1960s, should not obscure a basic fact: its political strategy for protecting itself from the forces of nationalism, as represented by Lumumba's government, ultimately proved to be a failure. First of all, Tshombe's Katangan secession turned out to be short-lived, so the insulation which this development had provided for the company against political currents in the Congo as a whole did not last for long. These political currents then took a hostile direction with the rise of Joseph Désiré Mobutu as the Congo's leader. Although Mobutu had the support of the west (he came to be regarded by America as a bulwark against Communism in the region), that did not stop him turning against Union Minière, whose holdings in the Congo he nationalized in 1967. Arguably no self-respecting Congolese leader – whether Mobutu or not – would have tolerated the continued existence of a foreign corporation which had played such a central role in their country's colonial past.

What ended the secession was both diplomatic pressure from abroad and increasingly robust physical attacks by United Nations troops against the Katangan forces. International opinion was against Tshombe, and the fragmentation of the Congo posed a clear threat to security in the whole region. Gone were the days when an imperial power – certainly one the size of Belgium – could operate "a sphere of influence" free from intervention from other foreigners. An attempt in 1961 by Dag Hammarskjöld, the UN Secretary General, to negotiate a cease-fire in Katanga came to a tragic end when his plane crashed *en route* to a meeting with Tshombe. Eventually, however, even the Belgian government and Union Minière were urging their erstwhile Katangan ally to surrender peacefully.[22] Tshombe finally declared an end to the secession on 14th January 1963.

There would be a few years yet of continued regional and tribal fighting before Mobutu's rise put an end to the country's fragmentation. The situation during this interregnum was complex, and alliances continually shifted. Tshombe put in another appearance, this time as the prime minister of the Congo itself, though his period in government was even more brief than it had been in Katanga. At one point, even Che Guevara came over to join the mêlée, helping to train various African comrades in revolutionary methods near Congo's border with Tanzania.

Although Mobutu's rule – which began when he seized power in a coup in 1965 – was shaped in unique ways by his own personality, his nationalization of Union Minière cannot be seen as a historical accident. It was rather one part of an inevitable reaction to the period of colonialism and the subsequent regional chaos. For the method Mobutu used to unite the country was common to other rulers of new or fragile nations. He instilled in the population a new national identity, a sense that they were citizens of Zaire (as he decided to rename the Congo), a country both whole and defiant of meddling foreign influences. Eventually Mobutu's 32-year regime would become notorious internationally for its corruption and disastrous economic policies – but all that concerns us here is what drove him, in the late 1960s, to throw out Union Minière.

During this initial period of Mobutu's rule, Zairians were encouraged to topple Belgian statues, which symbolized colonial rule. Mobutu's campaign to rid the country of reminders of Belgium was applied not just to the names of towns and cities (Léopoldville became Kinshasa, for example), but also to the president himself. No longer happy with "Joseph Désiré Mobutu", he opted instead for "Mobutu Sese Seko Koko Ngbendu Wa Za Banga", or "the all-powerful warrior who, because of his endurance and inflexible will to win, will go from conquest to conquest, leaving fire in his wake". Such was Mobutu's unabashed remaking of the national image, and his desire to create pride in Zairian history, that even Lumumba, the man whose grisly fate he had helped seal, was proclaimed a "national hero". News of Zaire's new-found confidence also reached international shores. In 1974 Kinshasa was chosen as the location for the "Rumble in the Jungle", the world heavyweight boxing match between Muhammad Ali and George Foreman, an event which was "as much a celebration of black pride as a sporting event".[23]

This was the climate in which Union Minière was nationalized, although Mobutu's motivations for the move were practical as well as ideological. By taking full control over the Katangan mining empire he could reduce the risk that his own political power would be threatened by any future moves to secession in the region. Following the nationalization, Mobutu also hatched the idea of building a 1,800 km power line from a hydroelectric power scheme near Kinshasa all the way to Katanga. Though hugely uneconomic, one advantage of this line is that it would allow Mobutu to turn off the lights in Katanga if ever the province became rebellious again.[24]

In the event, Union Minière lost little financially as a result of the nationalization. Strong protests by the company's bosses, as well as pressure on Zaire from the World Bank and the International Monetary Fund, ensured that Mobutu provided significant compensation to the Belgians for the loss of their assets.[25] Also, an arm of Société Générale, the Belgian holding company, was contracted to provide management services to the new Congolese mining entity which replaced Union Minière. But these financial concessions could not mask what amounted to a dramatic shift in political power. In the words of one historian, the nationalization "demonstrated that the [Belgian] financial groups could maintain their stake in the country only if they submitted to the objectives of the new regime and recognized it as a full partner in the decision-making process".[26] Or, put another way, for all their political maneuverings in the Katanga, the Belgian mining managers eventually walked away from the Congo well compensated, but bereft of their empire.

An Italian job

If the story of Union Minière illustrates that the forces of nationalism may be too powerful for a multinational to hold them back – at least not using the sort of heavy-handed, imperial-style tactics applied by this Belgian firm – what about the reverse approach? Is it possible for western firms to find ways to work in friendly co-operation with these forces, rather than attempting to resist them? This was precisely the strategy of the Italian energy firm Ente Nazionale Idrocarburi which in the 1950s and 1960s attempted to ride the wave of Middle East nationalism. The second half of this chapter provides a snapshot of ENI's approach, and of the limited nature of its success.

The Islamic country which was a principal focus of ENI's efforts, Iran, was no less susceptible to nationalist tides than was the Congo. Admittedly, unlike the former Belgian territory, Iran – or Persia as it was known until 1935 – had not been subject to decades

IRAN 1960s

of direct rule by a colonial power. Nonetheless it had experienced sufficient western interference in its affairs during the imperial period for some deep local suspicions of foreign influences to have taken root.

In the second half of the nineteenth century, as noted previously, Russia and Britain had vied for influence in Persia. Russia wanted to extend its empire southwards, while Britain was anxious to protect its local trade routes to India. As well as manipulating politics in the country, both imperial powers carved out for themselves generous trade concessions. In 1901, the British persuaded the then Shah, Muzaffar al-Din, to grant them a lucrative oil concession covering most of the country's territory (this was to be operated by a company called Anglo-Persian, later to be known as Anglo-Iranian, or as it was renamed in 1954, British Petroleum).

In the past, the apparent acquiescence of Iran's rulers to the wishes of foreign investors (who in turn used bribery and other unsavory methods to win them over) had fueled opposition to their rule on a local level – and particularly among Iran's influential Islamic clergy, who condemned all sorts of external, secular influences in the country. It was precisely the desire of a later Shah to be seen by his people to be less fawning to the interests of western investors which ENI – by proclaiming its respect for nationalist movements across the developing world – would attempt to turn to its advantage.

ENI's history is much briefer than Iran's but it also provides some important context for the story. Indeed, it was the fact that the company had little history in running an overseas empire that allowed it to promote itself as a friend of countries such as Iran. Unlike Union Minière, ENI was untainted by the brush of imperialism. However, like its Belgian counterpart it was strongly shaped by the culture of its home country. A state-owned company, ENI became a corporate manifestation of some of the hopes and insecurities of post-war Italian society, and above all of the fertile imagination of its founding boss, Enrico Mattei.

What Mattei offered to Italians through his ambitious leadership of the company was a proud vision of their country at a time when national self-confidence was in short supply. It was not just that Italy had suffered defeat in the Second World War. Long before then the

country had fallen behind in the process of industrialization that had
so transformed other European nations. This was in part due to
Italy's lack of indigenous energy resources – it had little of the high-
quality coal which drove the Industrial Revolution in Britain and
Germany, and nor had much oil or natural gas been discovered on
home soil. When the country's economy began to boom after the war
– the "Italian miracle", as it became known – ENI's buccaneering
boss became associated in the minds of many Italians with this
economic turnaround (even if the activities of the company itself
made only a modest contribution to the boom).

The son of a police officer, of small build, and often shy, Enrico
Mattei had already proved himself to be a wily commercial operator
before the war, running first a tannery and then a chemicals business.
He fought bravely with the resistance during the war and shortly
afterwards was appointed by the government to run Azienda
Generale Italiana Petroli (or AGIP), a defunct, public corporation,
which had been set up by Mussolini in 1926 to look for oil in Italy
and abroad. The post-war government wanted the company simply
to be wound down and its assets sold off, but Mattei – seeing AGIP as
an ideal vehicle for his ambitions – had other ideas. He gave the go-
ahead for an exploration program in the Po valley, in Italy's
wealthier north, where in the late 1940s – in a remarkable piece of
luck – AGIP discovered large quantities of natural gas.[27]

The Po natural gas fields provided a steady stream of profits
which helped Mattei build the rest of his empire. In 1953, he pulled
off a piece of political maneuvering as impressive as his actual gas
find. He persuaded the Italian government not only to grant his firm
a monopoly over the exploitation of the Po's hydrocarbon resources,
but also to enlarge his fiefdom. Mattei was put in charge of a new
state holding company, called ENI, which controlled not just AGIP,
but a variety of other state concerns. ENI's tentacles in turn began to
extend into a broad range of industries, including chemicals,
machinery, textiles, construction, motels and highways, as well as oil
and gas.[28]

Mattei's drive, and cheeky disregard for obstacles in his way, can
be illustrated by his strategy for laying pipelines in the Po valley,
which were needed to deliver the gas to customers. Rather than wait
for the approval of locals, Mattei preferred to present them with a

© David Lees/CORBIS

Enrico Mattei, charismatic president of ENI, in 1962. His ambition was to propel ENI into the league of the world's great oil companies.

fait accompli: he once boasted of having broken 8,000 ordinances and laws.[29] According to one of his biographers:

> It was said that in Cremona, where they [ENI] could not get the permit quickly enough, they dug the trench one night right through the town, and when in the morning the Mayor came screaming and asked for the damage to be made good at once, Mattei's henchmen replied calmly that they fully agreed, that an end must be put *prestissimo* to this nuisance, and that they would fill in the trenches just as quickly as they could put in the pipe which was all ready to hand. Nothing more was heard of the matter, and the gang moved on to the next location.[30]

Across the country, there sprouted AGIP filling stations, proudly proclaiming the sale of "Italian" fuel, and accompanied by "neat little bars and restaurants with bright-colored tables, and cheerful assistants in clean uniform",[31] a notable improvement on the dour outlets to which Italian motorists had become accustomed. Mattei's populist, egalitarian, image was further enhanced by stories that ENI had abolished executive dining rooms and private elevators for managers. Mattei was on the side of ordinary workers – or at least that was the impression he wanted to create. "[The Italian] people are wealth, an immense human capital", he once proclaimed.[32]

Mattei's political philosophy was sometimes difficult to pin down, but this allowed him to appeal to Italian politicians of all hues, from Communists to Christian Democrats. In winning over parliamentarians to his cause, it must also have helped that ENI owned one of Italy's most influential newspapers, *Il Giorno*.

Crude dealing in Iran

What drove Mattei to seek deals with Middle East governments was partly economics – the desire to secure for ENI, and thereby for Italy, a reliable source of oil – but partly also his personal psychology. He had made no secret of his dislike of the seven British and American oil companies, or the "Seven Sisters" as he called them, which then dominated the industry and also controlled most of the major oilfields in the Middle East. (The companies concerned were British Petroleum, Shell, Gulf, Standard Oil of New Jersey, Standard of California, Socony-Vacuum, and Texaco; the last four, all American, were together partners in Aramco, the subject of the next chapter.) It was said that Mattei had once been treated brusquely by the boss of Standard of New Jersey, and also that he was bitter ENI had been kept out of a deal in Iran in the early 1950s by both the British and Americans. On Italian television in the early 1960s, Mattei provided a vivid depiction of how, in his perception, ENI had been treated by the "Seven Sisters". Likening his own company to a hungry cat he had once observed attempting to eat a scrap of food at a meal being devoured by dogs, he elaborated:

> The cat slowly approached the dish and as he began to eat one dog put his paw on the cat's tail and the other flung the cat ten or fifteen feet, breaking his spine. We have been like

the cat in the hold of the dogs – such were the interests aligned against us.[33]

Seeing himself thus engaged in a David and Goliath struggle with the rest of the oil industry, it was only natural that Mattei should seek to ally ENI with other parties which felt similarly oppressed – notably the governments of countries eager to demonstrate their defiance of western imperialism. As he proclaimed in a speech in Tunisia in 1960, ENI "does not operate according to the obsolete pattern of nineteenth-century colonialist capitalism but looks toward financial co-participation and joint technical and commercial management in terms of perfect equality [...] Africa and Asia are no longer objects but subjects of history in its economic tomorrow".[34] In attempts to woo the nationalist leaders of developing countries, ENI offered to train their young engineers and geologists in its own laboratories and even funded a small foreign aid program, loaning money to India, Argentina and Brazil to help these countries develop their oil industries.[35]

It was in Iran where Mattei's strategy seemed – at least at first – to reap the most dramatic rewards. In Mohammad Reza Pahlavi, or the Shah of Iran from 1941, he found a ruler particularly receptive to the idea of a new, post-colonial basis for foreign investment. For the young incumbent of Iran's Peacock Throne, as mentioned previously, wanted to demonstrate his credibility as a nationalist leader, particularly to the country's powerful Shiite Muslim clerics who were deeply suspicious of secular, western influences in the country. In 1949, an Islamic extremist had attempted to gun down the Shah at Tehran University, an incident which, though he survived remarkably unscathed, must surely have continued to play on his mind.

Indeed, it was the perceived closeness between the Shah and the western imperial nations, and the local suspicions this raised, that now made him particularly keen to be seen to assert his independence. Educated in Switzerland, the Shah had been brought to power during the Second World War after Britain and the Soviet Union had deposed his father (who at the time had been showing worrying signs of support for Nazi Germany). He had depended again upon western intervention in the early 1950s to overcome a threat to his regime from Mohammad Mossadegh, an Iranian nationalist who had been appointed as prime minister by the Majlis, the country's parliament.

In spite of Mossadegh's feeble appearance – he was around 70 and issued many of his political instructions from bed in his pajamas – this brilliant politician for a time had become hugely popular, in part because of his decision to nationalize the assets of Anglo-Iranian, which ran the main oil concession in the country dating from 1901. (Interestingly, Anglo-Iranian – like Union Minière – had over time built up impressive social and welfare facilities around its commercial operations, including schools, hospitals, roads, and even cinemas and British-style sports-clubs. But rather than endearing the company to local people, it appears that these efforts had fueled the suspicions of some Iranians that Anglo-Iranian considered itself as a colonial-style state within a state.[36])

Mossadegh's efforts to combat the foreigners had been cut short, however. In 1953, with a little covert assistance from the CIA and Britain's MI6, he had been overthrown, the Shah had been allowed to reassert his authority, and a new set of western oil interests – dominated by the "Seven Sisters" – took over the old Anglo-Iranian assets (this was the deal that had so irritated Mattei). The one concession to local nationalists in this new set-up was that actual ownership of the oil was in the hands of an Iranian state firm, the National Iranian Oil Company, though the foreigners still managed the industry, profited handsomely from it, and had control over the important decisions.

Though the Shah owed his own survival partly to such imperialist meddling, he could not ignore the popular currents which had brought Mossadegh to power and which might once again threaten his regime. This was why Mattei's promises of a new basis for foreign investment, more respectful of Iranian national interests, proved so welcome to the Shah. In that sense, Mattei's reputed offer of an Italian princess in marriage was neither here nor there. What interested the Shah most was that Mattei was promising a 75% share in the profits from any oil venture with AGIP – as opposed to the 50% typically offered by the "Seven Sisters" in such oil deals – together with genuine participation for Iranians in the management structure.

It was on this basis, in 1957, that a contract was agreed between AGIP and the National Iranian Oil Company to undertake joint exploration for oil across a 22,700 square kilometer region along the Persian Gulf.[37] This appeared to be a moment of triumph both for Mattei and the Shah. British and American oilmen expressed their disquiet at the generous terms of the deal, but this must only have intensified Mattei's pleasure. A British diplomat in Iran chanced upon ENI's boss in the Italian embassy in Iran shortly after the contract had been signed. Mattei was relaxing under a tree, happily sipping a whisky and soda and expounding "on the thesis that the Middle East should now be industrial Europe's Middle West".[38]

Though Mattei's Iranian deal made the greatest waves internationally, he made himself busy in other countries too, including Libya, Algeria, and Egypt. In Algeria, it was widely rumored that he was negotiating with the rebel FLN movement for access to the Saharan oil reserves once the country had gained its independence. This did not endear him to the French, who had been fighting a bloody war to try to keep hold of their colonial territory. In Egypt, where Gamal Abdel Nasser's takeover of the Suez Canal in 1956 had struck pride into the heart of Arab nationalists across the Middle East, Mattei bought a 20% stake in the International Egyptian Oil Company (interestingly, he was able to increase this stake in 1960 when a Belgian company Petrofina sold its own shareholding in the company: as a result of the Congo crisis, Belgian investors were no longer welcome in Egypt).[39]

Flights from power

But for all Mattei's energetic maneuverings, were his tactics successful? One thing is for sure: they fell short of his own grandiose dreams. Few of his deals to explore for oil in the developing world resulted in substantial discoveries, although production in Libya began to take off in the 1960s. It was a sign of Mattei's failure to strike it big in the Middle East that, in the early 1960s, in order to keep up with the demand for oil from Italian consumers, Mattei came to an arrangement with the Soviets to import large quantities of their crude (this was a move which Italy's western allies found particularly provocative in the context of the Cold War). And even had the contract in Iran led to the discovery of a giant oilfield, returns to ENI

would have been kept in check by the profit-sharing terms Mattei
had agreed, which were generous by the standards of the time.

As an industrial group, ENI's fortunes over the next several
decades were mixed. The company's sheer size and growth gave
Italians some pride: according to a ranking of oil companies in the late
1970s, it was the 11th largest in the world, with a growing network of
petrol outlets in Italy. But few of its investments, which covered a
range of industries, proved to be as profitable as the original Po gas
development. Many outsiders complained that ENI's accounts were
opaque and confusing. Matters were made worse by regular meddling
in the company's affairs by the Italian government.[40]

Mattei's personal fate was even less happy. In October 1962, his
private plane crashed to the south of Milan airport, killing him, and
a journalist from *Time* magazine who was preparing a feature on the
Italian oil boss. Such was the controversial nature of Mattei's business
dealings that many at first suspected his death had been arranged –
perhaps by western intelligence agencies to prevent him from
pursuing his Soviet oil deals, perhaps by French extremists annoyed
at his attempt to muscle in on Algerian oil. But such suspicions
remained unproved; the crash had occurred in a fierce thunder-
storm, suggesting the possibility that it was a pure accident. Always
in a rush, Mattei may simply have be too impatient to wait for calmer
weather before giving instructions to his pilot to land.[41]

From the perspective of this chapter, the most important point is
that ENI's tactics failed to provide the company with immunity from
a further wave of nationalism in developing countries. Mattei's
attempt to identify himself as an anti-colonialist may have been a
clever gambit in public-relations terms, but it lacked substance. In
the final analysis ENI was still a western multinational, and could not
avoid being identified as such by populist leaders whose own power
depended on tapping xenophobic sentiment. Thus, for example,
Libya nationalized 50% of ENI's holdings in the country in 1972.
This was a few years after Muammar al-Qaddafi, a radical follower of
Nasser's writings, had seized power in a coup, and had ordered
resident Italians out of the desert kingdom.

Similarly, in Iran the Shiite clerics who deposed the Shah in
1979, proceeded to nationalize all foreign oil holdings. They
appeared to draw no distinction in this respect between ENI's assets

and those of other foreign companies; all were regarded as contemptible symbols of the west. "The oil industry of our country after 80 years is liberated from the claims of imperialism", proclaimed the Iranian Oil Ministry in 1981.[42]

The reasons for the overthrow of the Shah were varied and complex and need not be explained in detail here. The next chapter will provide an opportunity to look closely at the growth of anti-western sentiment in another of the region's oil superpowers. With respect to Iran, it is enough to note that one of the factors underlying the Shah's downfall was the hostility of traditional sectors of Iranian society to rapid economic and social change – a deeply-rooted reaction which it is difficult to imagine any western multinational finding ways to control or overcome, however carefully it had managed its political interactions.

The change in the country was driven partly by rising oil prices. Per capita income in Iran grew from around $176 in 1960 to $2,500 in 1978, bringing with it an influx of western material goods, a vast migration of the population from rural to urban areas, and growing levels of corruption in daily economic life. The Shah had also consciously accelerated the process of change, hoping to transform the country into one of the world's leading industrial powers. "Give me ten years and I will make Iran a great power again", he had told a French newspaper in 1959.[43] Under a set of reforms he proclaimed as the "White Revolution", the Shah redistributed land to millions of small farmers, to the irritation of the many religious leaders who were also major landholders. He also expanded the country's road and rail network, and set up literacy and health programs for the rural population. Shiite clergy who complained about this enforced westernisation, which they said was undermining Islamic traditions, were often dealt with brutally by the Shah's secret police.

For all the Shah's grandiose attempts to provide a sense of national direction for his people (this included, for example, inviting world leaders in 1971 to a lavish celebration at Persepolis of the founding of the Persian empire 2,500 years before and comparing himself to Cyrus the Great), it was Ayatollah Ruhollah Khomeini, a fiercely anti-western cleric, who provided the most powerful rallying cry for an Iranian population buffeted by such changes. The Shah fled the country in 1979, and when it became known that he was being treated for cancer in America, the response of many Iranians was fury with America for giving him refuge, rather than sympathy for the Shah over his illness. Supporters of Komeini's revolution stormed the United States embassy in Tehran and held 66 Americans hostage while chanting anti-western slogans. The Shah died the following year.

Even had Enrico Mattei been alive during the Shah's downfall, it is hard to imagine him persuading Iran's new revolutionary leaders that, as an anti-colonialist company, ENI was really on their side, and hence should be spared nationalization. Even with his charm, it seems unlikely that Mattei would have swayed the stern, demagogic Ayatollah Khomeini – just as Union Minière ultimately could do little to dissuade the self-confident Mobutu from his course of action.

As it was, both these companies, for all their reputed power, eventually had to accept that the current was against them. In the case of Union Minière, it will be recalled, the company's attempt to insulate itself from political instability by supporting the Katangan secession not only exacerbated the bloody chaos which engulfed the Congo after its independence but this tactic also failed to prevent the company's eventual nationalization. In the case of ENI, the friendly, anti-colonial mantle adopted by the company proved little more successful a tactic over the long term for guaranteeing protection against nationalist forces.

Confronted by unexpectedly strong political tides, in short, both companies saw some of their investments swept away. Multinationals being surprised by events beyond their control is a pattern which has repeated itself many times in this book. And it will repeat itself again in the chapters to follow.

SIX

Clash of the Titans
Aramco and Saudi Arabia

O, Slave of Aramco, stooge of imperialism,
You built Nasiriyah on sweat (and moving sand).
Ah, slave of Aramco, stooge of imperialism.
You did this with the sweat of the free in your land.
People shall have a hand in exploiting their land
And the day is at hand when they will have their revenge.
They live in your prisons, tortured and behind bars.
Now you no longer pray, but kneel to the dollar;[...]
You have nightly soiled the land of the Prophet
O, Symbol of debauch, baseness, and treachery;
You are true corruption, disgrace, and lechery [...]

Poem denouncing the Saudi royal family, broadcast in 1958 by "Voice of
the Arabs", an Egyptian propaganda radio station.[1]

There were headlines and excited news bulletins the world over when Sheik Ahmed Zaki Yamani, the Saudi oil minister, and a number of other OPEC oil officials were kidnapped in Vienna on 21st December 1975, and bundled into a plane bound for Algeria. For Sheik Yamani had become famous internationally, his brilliance and confidence a symbol of the growing power of the Arab world and of OPEC, the oil cartel which had held hostage the entire western economic system with a series of embargoes and price hikes.

To some westerners, it must have seemed as though Yamani was receiving a taste of his own medicine, even if his kidnappers' methods were shockingly brutal. They had taken their hostages in Vienna after storming OPEC's offices in the city, spraying gunfire and throwing grenades at anyone who tried to stop them. One of the kidnappers, a 25-year old woman, coolly shot a policeman dead with a bullet through the neck. Their leader was a young man wearing a leather jacket and brown beret who called himself "Carlos". Originally from Venezuela, Carlos or Carlos the Jackal, as he was also sometimes known – had been trained in far-left, subversive activities in Cuba, in Moscow (at the "Patrice Lumumba Friendship University") and also with an extreme Palestinian group in the Middle East. He had a history of successful terrorist attacks behind him. The Austrian authorities had thus complied when Carlos demanded safe passage to Vienna airport and a plane on the tarmac ready to leave.[2]

Before boarding the plane with his hostages, Carlos coldly informed Yamani: "We respect you. But you will be killed because what we are doing is directed against your country." What grudge did Carlos hold against Saudi Arabia? He seemed to resent the fact that Saudi oil was being developed with money and investment from America, an ally of Israel, rather than – as he saw it – solely for the benefit of the Arab people. This outlook became clear in a radio message, a manifesto of the self-proclaimed "Arm of the Arab People", which Carlos insisted be broadcast on Austrian radio, and which denounced "American imperialism" and "Zionism".

Whatever Yamani thought of Carlos's political philosophy, he must surely have taken his threats seriously, perhaps contemplating the possibility that he would never see his family again. Earlier that year, the Saudi oil minister, still boyish-looking at the age of 45, had married his second wife, a beautiful young Saudi woman who studied biology at the American University in Beirut. He once said how much he looked forward to the decades ahead with her.

Those who had worked with Yamani often remarked not just on his charm and politeness, but also on his unruffled nature under pressure, his ability to look interrogators calmly in the eye, even while his hand worked away at worry beads (a habit that had become one of his trademarks in the media). This time, however, it is known from the reports that Yamani found it difficult to remain unperturbed. He whispered to himself verses from the Koran and before boarding the plane he scribbled out a will and a farewell message to his family. "I cannot deny that waiting for death is a frightening and painful thing", Yamani admitted.[3]

22nd December 1975, Vienna airport: at gunpoint, the kidnapped OPEC oil ministers – Sheik Yamani among them – are ordered onto the plane which will take them to Algiers, and to an uncertain fate.

The Austrian Airlines DC9 lifted off from the tarmac of Vienna airport at around 9.15am on 22nd December 1975. Inside, one of Carlos's men kept a submachine gun pointed at the pilot throughout the flight to Algiers. Yamani and his fellow hostages sat in the back, ashen-faced. The world waited with bated breath. But little known at the time was that as the plane carrying the kidnappers and the hostages streaked across the morning skies of North Africa and the Middle East it was shadowed by a private plane, a Learjet, owned by the Arabian American Oil Company, or Aramco for short, a firm controlled by American interests and with vast operations in Saudi Arabia.[4]

The order for this mission, which aimed to keep track of the kidnapping, and to provide assistance to Yamani if possible, had come from Aramco's top boss. Yamani may have appeared anti-western to the public in America and Europe. But, for the same reason that Carlos wanted to kill him, the American oil managers wanted to protect the Sheik – for they knew him to be moderate by the standards of other politicians in the Middle East, men such as Muammar al-Qaddafi, for example, who had recently taken power

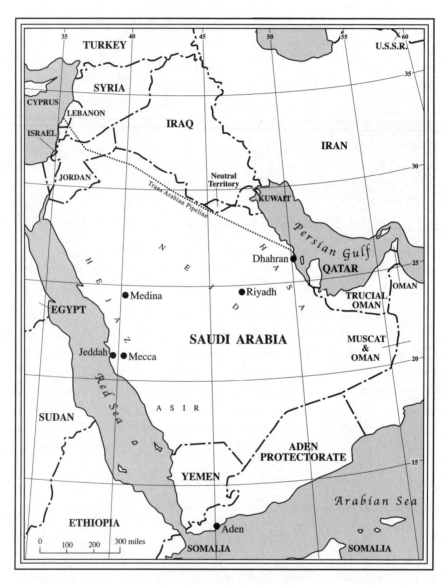

SAUDI ARABIA 1950S/1960S

in Libya. In fact it was later claimed that Qaddafi himself had commissioned Carlos to undertake the kidnapping. As the two planes prepared to land at Dar al Beida airport in Algiers, it was anyone's guess how the crisis would end. One of the only certainties was that Aramco would help Yamani if it could: despite appearances, he was one of their greatest assets.

A record loss

Yamani's kidnapping, with Aramco's jet following silently behind, symbolizes perfectly the delicate nature of multinational management in the age of "backlash". Aramco, like other western firms in the period, found itself having to support political leaders who were moderately nationalistic for fear that more extreme figures might take power. At the same time it felt it had to keep a distance from all politics, or at least give that impression, lest knowledge of its interference fueled the fire of anti-imperialism, and thereby local opposition to its activities. This sort of diplomatic, delicately balanced political strategy was typical of the approach of many other western multinationals at the time. It can perhaps best be seen as a middle route between the extreme political tactics adopted by Union Minière and ENI which were described in the previous chapter.

Yamani's kidnapping is actually just one of the finishing flourishes of a larger narrative. This is the story of how, over the space of several decades and in spite of the maneuvers of their Learjets and other such carefully calculated tactics, the group of American multinationals that originally owned Aramco were forced to surrender this prized asset to the Saudi government.

Aramco was not any old oil firm. It was the largest oil concession in the Middle East, an investment once described by one of its directors – and with some justification – as "by far the greatest, most important and most dramatic overseas American enterprise which has ever existed".[5] As noted in the introduction to this part of the book, the interest of foreign oil firms in re-entering Saudi Arabia in recent years, in spite of the political risks involved, provides some hint of the wealth they lost when they were forced out of the kingdom; and the attack on the World Trade Center in 2001 is an indication of the virulence of the anti-western sentiment which has some of its roots in the changes which Aramco wrought in Saudi society.

As with previous chapters, the aim here is tell a story which is true to its time and teases out themes which are relevant to the present. It will be shown that Aramco's experience provides a perspective not just on Middle Eastern politics in the 1960s and 1970s, but also on the problems encountered by any multinational trying to protect a large, profitable asset in the developing world in the post-imperial period. Like many developing countries in the modern era which are apparently eager for western capital, Saudi Arabia's attitude to foreign investment was originally relatively welcoming; and like many modern-day companies, Aramco tried hard to maintain stable, en-lightened, relations with the rulers and people of its host country. And even so, in spite of this promising context, the concession was lost.

The reason lies in a series of timeless dynamics, some of which have also surfaced in previous chapters. These include the way in which multinationals often trigger far-reaching social changes in the countries in which they invest, yet struggle to predict these changes, let alone to manage them. Another recurrent phenomenon is the challenge which rapid industrialization poses to the stability of tradi-tional regimes, and the maneuvering which these regimes may find necessary in order to preserve their power. A third is the tendency of western observers to perceive all events through western goggles, and to respond to them in a way which may increase their volatility.

Then there are phenomena which will be encountered for the first time in the period of "backlash" – cycles of competition between developing countries to wring ever greater concessions from foreign investors, for example, and the problems faced by multinationals in persuading these countries that they are not agents of their home governments. All these phenomena will be examined at some length, for they are patterns which easily could repeat themselves in a future era.

The first embrace

For the first several decades of the Aramco concession, it might have seemed that the problem of nationalism would be avoided, or at least kept submerged under a tide of money which gushed from the operation. It will be useful to start by describing the *modus operandi* that emerged between the Saudi rulers and the American oilmen in this early period. Although the relationship was initially stable – it might be pictured as an embrace of friendly giants – from an early stage it also contained the seeds of future tensions, which by the 1960s and 1970s would have these Titans engaged in an earth-shaking wrestling match. This later, more fraught period, which includes Yamani's kidnapping, will be returned to later in this chapter.

The Saudi oil fields would turn out to be worth trillions of dollars, but there was little excitement or expectation in the oil industry when the first concession was signed. The deal in 1933 between the Standard Oil Company of California and King Ibn Saud gave the Americans the exclusive right to explore and produce oil across much of Central and Eastern Saudi Arabia (following a supplemental agreement in 1939 the concession area was extended to cover 440,000 square miles, or an area about the size of Texas and California combined). But though the territory was vast, as yet there were few indications that much oil lay below the kingdom's barren and forbidding deserts. Under the concession agreement the government of Saudi Arabia, that is to say, Ibn Saud, would receive four shillings of gold, for every ton of crude produced.[6]

The fixer for the deal was Harry St John Bridger Philby, a British adventurer and writer fascinated by the Arab world who had struck up a close friendship with Ibn Saud (and whose son, incidentally, was Kim Philby, the British spy who was famously exposed during the Cold War as being a double agent for Stalin). Like son, like father, at least in their taste for treachery to the British crown: Philby the elder was happy to secure the deal for an American firm, even though he knew the British government would perceive such a development as a threat to its sphere of influence in the Middle East.

Article 35 in the concession which Philby helped negotiate was an "anti-imperial clause", which prohibited the company from interfering in "administrative, political or religious affairs within Arabia". According to Philby, Ibn Saud at various points dozed off while the lengthy concession document was read out to him by his finance minister. But it was eventually signed and the following night

Ibn Saud's "privy council devoted its sitting to a long discussion of women and their ways: the King did not sleep on this occasion, and was the life and soul of the party".[7]

The culture of Ibn Saud's court and his kingdom will be explored in more detail further on. But the culture of the American oil companies which came to be involved in the concession is equally important to the story. These expanded in number following Standard of California's initial deal, as the quantity of oil beneath the desert proved itself to be beyond the capacity of a single entity to exploit. First, the Texas Company (later Texaco), and then Standard Oil of New Jersey (later Exxon) and Socony-Vacuum Oil Company (later Mobil), bought stakes in the deal. Together these four companies came to control the concession, which itself became known in 1944 as Aramco. Although these Aramco partners made considerable efforts to stay on good terms with the Saudi elite, and to embed their business successfully within Saudi society, their approach was sometimes naïve and inward-looking. And some cultural problems they encountered were simply inescapable.

Cultural legacies

Even though Aramco's ownership structure meant that no one parent firm was in charge – in the words of one oilman, "Aramco was, in effect, the neurotic child of four parents, subject to the whims, qualms and jealousies of each"[8] – the companies involved shared a broadly similar cultural outlook on the external world, for not only were they all based in America, but also three of the four firms were descendants of Rockefeller's old empire. This common legacy made them particularly aware of the potential for popular anger against the oil business – though it did not make them experts at dealing with such political antagonism in a developing country.

The typical senior manager of Standard of New Jersey, the largest of the parents, for example, was more likely to be a brilliant chemical engineer rather than a seasoned diplomat, with experience of running a refinery in America's deep South rather than a concession in the Middle East. Anthony Sampson, a British writer on multinationals, visited Standard of New Jersey's towering headquarters in New York in the 1970s and even then found the globe-trotting directors more at ease in the security of their offices than in dealing with the outside world: "once outside their own territory, their confidence easily evaporates", he noticed. "Confronting their shareholders they seem thoroughly nervous, sitting in a row, their fingers fidgeting and their cheekbones working [...] They know well enough that their company, while one of the oldest, has also been the most hated."[9] In an attempt to overcome the American public's profound dislike of "big oil", the directors had initiated a major PR and "corporate responsibility" program in the 1940s, which included funding various educational programs[10] – though there is little evidence that the company became much more popular as a result.

As for the "child" – Aramco – it made even greater efforts to present itself as a progressive entity though its approach, like that of Standard of New Jersey, also sometimes lacked sophistication. What made Aramco's managers particularly keen to develop an enlightened relationship with the Saudi people was not just article 35 of the concession, but also their slightly self-conscious belief that, as Americans, they ought to be behaving in a less colonial way in the region than had the British. New American recruits to Aramco, for example, were given briefing sessions on Saudi customs and on how to avoid misunderstandings. Among other things, they were advised against offering Arabs lifts in their cars; some locals, accustomed only to travel by camel, had stepped out of vehicles travelling at full speed.[11] Aramco also produced a bulky handbook for American employees providing information on the history and culture of the Middle East that proclaimed the company as "a great proving ground for the ability of people of widely different cultures and backgrounds [...] to work together harmoniously in projects of great mutual advantage".[12] And there was *Aramco World*, a glossy magazine with regular features on aspects of Arab life, including, for example, a long article by one of Aramco's senior lawyers in one issue in praise of Shari'ah law.[13]

Though Aramco was reluctant, naturally, to surrender much of its profits to the Saudi government, its cross-cultural efforts went beyond public relations. It established various hospitals, clinics and schools in the kingdom (by the mid-1970s, it had built 54 schools in total[14]), for example, and awarded scholarships to hundreds of

Saudis to study in the United States. Experts in politics and diplomacy, including various PhDs, were drafted into the government relations department to guide interactions with Ibn Saud's court. One such expert was the late William Mulligan, who had been sent by the company to study classical and Islamic studies at the Hartford Seminary Foundation in Connecticut, and whose recently discovered papers form the basis of an interesting account of Aramco's history by the writer Anthony Cave Brown.[15]

Another revealing source on the company's relations with the Saudis is Michael Sheldon Cheney, the son of a New York drama critic who worked as a public-relations officer for Aramco in the 1950s, and who later wrote up his experiences in a frank memoir, *Big Oilman from Arabia*. Cheney supported the intention behind Aramco's philanthropic efforts, that is, "to prove that a private Western concern can develop the oil resources of an 'underdeveloped' Eastern country with equal profit to company and country, and without abridging the host nation's sovereignty or the interests of its people". But he could not help remarking that "set against the popular picture of the big bad oil industry, this little band of altruistic executives, carrying their shining doctrine through the Stygian night of Middle Eastern politics, strongly suggested a troop of Boy Scouts set adrift in a brothel".[16]

One relatively minor cultural problem in the company's early days was that its Saudi employees, accustomed as they were to the natural rhythms of life in the desert, often found it difficult to understand the American managers' demands that they work according to a fixed timetable; and likewise the Americans often became frustrated with what they saw as the Saudis unreliability. Eventually it was possible to smooth over such problems, with some give-and-take and pragmatism on both sides. This was also true with regard to language difficulties. In the early years of the concession, for example, few American managers spoke Arabic, and likewise few of their Saudi employees spoke English, so in day-to-day interactions a form of dialect emerged – a combination of simple words, and grunts and gesticulations – to allow for communication.[17]

Other cultural differences between the Americans and Saudis, however, remained stark over time. The main way in which Aramco succeeded in attracting good expatriate managers to what otherwise would have been considered a hardship posting in the desert, for example, was to create enclaves of American culture around its rigs, refineries and other facilities. These were not dissimilar to the banana enclaves created by United Fruit or to Elizabethville, Union Minière's mining town. Around Aramco's headquarters in Dhahran, on the country's east coast, for example, "bungalow houses sprang up in neat rows, with creepers up the walls and green lawns alongside the desert, and a complete suburb formed itself with a baseball park, a cinema, swimming-pools and tennis courts. It was an astonishing optical illusion, looking like a small town from Texas or California", observed Anthony Sampson.[18]

The differences between corporate life and the local society were thrown into particular relief on the occasions when members of the Saudi royal family, travelling with their entourage of servants, princes, wives, and falconers, would pay interested visits to Aramco's facilities. Tents would be set up amid the bungalows and company buildings, and the Saudis innocently would dig up the neat lawns to create their evening fires. It was at one point Cheney's job, as a public-relations official, to facilitate these visits. While the Saudi dignitaries were well cared for, as soon as they had left, the compound's surroundings would be returned to the state in which their American residents preferred them kept.[19]

In Aramco's day-to-day operations, too, the perspective of the Americans was inevitably different from that of many local people, and many of the company's managers were imbued, as were United Fruit's bosses, with a sense that they were taming a wilderness. Aramco's exploration geologists, for example, would travel for days across the so-called Empty Quarter or the many other vast and barren expanses in the country's interior. Buffeted by fierce sandstorms, and encountering occasional groups of Bedouin along the way, they would map the lie of the land, drill into the rock, and take samples. When oil was discovered, as it often was, in far greater quantities than anyone dared imagine (the great Ghawar field, for example, was a veritable underground ocean of crude, 241 kms long and 35 kms wide), there would roll into the desert further evidence of the modern world – trucks, rigs, pipelines, pumping stations, even airplanes. And the Bedouin often would be watching with a combination of shock and amazement.

Band of brothers

The sight of giant, western machines was just one of the unsettling new experiences for many local inhabitants. If Aramco's early cross-cultural efforts faced some inherent obstacles, this was no less true for Saudi society itself during the first several decades of the concession's existence. For the Saudi nation was not only a recent, and hence relatively fragile, creation. The very nature of its founding had raised a question which would create endless internal tensions in the future: should the country be open to, or should it cut itself off from, western influences?

It was Ibn Saud who was directly responsible for creating the country (and it was named after his own clan, the House of Saud). He had achieved his victory in 1932, having successively conquered and united various tribal territories. The king was a brave warrior, originally from Riyadh, a desert town roughly in the center of the Arabian peninsula. After an early period of exile in Kuwait, he had returned to recapture his home province, the Najd, from a rival faction, and from there had subdued both the Al Hasa province to the East, and the cosmopolitan Hijaz province, with its holy cities of Mecca and Medina, to the West.

Though a pragmatic man, Ibn Saud was a member of the Wahhabi sect, a puritanical branch of Islam, and his conquest of the various provinces of the peninsula had been undertaken with the help of the Ikhwan, or "the brethren". These were the strictest group within the Wahhabis, and Ibn Saud had had a hand in their creation himself, even if he no longer controlled them entirely: their origins lay in an elite fighting force, educated in fundamentalist Islamic precepts, which the king had recruited from among the Bedouin of the region in the 1910s.

Clearly recognizable in the towns of Saudi Arabia – the men wore white robes, pointed beards and black antimony paste around their eyes[20] – the Ikhwan denounced western influences, including music and unveiled women, and dealt violently with fellow countrymen who strayed from the path of pure Islam. Towards the end of his campaigns, Ibn Saud had forcibly disbanded his band of religious fighters, for they had begun to turn on him for allowing such western innovations as automobiles and telephones. Even without official support, however, the Ikhwan's influence in the country remained significant.

Demonstrating his virility off as well as on the battlefield, Ibn Saud fathered a large number of offspring (including 45 recorded sons) by his many wives during the course of his life. But the costs of maintaining this exponentially growing family became particularly difficult in the early 1930s when revenues from pilgrimages to Mecca, one of his government's principal sources of income, declined sharply. These tight circumstances were what encouraged him to sign away the oil exploration rights to the kingdom in 1933, to a western company no less. But Ibn Saud's pragmatic nature was to the fore now, and he hoped the deal would help tide him over till better times.

For the time being his kingdom's population (which had reached an estimated five to six million by 1960) continued to live as they had for centuries, a lifestyle in which survival and the search for water were the primary concerns, and in which Islam provided spiritual sustenance. Roughly half of the king's subjects engaged in subsistence farming, their homes clustered around oases; and many of the rest were Bedouin, desert nomads whose seasonal migrations across the wilderness accompanied by their herds of camels and other animals were determined by the patterns of rainfall across the land.

Oil development would have various long-term impacts on the Saudis, but there were numerous immediate effects too. An example would be the changes brought by the Trans-Arabian Pipeline, a 1,068-mile stretch of metal tubing interspersed with pumping stations which Aramco laid across the desert to export oil from the fields near the Gulf coast in the east to the Mediterranean in the west. Tapline, to give the project its abbreviated name, crossed various Bedouin travelling routes, and in order to persuade the Saudis to grant the company permission for construction, Aramco had drilled dozens of deep wells along the line to provide water for the passing nomads.

Overnight, these wells altered centuries-old migration patterns: by 1950 they were playing host to an estimated 100,000 Bedouin and 150,000 of their camels. Cheney journeyed along Tapline in the 1950s and describes a visit to one of the wells:

We drove in at sunset to find thousands of skittery, sham-
bling, bawling beasts milling around the troughs. It was a
scene of indescribable noise and confusion, overhung by a
haze of dust turned blood-red by the setting sun. [...] The
cameleers somehow preserved a sort of order among the
shifting herds, leading their animals up to drink as space
opened at the troughs, calling them away again with signals
recognized only by their own beasts.

Nearby, Cheney visited a new town adjacent to a pumping station.
Planned with the help of Tapline's engineers, it was laid out in "neat
blocks, with strangely broad streets" and hosted a growing population of local contractors, artisans and merchants, all dependent on
business with the company.[21]

Another immediate manifestation of the effects of oil was in the
behavior of Ibn Saud's family. Once camels or other traditional
goods would have sufficed as symbols of patronage and status for the
ruling dynasty. Now, with revenues generated by Aramco for the
Saudi government rising fast (in the period leading up to 1950, the
company had paid the government less than $150 million in
royalties, whereas between 1950 and 1964, its contribution to state
coffers totaled $4.5 billion),[22] only palaces, Cadillacs, and feasts of
unimaginable lavishness would do. Ibn Saud built himself a $25
million palace complex in Riyadh complete with a 200-bed hospital,
a university, and a large harem surrounded by an exotic garden. It
is an indication of the lax nature of budgetary controls that the Saudi
politician who built in his own palace "a submarine nightclub with
walls of glass, through which the circumambient fish could watch the
dancing" was none other than the king's finance minister. It was also
said that some Saudi princes would throw away their newly bought
Cadillacs once the ashtrays became full.[23]

Another common, though more sensible, use of the oil money
was sending bright young Saudis abroad to study. One of the
beneficiaries of this trend was Sheik Yamani. Born into an eminent
family from the Hejaz province and the son of an Islamic judge, the
young Yamani was dispatched by the Saudi government in the 1950s
to study law in America, first attending New York University and
then Harvard Law School. But whereas Yamani appeared to adapt

relatively easily to American culture, other young Saudis who studied abroad seemed unable to establish for themselves a psychological middle ground between their Islamic roots and the temptations on offer in the west. The experiences of Prince Faisal Ibn Musaid, one of the grandsons of Ibn Saud, provide an example of this. While a student in America, Prince Faisal was arrested in possession of LSD. He moved from college to college, and once became involved in a bar-room brawl. Once back in Saudi Arabia, however, he not only rediscovered Islam, but became convinced by the puritanical, furiously anti-western beliefs of the Ikhwan.[24]

This unstable prince will return again later in the story. But one initial conclusion can be drawn from his early experiences, from the continued influence of the Ikhwan in the country, and also from the profligacy of the royal family: that the wealth brought by oil, rather than helping to resolve the underlying ideological tensions within Saudi society, had the potential to exacerbate them too.

Shifting sands

With this context in mind it is now possible to begin tracing the processes which, over time, forced the four American companies that owned Aramco to surrender their giant concession. This did not occur as the result of a revolution, in which the Saudi regime was overthrown by radical nationalists or religious extremists, though at times that may have appeared a likely outcome. What happened instead was a largely peaceful, but no less seismic, transfer of power in which demands for nationalization within the regime itself built up an unstoppable momentum. And this was in spite of the benefits which Aramco had brought to Saudi Arabia, or at least to its rulers, underpinning not just a vast increase in their wealth but also bringing them close economic and political ties with America, the world's leading capitalist power.

One of the interesting aspects of this story, as mentioned at the start of the chapter, is that it is possible to detect in it various timeless phenomena: the problems faced by modern multinationals in coping with the social and political changes triggered by their own activities, for example, and the susceptibility of otherwise pro-western regimes to be swept along by anti-western currents.

What were the underlying pressures on the Saudi regime? A driving factor within the kingdom was an expectation of ever-increasing wealth which had built up both within the royal family, and also among many ordinary Saudis. Financial claims on Aramco were outpacing oil production, which itself was rising at a steep rate. Among the royals, greed and profligacy played a part in this, but an appetite for material goods was also an understandable reaction from a local population suddenly exposed to western-style media. Observing the introduction of televisions in the kingdom, for example, Aramco's political agent in Riyadh observed:

> The appearance of beautiful homes, fancy cars, modern appliances and beautiful dresses, in both Western and Arabic movies, instils a desire in many of the viewers to possess things which they are not able to afford. This has been excellent for business in the Eastern Province in the short term, but may cause considerable social discontent over the long term.[25]

Aramco's Arab employees began to experience similarly ambitious aspirations, and hence frustrations. Their wages were far above the average income in the country (the average Saudi employee's income was $1,300 in 1957, according to Cheney, compared with less than $50 for the ordinary Saudi citizen).[26] Yet by dint of their relative lack of technical experience and skills, an effective apartheid emerged between them and their foreign managers. Perhaps the most grating manifestation of this for the Saudis was in Aramco's provision of accommodation, where their own spartan blocks contrasted with the well-tended private houses, and even swimming pools, enjoyed by their bosses. The company had committed over time to train Arabs to take management positions but many Saudis said the process was not moving fast enough.

Feeding these domestic pressures, in turn, were nationalist developments across the Arab world, some of which have been described previously. Throughout the region, regimes supported directly or indirectly by the old imperial powers were coming under threat. The Saudi royals worried that they might be next. In Egypt, Gamal Abdel Nasser's calls for pan-Arab unity and for "the reconquest by the people of real decision-making power" and of "an identity crushed by colonialism"[27] resonated with many Saudis, though they made the royal family nervous, especially when Nasser's propaganda radio station accused them of being a "slave of Aramco" and "stooge of imperialism" (see the poem quoted at the start of this chapter).

What made co-operation with the American oil industry even more politically awkward for the Saudi royals was America's support for Israel. Opposition to the Zionist state was one issue that united otherwise quarrelsome Arab countries. King Ibn Saud himself was fiercely anti-Zionist. In the early 1940s, for example, he wrote to America's President Roosevelt about the long-standing "enmity" between Arabs and Jews, enmity which "is well known and mentioned in our holy books". But in the eyes of Arab opponents of his regime, Ibn Saud had sold out to Zionist forces merely by working with American companies, and his critics would not let him, or his successors, forget it.

Influences on the Saudi regime from other Arab countries were not just ideological. Practical tactics were beginning to be used elsewhere to extract more money, at least in the short term, from domestic oil reserves. OPEC, established in 1960, provided a means by which the oil-rich countries could present a united front to the western companies. What particularly worried the companies was the process of "leapfrogging" whereby a deal struck with one developing country would lead to demands for an equivalent, if not more generous deal, from other countries. And it did not help that upstart firms such as ENI were happy to compromise with Middle East rulers in order to secure oil concessions of their own.

In the future, the Saudi regime would often play a moderating role in debates within OPEC, urging caution on price rises for example. However, this was less because of any inherent sympathy with the west and more because Saudi Arabia's vast reserves – bigger than any other country's – gave it a greater interest in the long-term stability of the oil market (too high a price, it feared, would turn the consuming nations off oil in decades to come). When it came to nationalization, meanwhile, the Saudi regime would find the herd instinct among OPEC nations difficult to resist.

Early skirmishes

These, then, were the underlying pressures. But what did they mean in practice for Aramco? What were the flashpoints on the ground? And how did the company respond? An early issue was King Ibn Saud's demands for a greater share in the profits of the venture, though here it was possible, at least at first, to respond favorably to the Saudis at little cost to shareholders. In 1950 Aramco agreed to award the king a full half of the profits. However, by convincing the American government that this constituted a tax which should be deducted from its tax liabilities at home, Aramco was able to keep its own profits intact.[28]

Occasionally, too, other opportunities presented themselves to curry favor with the Saudis at little cost. In the early 1950s, for example, the company provided assistance – including advice from its political experts and the supply of reconnaissance vehicles – to the Saudi government in its dispute over a patch of territory near the country's south-east border. This territory was also claimed by the British-protected Sultanate of Muscat and Oman; Aramco had little hesitation in siding with Saudi Arabia against the British and their imperial ways.[29]

But such maneuvers by the company, however astute, could serve only as temporary responses to the changes under way in Saudi Arabia. It is not that Aramco's managers were blithe to what was happening in the kingdom. In fact, even a few far-sighted people in the American government were predicting problems ahead. In 1950, an internal US State Department paper on Middle East oil worried about the increasingly "anti-American undertone" in relations between the Saudis and Aramco and about the Saudis' incessant "nibbling" at the terms of the original concession. It also expressed the fear that the forces of nationalism and Communism might combine throughout the Middle East to dangerous effect.[30] But there was a difference between pinpointing and predicting broad socio-political trends which might threaten the concession, and dealing sensibly with them. It was difficult enough for Aramco to keep track of the shifting political alliances within the Saudi royal family; influencing the development trajectory of an entire nation was another matter entirely.

Even simple initiatives intended to assist the population, by which Aramco hoped to prove its post-imperial credentials, could provoke suspicion. At one point, for example, the company produced a film to raise the awareness of local people about insect-borne diseases and the importance of sanitation. But it was banned by a Saudi provincial governor who, in Cheney's words, "took one look at the sneak preview and turned thumbs down. He didn't, he said, see why we chose to go to such lengths to portray the Saudis as filthy people".[31]

Even in employee relations, an issue over which the company had significant control, it was finding it difficult to keep Arab resentments in check. This reached an initial climax in 1953 when a group of young, well-educated Saudi employees issued a petition to Aramco demanding pay increases and other benefits. This was an unprecedented move – unions were unheard of in Saudi Arabia – and the government seemed unsure as to how to respond. Ibn Saud was reluctant to undermine the company that generated most of his kingdom's income, yet equally felt obliged to uphold Saudi national pride.

When a Royal Commission, specially appointed to temporize between the company and the employees, slung the workers' representatives in jail because of their forthright manner, a full-scale strike broke out. A crowd of angry Saudi employees hurled rocks at the local police station where their leaders were being held and Aramco's American managers began to worry that the mob might turn on them. Eventually, however, the Royal Commission opted to appease the workers rather than provoke them further. It insisted on a string of concessions from Aramco, including higher pay for Saudis, a doubling of their vacations, and more subsidized houses and schools. In Cheney's eyes, the government had opted to "show Aramco as the villain of the case" in order to preserve its legitimacy.[32] It was a politically expedient tactic which the royal family would call upon again in the future.

Crude maneuvers

The events surrounding the formation of OPEC in 1960 provide another indication that developments were beginning to spiral out of

Aramco's control. Indeed, the oil cartel might not have come into existence were it not for the politically inept maneuvers of Standard of New Jersey, Aramco's largest parent. A key character in this episode was Abdullah Tariki, who came to be known as the "Red Sheik" among western oilmen because of his radical leanings. The son of a camel owner from the Najd province, Tariki had excelled in science as a student, won a scholarship to study oil geology in America, and also worked for a time for Texaco in Texas and California. In 1955, back in Saudi Arabia, the government appointed him to run the newly created Directorate of Oil and Mining Affairs.

Tariki, it soon became clear, was a fan of Nasser's nationalist writings, and began trying to put his political ideas into practice in his dealings with Aramco. He accused the company of manipulating its figures to reduce its taxes, for example, and demanded positions for Saudis on the company's board (he himself was appointed an Aramco director in 1959). In the late 1950s, William Mulligan, one of Aramco's resident Arab experts, had given a presentation to the company's managers explaining the suspicions of men like Tariki about the very basis of the Aramco concession. In their view, according to Mulligan, "the Saudi Government was hoodwinked into giving concession rights to an enormous area for a song, because the Company was sophisticated and the Government negotiators were simple 'barefoot' boys who did not realize what they were doing".[33]

Such warnings concerning Arab resentment were not sufficiently understood by the bosses of Standard of New Jersey, or Jersey for short. In 1960, in response to a recent weakness in global oil markets, Jersey decided to cut the "posted" price of its crude oil. This "posted" price was used to calculate the revenue due to governments of producing countries, and the cut thereby reduced the Saudi government's income by $30 million for the year 1960–1961.[34] What really incensed the producing countries was that Jersey announced the cut unilaterally, without consulting them.

Though Jersey's move was largely the result of political naïvety, in Tariki's eyes it symbolized the arrogant, patronizing attitude of the western oil firms. "They treat us like children", he fumed. "Now it's about time for the oil companies to [...] work for the governments and peoples of the countries in which they are operating".[35] In September 1960, he presided over an emergency congress of Middle

East oil ministers at which OPEC was formed, its initial membership consisting of Saudi Arabia, Iraq, Iran, Kuwait and Venezuela.

Within a few years, much to Aramco's relief, Tariki found himself out of a job in Saudi Arabia. This was the result of changes at the top of the ruling dynasty. Ibn Saud had died in 1953, and had been succeeded by one of his sons, Saud, who in turn had been deposed by his half-brother, Faisal, in 1964. Faisal (not to be confused with the young prince of the same name who was encountered earlier) was an interesting-looking man – "his gnarled face – the mean-looking downward twist of his lips – seemed symptomatic of his deep cynicism, till he smiled, when he radiated kindness and warmth"[36] – and it was he who took a dislike to Tariki, and who appointed Yamani in his place as oil minister. Faisal had been impressed by the young Yamani's soft-spoken intelligence, and over time a strong friendship evolved between the two men: "I thought of him as a father", Yamani would later say.[37]

Some within Aramco interpreted this appointment as a sign of Faisal's moderation, for his new oil minister's charm and diplomacy contrasted sharply with Tariki's brash denunciations of the western oil companies. Certainly Faisal, like Ibn Saud, was a pragmatist. Though a devout Muslim, he understood well his regime depended on the revenues which flowed from the concession, and was reluctant to take precipitous action in this regard. He was also astute, knowledgeable about international affairs, and intent on curbing corruption within his government. But again, like Ibn Saud before him, the new king could not ignore the pressures on the regime at home and abroad. Shortly after his accession to the throne, for example, a shoot-out had occurred in Riyadh after Saudi police had tried to stop religious activists dressed in the garb of the Ikhwan trying to wreck a new television station. Meanwhile, Tariki, though no longer welcome in Saudi Arabia, was continuing his nationalist maneuvers elsewhere, offering advice on oil issues to the Iraqi and Algerian governments.

Any hopes within Aramco that Faisal's reign would see a return to the original harmony between the company and regime were dashed in June 1967, when there erupted the latest in a series of conflicts between Israel and its Arab neighbors. It was at times like this that the regime's political balancing act – supporting American investment in the country, and yet siding with other Arab countries in their opposition to Israel – appeared most precarious. On 6th June 1967, to a chanting crowd of angry Saudis in Riyadh, Faisal insisted that: "we will regard any state or country which supports Zionist and Israeli aggression against the Arabs as an aggressor against us". He also demanded that Aramco stop shipments of oil to America and Britain, as part of a co-ordinated Arab embargo against these western supporters of Israel. Yet at the same time, in private conversations, he and Yamani were asking the Americans to stay in the country, and promising them protection from the angry mobs which were now surrounding Aramco's facilities too.

For Aramco's American employees these were fraught days, for at first the promised protection did not arrive and local Saudi police began to join with the protestors rather than holding them back. At the American consulate in Dhahran, that oasis of American culture in the desert which was also home to Aramco's headquarters, a Saudi mob over a thousand strong threw rocks and chanted anti-western slogans. Aramco began to prepare planes to evacuate American personnel. To the company's relief, however, the protests soon abated and, following a cease-fire agreement between Israel and Egypt, a well-armed – and pro-American – Saudi protection force arrived at its facilities.[38]

The significance of this episode is not just that it was a fleeting moment of tension for Aramco: it also symbolized an historical shift. For this was no longer the imperial era in which companies could call without hesitation upon their own armies for protection. In future moments of extreme crisis, it is true, American troops would be sent *en masse* to protect Saudi oilfields – as happened in the Gulf war. But for the time being, as was now frighteningly apparent to Aramco's managers, their lives depended on Saudi security. And this made them all the more eager to co-operate with moderate Saudi leaders, men such as Yamani who, though nationalists, at least were not baying for their blood.

Giant negotiations

Among the key goals of Aramco, as set out by Tom Barger, who became the company's president in the early 1960s, was "To preserve the Concession and to optimize the returns to the Shareholders over the term of the Concession".[39] From the late 1960s onwards, Aramco's hold over the concession shifted, in a stage-by-stage process, from total control to total surrender, at a huge loss to shareholders.

The early skirmishes between Aramco and Saudi Arabia, and the tensions which underlay them, have been described. From the late 1960s, the showdown itself – the battle of the Titans – begins in earnest. But it is waged not with weapons, but through peaceful negotiations, through countless meetings between company managers and their Saudi opponents in offices, palaces, and luxury hotels across the globe, at which prices and percentages and compensation terms are hammered out in painstaking detail. What gives the battle added momentum, however, is a series of startling events, including an oil price shock and Yamani's kidnapping, running in parallel. And another parallel development, which chimes with the themes of this book and which will be explored in more detail later, is the way in which the Middle East oil crises of the 1970s helped trigger angry, but also curiously disconnected, debates in the west.

Yamani's strategic thinking, and skills as a negotiator, determined the nature of the battle from the start. His ultimate aim, though he kept this to himself, was full Saudi ownership of Aramco in the long term. But like his patron, King Faisal, whom he kept closely informed on oil matters, he wanted to avoid any sudden nationalization, as this might disrupt the country's revenues. He also wanted to maintain the inward flow of American technology, and management expertise until his countrymen were fully sufficiently skilled and prepared in this respect. So he proposed Saudi "participation" in Aramco – that is, the government taking a small percentage stake in the company – rather than its outright "nationalization", a formula that was liable to panic the American oilmen. With this aim in mind, Yamani secured an OPEC resolution in 1968 stating that "each government may require a reasonable participation" in the exploitation of its own oil.[40] "Give me the rantings and ravings of Tariki any day", an American oilman once exclaimed, "Yamani drives you to the wall with sweet reasonableness".[41]

In February 1972, Aramco's negotiators, led by Frank Jungers, a politically-astute American engineer who had taken over as the company's president in the late 1960s, met with Yamani in Jeddah for the latest round of their talks. At the time, thousands of pilgrims, recently returned from the *hajj* in nearby Mecca, were thronging the port city. One western observer noted at the time:

> One of the small pleasures of attending the Aramco–Saudi confrontation was to watch the preoccupied businesslike expressions on the faces of the American oilmen soften ever so slightly as they pushed their way to the morning conferences through the merry hordes of giggling, frizz-haired girls from Nigeria, nomads from the Sudan, bare-dugged old ladies from Abidjan, and smiling sari-ed men and women from Bali, the Philippines, Malaysia and India. Here were human beings at peace with themselves, happy and relaxed, and even momentary contact with them was a relief from the tense business in hand.[42]

By the end of that year, the American oilmen had made their first significant retreat. Aramco, in common with some other foreign-owned oil concessions in the Gulf region, would permit 25% participation by the respective host government, a proportion gradually increasing to 51% in 1983. It was fear of a worse outcome, such as sudden nationalization, and the possibility of further instability within Saudi Arabia – all of which was deftly suggested by Yamani, even if not explicitly threatened by him – which awoke Aramco to the inherent weakness of its position.

This process of "participation" was then forcefully accelerated as a result of a combination of events outside Saudi Arabia. Even more dramatic terms began to be demanded by other Middle East countries. In Libya, for example, Qaddafi – who had recently toppled King Idris in a coup – began nationalizing foreign firms. With global demand for oil now rising faster than available supplies, OPEC's calls for higher prices could no longer be brushed off, as they once had been by the western companies. Then, in October 1973, there erupted another Arab-Israeli war, with an attack on the Jewish state by Egypt and Syria. In protest at western support of Israel, the Arab nations imposed another oil embargo, sending the oil price rocketing – the first oil "shock" – and inducing a crisis in the global economic system.

Ideological webs

For all the western oil companies this was a period of extreme political tension. Those firms still in control of Middle East concessions faced demands from Arab governments that they help enforce the embargo against the very countries in which they were headquartered; meanwhile the governments of consuming countries, their entire transport systems under threat, applied heavy pressure on the oil companies for a larger share of available supplies.

Aramco, too, found itself caught in a web of irreconcilable political demands. Believing Aramco's parent companies to have significant influence in Washington, King Faisal demanded that they try to bring about a shift in American policy on Israel, at one point in 1973 threatening to cancel the concession if this was not achieved. Following one audience with the King, Frank Jungers nervously noted in an internal Aramco memo: "He mentioned that except for Saudi Arabia today it was most unsafe for American interests and in Saudi Arabia, where he emphasized that a deep-seated friendship had always and still existed, it would be more and more difficult to hold off the tide of opinion that was now running so heavily against America".[43]

Aramco tried to carry out the king's wishes. In a whistle-stop tour of America, for example, Jungers paid visits to over 30 chief executives of large domestic corporations, trying to impress on them the need for a more "even-handed" (i.e. pro-Arab) American policy in the Middle East. In October 1973, the bosses of the four Aramco parents even wrote directly to President Nixon warning, among other things, that increased US military aid to Israel could upset "our relations with the moderate Arab producing countries".[44] In spite of Faisal's hopes, however, there is little evidence that these political interventions by Aramco brought about any shift in American foreign policy – though they did provoke hostile comment in the domestic media about the oil firms' pro-Arab stance.

Whatever the rights and wrongs of Aramco's frantic maneuverings, it is worth noting a general lesson that all multinationals in the post-imperial era can draw from them: however hard companies try to work in sympathy with the developing countries in which they invest, or however hard they try to present themselves as non-political, a perception will always persist in these countries that they are agents of their home governments. When political disagreements arise between home and host country – as inevitably they will – multinationals can expect to be caught in the cross-fire, and to be called upon to serve the incompatible interests of both sides.

In the angry public reaction in the west to the oil crisis of 1973 lies another timeless phenomenon worth noting (and one which has been observed at regular intervals throughout this book, starting with British "ethical" pressure on the East India Company): the tendency of western debates to reflect more the habitual concerns of the western mind, rather than the situation on the ground. Two of the most widespread western reactions fit this pattern well. The first was a theory that became popular for a time in both America and Europe, that the oil price rise was the result of explicit collusion between the Middle East countries and profit-hungry western oil companies. In America, a series of official investigations were launched into the behavior of the oil companies. Among these was a Senate investigation chaired by Senator Henry Jackson, a skilled populist with strong suspicions of the industry. "The American people want to know if this so-called energy crisis is only a pretext; a cover to eliminate the major source of price competition [...]", he declared.[45]

Without doubt, the profits of the western firms had been swelled dramatically as a result of the price rise, while the negative effects of "participation" and nationalization would often take years to feed through into their bottom line. Nor were the companies unhappy about this. But there was a difference between profiting from the price rise, and colluding in it, and the mistrusting relationship between the firms and the Middle East countries certainly precluded any major attempt by them to rig the market in unison. The oil "shock" was the result of collusion yes, but most likely collusion between the OPEC governments alone.

For the American consumer, however, with long queues forming at gasoline stations across the country, the villainy of the oil industry must have been an obvious conclusion to draw. It was evident, in the eyes of many Americans, that the firms were putting profits before principles and before their duty to the nation. An added appeal of this notion was that it required no knowledge of the confusing politics of various far-flung Arab countries.

The oil shock also gave great momentum to another idea (and this is the second key western response): that the world's natural resources were being over-exploited. Already an article of faith among environmental activists, the fear here was that the capitalist system, with its never-ending quest for profits, was leading to levels of consumption of material goods which could not be sustained over the long term. "The Club of Rome", a respected body of experts, issued a widely acclaimed report which gave warning about the dangers of resource depletion and other "Limits to Growth", as the publication was entitled. And "Small is Beautiful", an environmental tract recommending a return to community-based economic organization in place of "an industrial system that consumes so much and accomplishes so little",[46] became wildly popular. There may be some irony in the fact that this ideological attack on large-scale production had sold over 750,000 copies by the late 1970s.

The point here is not to dispute these environmental concerns (though it is true that resource prices have followed a broadly downward trend since the 1980s, indicating that global supplies of minerals have in general more than kept up with demand so far – contrary to the warnings in the 1970s of impending scarcity). What is of interest instead is how a global crisis driven largely by nationalism in the developing world and by a conscious decision on the part of Arab countries to restrict oil supplies, rather than by any physical scarcity *per se*, became reinterpreted in western debates in a way which chimed with western concerns. For many people in America and Europe, the oil shock seemed to prove a long-held suspicion that there was a price to pay for their own society's rampant materialism.

A tumultuous end

This complex and intriguing relationship between western perceptions and the situation faced by multinationals on the ground is a subject that will be taken up again in the last part of the book. For now, the story of Aramco's losing battle with the Saudis needs to be brought to its *finale*. Even without the further dramas that were to unfold in 1975, there was now a strong momentum for additional government "participation" in the company. Early in 1974, Kuwait and Qatar rejected as too weak the proposal for a 25% government stake in their foreign oil concessions, and announced instead a takeover of 60%. Partly as a matter of pride, Saudi Arabia had to follow suit.

Even though the oil embargo had failed to secure Israel's military defeat, the confidence of all the Middle East oil-producing countries had been inflated by the dramatic increase in their revenues as a result of the oil prices rise. There was heady talk of a "new international order", in which the dominance of the rich, industrialized countries was supposedly starting to crumble. Some Middle East politicians began to fashion an image of themselves as champions of the "South" (although, as soon became apparent, those developing countries not endowed with oil were facing as severe an economic crunch as any industrialized nation).

In Saudi Arabia, where Aramco's payments to the government had reached at times in excess of $2 billion a month,[47] a consumption boom of staggering proportions was under way. The capacity of ports was overwhelmed, and off the coast at Jeddah hundreds of ships laden with cargo waited in long queues to dock. Across the kingdom there sprouted lavish new buildings and mosques. One of the construction companies thriving at this time was the Bin Laden Corporation, established by Muhammad bin Laden, originally a small-time builder from Yemen. Witnessing the boom in the country and the corruption which attended it, one of Muhammad's 50-or-so offspring, Osama, became attracted by the idea that "only an absolute and unconditional return to the fold of conservative Islamism could protect the Muslim world from the inherent dangers and sins of the West", as a biographer of the terrorist mastermind later noted.[48]

The growing pressure on the Saudi government to be seen to deal harshly with the western oil firms was thrown into stark relief by two events in 1975. The first occurred on 25th March 1975 at the royal palace in Riyadh. King Faisal, with his trusted adviser Yamani by his side, was being paid a visit by the Kuwaiti oil minister. Suddenly there burst into the room a young member of the royal family – Prince Faisal Ibn Musaid, the Saudi mentioned earlier in the chapter who had returned to Saudi Arabia, and to Islam, following his arrest on drug charges as a student in America. The prince shot the king three times, at close range. Yamani rushed out of the room screaming for a doctor. But medical help was to no avail: the king had been grievously wounded, and died shortly after.

Among the young prince's grievances, according to one of his friends, was that "the Saudi royal family was interested primarily in co-operation with American oil interests". He was later beheaded in punishment for the murder. Meanwhile another of Ibn Saud's sons – Khalid – was appointed king in Faisal's place. Yamani was deeply distraught by Faisal's death, for he had lost not only his king, but his father-figure.[49]

The second event, in December 1975, was the kidnapping of Yamani and other OPEC ministers by Carlos, the Venezuelan assassin who had an equally virulent dislike of "American oil interests". The kidnap plane – which, as mentioned earlier, was being shadowed by Aramco's Learjet – landed at Algiers airport where it sat on the tarmac for many hours. Yamani and his fellow hostages remained imprisoned while Carlos negotiated his terms. But if Yamani thought his ordeal was to end there, he was sadly mistaken. He was too valuable to Carlos. Some of the hostages were released, but a group of them including Yamani and Jamshid Amouzegar, the Iranian finance minister, continued to be held at gunpoint by the kidnappers on the plane. Carlos then instructed the plane to take off for Libya, the country which some suspected had commissioned the kidnapping. And it was on the tarmac at the airport in Tripoli that Carlos's plans began to crumble. From there, he had intended to fly on to Baghdad, but the Libyans, for some reason, did not have a jet ready for him which would make that distance. Enraged, Carlos decided that the plane should return to Algiers.

At 5.45am on 23rd December, after another agonizing wait at Algiers airport, Yamani and the remaining hostages were set free. Before letting them go, Carlos had warned icily, "If you escape death this time, our hands in the future will stretch to wherever you might be". Once off the plane, Carlos and his co-conspirators were allowed to go free. This appears to have been the *quid pro quo* agreed with the Algerian authorities for their release of the hostages. There were rumors that a large ransom had also been offered, either by the Saudi Arabian government or by Aramco. Certainly, Aramco's Learjet was ready and waiting for Yamani on his release in Algiers.

From there, the exhausted and relieved Saudi oil minister was whisked off to Switzerland where his young wife and children were waiting for him.[50]

While Carlos escaped unscathed from this event, and went into hiding, it is worth noting as an aside that he was finally tracked down in Sudan in 1994. Wanted for terrorist attacks in at least five European countries, he was then brought to France in a sack, and there tried and sentenced to life imprisonment.[51]

But while Carlos, as it turned out, would never fulfil his threat to hunt down and kill the freed hostages, Yamani was clearly shaken by the kidnapping at the time. It had dramatized for him, as nothing else could, the dangers in not pressing ahead with nationalization of Aramco. Now insisting on a retinue of bodyguards wherever he went, the Saudi oil minister held a series of further meetings with Aramco's owners, and by the spring of 1976, the American oilmen had agreed to surrender their cherished concession entirely. "Let's face it", as a senior manager of Standard of New Jersey who attended the negotiations later remarked, "he [Yamani] was holding the cards. If you want to know what cards we were holding I'd have to say, not many".[52]

As Yamani had always intended, the deal for 100% Saudi ownership involved no sudden rupturing of ties. Aramco's parent companies would continue to have guaranteed access to Saudi oil, which they would sell through their worldwide marketing networks; they also would continue to operate the concession for the time being, training a cadre of Saudis eventually to occupy the senior management positions. Other oil nationalizations in the Middle East had involved more abrupt ejections of western oil companies; so Aramco's efforts over the decades to stay on good terms with the Saudis at least may have helped to moderate the nature of the defeat in this way. It was a full twelve years before the Saudi regime, under King Fahd (who had since replaced Khalid), announced the formal transfer of Aramco to the government, re-christening it the "Saudi Arabian Oil Company".

But crucially, the 1976 agreement meant that Aramco no longer owned the oil under the ground, which was a point of principle for the Saudis, and a loss for which the company's shareholders received little compensation. The government paid out around $1.5 billion for "crude oil assets", whereas the value of Saudi reserves has been estimated at over \$100 billion.[53] As the manager from Standard of New Jersey put it, "We never got any payment for the reserves, which had a terrific value".[54] This loss was shared between four companies, and masked for a time by the effect of high oil prices. Also, in spite of the nationalization, Aramco had clearly not failed in one respect: it had generated considerable returns for its owners in the decades when the going had been good. Even so, its political goal of holding on to the concession now lay in tatters. And, given the limited compensation granted by the Saudis, the nationalization amounted to one of the biggest losses of corporate property in history.

Seeds of a re-birth

The story of Aramco can be left there, for sufficient light has now been shed on the processes by which the American firms were forced to surrender the concession, processes which may repeat themselves at some future stage elsewhere in the world. For the American managers remaining with Aramco in Saudi Arabia, the period after 1976 was often dispiriting. Their long-term career prospects were limited by the agreed "Saudisation" of the workforce. The puritanical pressures of Saudi life even began to permeate the company's compounds, once enclaves of American culture. As one long-serving western manager remarked, "If you had a cocktail party at home, you did not sit outside in plain view with glasses; you had the party inside or in an enclosed patio, where you had privacy. Generally, things became more and more unpleasant. The pressure was on, and the feel of total freedom just vanished".[55]

Extremist threats to the Saudi regime continued to mount, reinforcing its decision to nationalize the concession, although at the same time forcing it to turn increasingly to the west for military protection. Saudi royals watched with concern as the Shah of Iran was overthrown in 1979 by the Ayatollah Ruhollah Khomeini. Later that year, in Saudi Arabia, a group of around 1,500 disaffected Saudis and "religious warriors" from other Middle East countries stormed and seized the Grand Mosque in Mecca, an insurrection eventually put down by the regime with the help of French special forces.

The Shah's deposition and a subsequent war between Iran and Iraq disrupted oil supplies, leading to another hike in prices – the "second oil shock" of 1979–81. A decade later, in 1990, Iraq invaded Kuwait, creating fear in Saudi Arabia that the kingdom, too, would come under attack from Saddam Hussein. It was in this fraught atmosphere that King Fahd invited in the American-led coalition forces to wage their war against the Iraqis – in spite of the protestations of Osama bin Laden and others about "infidel" troops being allowed onto sacred Saudi soil.[56]

Yamani's career as oil minister had come to an end several years before, in October 1986. The circumstances of his downfall make an apposite end note, for they set the context for the next part of the book, the modern period, in which multinationals are once again welcome in the developing world. What helped bring Yamani's long period of service to the Saudi government to a close was not a terrorist outrage, nor a second visit from Carlos, but a collapse in the oil market brought about by over-ambition on the part of OPEC. By the mid-1980s, the cartel which once was thought to pose a terminal threat to western hegemony was in trouble – and with it, the idea that developing countries could grow wealthy alone, without western investment, had begun to appear less plausible.

The oil shocks of the 1970s had encouraged western firms to invest in less-politically risky fields outside the Middle East – in Alaska, for example, and in the North Sea. Surging supplies from these sources, together with conservation efforts by consumers and bickering among OPEC members, had brought about a glut in the oil market by the mid-1980s. In earlier OPEC negotiations, Yamani had warned other producing countries about the dangers of pushing the price too high, but his cautions went unheeded.

The oil shocks helped set the scene for the reopening of the developing world in another way too. During the 1970s, billions of dollars in Middle East oil revenues were recycled through the western banking system as loans for poor countries outside OPEC. Many of these countries accumulated unpayable debts, debts which eventually would help force them into the arms of the World Bank and International Monetary Fund. The *quid pro quo* offered by these institutions was to bail the countries out on condition, among other things, that they reopened themselves to western investment. But these are issues for the next part.

By 1986, Yamani was under increasing pressure from King Fahd, whose trust in his oil minister was less than that of King Faisal. Fahd wanted Yamani to secure both a higher oil price through OPEC negotiations and also an increase in Saudi Arabia's output of crude. For all his political skills and inside knowledge of OPEC, however, Yamani knew that he could not achieve both goals simultaneously; the existing glut on the market made that an impossibility.

Though the reason for Yamani's removal from office was never made explicit, it is likely that Fahd fired him in sheer frustration at the low oil price. Yamani learnt of his dismissal from Saudi television while playing a game of cards with some friends. He might have been expected to feel humiliated and furious at such brusque treatment, but this was not so. According to Yamani's biographer, Jeffrey Robinson, "Some people in the room were said to have been shocked by the announcement. But Yamani is said to have sighed deeply, as if a great weight had finally been lifted from his shoulders. He went right back to his card game."[57] The clever, unruffleable oil Sheik, once perceived in the west as a symbol of Arab might, must have known for a while that his era was drawing to a close.

Resurgence

INTRODUCTION

There are many ways of illustrating the contradictory pressures facing modern multinationals in developing countries, and there are many instances of western consumer goods triggering unexpected responses in local societies. But few examples are more curious than the phenomenon of Coca-Cola drinking in the Mexican village of San Juan Chamula.

A visitor might not expect the village – located in the beautiful, but poverty-stricken highlands of Chiapas, in southern Mexico, and inhabited by indigenous Mayan Indians – to be an enthusiastic market for such western goods. Chiapas was the launch-pad of a fierce left-wing Indian uprising, the Zapatista rebellion, which began in 1994. One target of the rebellion was the unpopular non-Indian landowning elite in Chiapas. But the Zapatistas' leader, Subcomandante Marcos, a media-savvy, balaclava-clad, former university lecturer, insisted they were also protesting against the Mexican government's neo-liberal policies and globalization in general. This helped their campaign gain widespread international attention and support from dozens of anti-capitalist western groups.

The government policies against which they were protesting, which included the negotiation of NAFTA, the free-trade agreement with America and Canada, brought about a surge of foreign investment in Mexico during the 1990s, particularly by American multinationals, and particularly in the region bordering the United States. While these changes were welcomed by many in Mexico – and an indication of this lies in the election in 2000 of Vicente Fox, himself a former local executive of Coca-Cola, to the country's presidency – little foreign investment or economic growth trickled down to Mexico's poor southern states, such as Chiapas. This helps explain some of the resentment against reform in the region. All of which makes the behavior of the Indians of San Juan Chamula so difficult to interpret.

Admittedly not all Indian communities backed the Zapatistas and their left-wing agenda, but few would have gone so far as to worship a symbol of western capitalism. And yet, at the time of this author's visit to San Juan Chamula in the late 1990s, the local people had not only painted large signs advertising Coca-Cola over the walls of the main square; they had actually elevated the American beverage to the status of a religious elixir. Inside their church, a brightly colored Spanish colonial construction whose original Catholic purpose had long been subverted by its use for indigenous rituals such as exorcisms and animal sacrifices, villagers were regularly taking swigs from Coca-Cola bottles. It became clear that the Indians of Chamula had somehow come to believe that drinking the brown liquid, and the belching it induced, would help rid them of evil spirits.

The occurrence of this ritual has been corroborated by other visitors to the village.[1] What remains open to dispute is how it should be interpreted. Is it an example of a perversion of indigenous religious practices by western consumerism, of a culture being undermined by globalization and local capitalist power structures? Or is it instead an illustration of a community retaining their unique way of life by adapting western commodities to their own purposes? Either way, it is the sort of unexpected, fine-grained social phenomenon which triggers endless debates among anthropologists and about which Coca-Cola's American bosses are unlikely to have received much instruction at business school.

This story is more than just a curiosity. It encapsulates the main underlying forces at work in this, the last, part of the book: the return or "resurgence" of foreign investment in a number of developing countries, the emergence of countervailing pressures and protests in both rich and poor countries, and the resulting series of encounters between multinationals and local societies which defy any simple interpretation or resolution.

Coca-Cola is not featured in the following chapters, but three other prominent symbols of western capitalism are: Nike (the American sportswear giant), Shell (the Anglo-Dutch oil multi-national), and News Corporation (Rupert Murdoch's media empire). The chapter on Nike focuses on its use of cheap labor in the developing world. The chapter on Shell examines its controversial operations in Nigeria. The chapter on News Corporation looks at

Murdoch's turbulent relationship with governments in China and India. All these multinationals, it will be seen, have become embroiled in issues which make the phenomenon of Coca-Cola drinking in San Juan Chamula seem only mildly perplexing.

Force fields

Once again, before turning to the stories of the companies themselves, it will help to outline in a little more detail some of the broad, underlying forces in operation during the timeframe in which the chapters are set. The most powerful trend – the return of western firms to many poor countries – can be encapsulated well enough in the figures. Foreign direct investment in the developing world rose from roughly $20 billion a year during the 1980s to over $200 billion a year by the late 1990s. By this point these flows dwarfed the rich world's official aid budget by a factor of four. This foreign investment was not evenly spread. The bulk of the flows went to a handful of developing countries, including China, Mexico, and Brazil, leaving entire regions – especially Africa – relatively untouched. Nonetheless attitudes had changed throughout the developing world. Whereas in previous decades, western firms were held back by general hostility in potential host countries, governments across Latin America, Africa, and Asia, were now liberalizing their investment laws and offering perks to the multinationals, even if these moves did not always succeed in attracting the companies as hoped.

What explained this shift from suspicion to apparent enthusiasm on the part of the governments? Partly it was a voluntary move, a reasoned reaction to a number of observable events. One of these was the failure of OPEC to sustain a high oil price during the 1980s, and also the collapse of a number of other attempted commodity cartels. Such disappointments extinguished the hopes of many developing countries that the end of colonialism would lead inevitably to a reorientation of the world economic system in their favor. Disillusionment had also set in over "import-substituting industrialization", a popular economic strategy of the post-1945 era which involved protecting domestic firms and raising barriers to trade, and which had achieved little in many countries except to notch up levels of inefficiency and corruption.

Then there was the success of the south-east Asian "tiger" economies such as Hong Kong and Taiwan – among the few developing countries which had actually taken off economically – which seemed to be due in part to their openness to trade and global markets. Rather than viewing western multinationals as exploitative agents of imperialism, elites in developing countries thus began to entertain new notions. Some argued that such firms actually held the key to success, as they could be used to import capital, modern technology and the latest management skills.

Such attitudes were fed, of course, by ideological currents of the time. Neo-liberal economic theories were becoming more fashionable in western universities (where developing country elites still often received their education). Events such as the elections of Margaret Thatcher in Britain and Ronald Reagan in America, and at a later stage, the collapse of Communism in the Soviet Union, gave powerful impetus to such ideas. The policy of privatizing state enterprises, begun in Britain, spread across the world, and reached developing countries, creating new opportunities for foreign investors. Interestingly, a fast-growing minority of these investors were now based in developing countries, particularly in south-east Asia where industrialization had created a vibrant private sector. By 1998, there were almost 8,000 such "indigenous" multinationals (however, the rich world, with 36,000 multinationals, still dominated investment flows).[2]

The conversion of many governments to the merits of foreign investment was only partly voluntary. Many had changed their policies as a result of World Bank and International Monetary Fund programs in which financial support or bail-outs were provided on condition that they liberalized their economies. During the 1990s the Bank and the IMF tried increasingly to create a sense of "ownership" in developing countries regarding such economic reforms. But it was difficult for these Washington-based institutions to hide the fact that governments had little choice in the matter if they were to receive the desired-for financial support, and this often bred resentment and accusations of "neo-imperialism" in developing countries.

This was just one element in a swirl of often-conflicting social pressures facing those western multinationals that took advantage of the new investment opportunities. For a start, ideological debates about the merits of liberalizing were far from over. New academic research in the west, for example, appeared to indicate that the success of the south-east Asian economies lay in the subtle way in which their governments had intervened in the private sector, and not just in a simple reliance on market forces. The fragility of the neo-liberal model appeared, at least to its critics, to be further confirmed by the financial crashes of Mexico in 1994, and the south-east Asian "tigers" themselves in 1997–98, and also by the chaotic state of Russia's newly "liberalized" post-Communist economy. Concerns about capitalism in the west were later heightened by financial scandals at a number of large American firms, including Enron and WorldCom. A challenge of another sort struck the western capitalist system in 2001 with the terrorist attacks on the World Trade Center. These provided a graphic demonstration that the forces of backlash were alive and kicking.

One further, less violent, but nonetheless challenging, phenomenon confronting foreign investors in many developing countries in the 1980s and 1990s was the emergence of local activist and non-governmental organizations (NGOs) focusing on such issues as the environment and the rights of indigenous people. These were not just local branches of western-based groups such as Greenpeace and Amnesty; they also included some genuinely ground-level movements – such as, for example, the Zapatistas in Mexico – and they were eager to take up the baton of opposition to neo-liberalism which their governments had recently dropped. In the past, western multinationals eager to maintain smooth relations in host countries needed only to keep on the right side of the relevant governments, though this in itself could be a difficult task, as has been seen. But now they were having to deal with local activists as well, whose demands sometimes conflicted directly with government policies, but whose potential to inflict damage on the corporate reputation was sometimes just as significant.

The growth of campaign groups was even more marked in the west. Between 1990 and 2000, the number of "international NGOs" headquartered in rich countries rose from 7,786 to 10,277.[3] Ethical investment funds – which channeled peoples' savings into the shares of companies judged to be "responsible" – also began to take off in many western countries in this period. Among the activists themselves, the noisiest groups were the "anti-globalization" protestors. Attacking multinationals, the World Bank, and the IMF (which were often lumped together as the principal, demonic symbols of globalization), and striking alliances with like-minded activists in developing countries, these groups helped block an attempt in the late 1990s to negotiate a set of rules to encourage and govern foreign investment known as the Multilateral Agreement on Investment. Emboldened by this and other victories, the "anti-globalizers" took to the streets in protest at a series of official summits in the late 1990s and early 2000s in such cities in Washington, Genoa, Seattle, and London. Their message was sometimes incoherent, for the movement included campaigners focusing on a range of issues, from the environment, to union rights, to poverty, but their energy, enthusiasm and ability to cause havoc could not be ignored.

The response to all this by many western multinationals, particularly those targeted for criticism, was what became known in the jargon as "corporate social responsibility" or "CSR", a strategy which covered a range of activities, from the production of glossy "social and environmental" reports to genuine changes in corporate behavior. Among managers and also among some campaigners, there emerged a standard line of reasoning for CSR. The increasing scrutiny of companies by activists in both rich and developing countries, it was argued, together with their use of the internet and emails, meant that bad deeds could no longer be hidden anywhere in the world. The only option for multinationals was therefore to behave "responsibly" wherever they operated. One tangible result of companies' CSR activities was a flurry of business codes of conduct, the emergence of the practice of "social auditing", and the launching of various international initiatives aimed at improving corporate behavior. Some activists welcomed these moves; others argued they were inadequate and needed to be enforced by government regulation.

Structural faults

The way in which CSR can obscure the complexity of the underlying situations will be explained fully in the subsequent chapters on Shell and Nike. These are both firms which had been savaged in the west over their behavior, and hence had both developed elaborate programs in response. However, it is worth introducing briefly here just a couple of typical obfuscations in debates about CSR.

One is a common assumption that critical scrutiny applies uniformly to all multinationals, and to all their activities, and that it involves a simple relaying of local situations to a global audience. What makes this view simplistic is the structural pressures faced by the non-governmental sector. Western activist groups typically rely on public contributions to fund their activities. Hence they tend, understandably, to focus on issues which can be packaged as attention-grabbing campaigns for western audiences. On the one hand, this means that many multinationals, and many worrying local situations, remain un-monitored because they do not involve high-profile western brand names, such as, for example, Nike or Shell. But on the other hand, it also means that those issues which do become the subject of campaigns are tailored in a way which makes them easily comprehensible to a lay, western audience. The impression is created that there are clear rights and wrongs, and that it is obvious how a "responsible" corporation should behave in the circumstances.

A second, related, assumption in the CSR debate which needs some initial unpicking is that there is a simple congruence of interests between anti-multinational activists in rich countries and their allies in developing countries. Rich-world and poor-world campaigners do indeed often adopt similar lines of attack against companies, both criticizing environmental destruction, for example, and both condemning collusion in human rights abuses. But that has something to do with the structure of power within international civil society. Just as there are many rich-world campaign groups competing for the limited attention of the public in the west, so there are innumerable local problems and conflicts in the developing world on which western groups such as Human Rights Watch or Friends of the Earth potentially might focus their efforts. It is in the interests of local activists to attract the attention of these western campaigners who can help bring financial resources, political clout, and international coverage to the particular cause which they hold dear. But only those developing-country activists who have framed their arguments in terms which appeal to the rich-world NGOs –

highlighting the environmental or the human-rights aspect of the problem, say, rather than its other manifestations – are likely to succeed in this respect.[4]

The point here is not that environmental or rights abuses are not of serious concern to local people. But rather that there may also be other, underlying factors driving local protest, such as ethnic disagreements, conflict over the regional distribution of economic resources, or broad dissent against a local regime for ideological or other reasons. This phenomenon will be explored in more detail in the chapter on Shell in Nigeria. The point to bear in mind for the moment is that apparently simple calls for multinationals to behave more "responsibly" may hide a myriad of motivations and hoped-for outcomes.

So, how have companies dealt with this flux of forces? Based on the multinationals examined in this part of the book the short answer is not very well. In the case of Nike, it will be seen that many of the company's managers appear to have been oblivious at first to the ethical dilemmas involved in its expansion in the developing world; then, faced with a barrage of criticism, they struggled to respond in a way which would both satisfy western activists and actually improve the situation on the ground.

In the case of Shell in Nigeria, the company's original approach of embedding itself in Nigerian society and keeping on good terms with local rulers and dictators was precisely what opened it to attack from the west; but its new "responsible" strategy involves more active intervention in local politics, which raises some awkward reminders of the era of imperial multinationals. On a practical level, Shell's new approach has also failed significantly to dampen violent local unrest.

As for Rupert Murdoch's activities in China and India, these provide a classic example of a western multinational initially underestimating the potential for backlash from indigenous cultures. Murdoch subsequently made every effort to appeal more to local tastes and to stay on the right side of local politicians (and Chinese leaders in particular). But, while his problems have temporarily abated as a result, the relatively unsophisticated nature of this new approach given the complexity of the underlying situation suggests that his company will not entirely avoid political turbulence in the future.

All these stories, in short, confirm the basic message of the book: that multinationals, however powerful, are often ill-equipped to understand or shape the social environment in which they operate, and that the tools they use are too blunt for the task at hand. Each chapter necessarily focuses on one particular company, which means that not all controversial modern-day multinationals receive the attention they deserve (among those not featured in detail, for example, are the western drugs firms which were heavily criticized in the late 1990s and early 2000s over the high price of their HIV medicines in Africa). Nonetheless, the general phenomena described in each chapter are relevant to many other contemporary cases. Shell's struggles, for example, parallel those of other giant oil and mining companies embroiled today in violent conflicts and ethnic disputes in developing countries. Murdoch's experience is a warning to all media, and information-based firms which may be tempted to assume that "new economy" companies somehow will avoid the political problems of traditional industry. And, as will be explained, one of the knottiest problems for Murdoch's businesses – the protection of intellectual property rights – applies to many other companies, and indeed underlies the debate about HIV drugs in Africa.

Finally, it is worth noting briefly the fascinating experiences of one other controversial multinational – Monsanto, the American life-sciences company. Monsanto's principal political crisis arose in Western Europe rather than in developing countries, but even so, in terms of this book, it still acts as an excellent illustration of how apparently clever corporations can misread cultures.

In the 1990s, Monsanto had employed legions of top scientists to create some of the world's first genetically modified crops. Its managers, including its boss, a Harvard-educated lawyer called Robert Shapiro, appeared to be genuinely convinced not only that these crops would generate large profits for the company, but that they would bring major social benefits, and even help save the world from future famines. The American public had broadly welcomed the introduction of Monsanto's new-fangled seeds. In Europe, however, and to the managers' surprise, they met with furious public opposition. Fields of the crops were trashed, supermarkets refused to buy them, celebrity chefs denounced them as "Frankenstein foods", and governments denied them regulatory approval. Not only was Monsanto's expansion in Europe blocked; the entire European agricultural biotechnology industry became stalled for years.

Debate continues as to why Europeans were horrified by an innovation that had been accepted by many Americans, whether this was a result of their differing cultural beliefs about the sanctity of nature, for example, or the differing degree to which they would accept risks associated with new technology. But whatever the explanation, here was an example of corporate managers from one wealthy part of the world fundamentally misreading the social and political dynamics of another wealthy region. What would happen when western companies tried to expand in developing countries, where capitalism was less firmly embedded and where cultures were more different still? How much greater would be the scope for chaos and confusion? Some answers lie in the following chapters.

SEVEN

The contortions of corporate responsibility
Nike and its third-world factories

How much do we really know about issues in all of these factories? Not enough.
Every time we look closer, we find another thing wrong.

Todd McKean, Nike's Director of "Corporate Responsibility Compliance".[1]

A visitor to one of the factories in Indonesia which manufactures shoes for Nike can easily begin to suspect that what is on show is too good to be true, a version of reality staged to persuade westerners that this is an enlightened workplace. For when this author paid a visit to one such plant in May 2002, he found what appeared to be not a dark satanic mill – the image of Nike factories which might be expected given the critical media coverage the company has received – but rather a bright, modern facility whose management waxed lyrical about "corporate responsibility".

It may have been the rainbow colors which contributed to the impression of unreality. Within a vast hangar-like structure, the floor crisscrossed with multicolored lines denoting safe and unsafe areas, sat hundreds of young women, all dressed in light green overalls and pink headbands embossed with Nike logos, bent silently over their stitching machines. Next to each team of workers, an electronic billboard displayed to the rest of the factory their output of shoes so far that shift – a stark reminder of the relentless pressure to work fast (the plant produces some 25,000 pairs of shoes a day). But also posted prominently in the factory was Nike's "Code of Conduct",

translated into Bahasa Indonesia, the local language. This claims that
Nike prohibits child and forced labor, and sets limits on hours of
work and basic safety and health standards. But, for the suspicious
visitor, it was tempting to wonder: had this document been posted up
simply for show?

Next to the factory was a new clinic, immaculately clean (perhaps
suspiciously so?) and well equipped. Here, the author was told by the
director of the factory, workers and their families receive free health-
care. The director also insisted he has no problem filling vacancies
when they arise, an apparent indication that the jobs he provides are
considered desirable by local people. Meanwhile, according to an
official working in the factory's "corporate responsibility" team, many
supervisors, or line managers, have recently undergone a special
training program to teach them to be less authoritarian in their
approach. To the astonishment of their workers, some previously
gruff supervisors – or at least so it was claimed – are now greeting
them with a smile and an American-style "how are you today?"

So is all this too good to be true: a public-relations mirage? Are
the smiles false? Do the factory bosses exploit their workers once
visitors are gone? Whatever the answer to these questions (and most
likely the plant is neither an abusive sweatshop nor an industrial
utopia, but somewhere in between), the important point from the
perspective of this chapter is that it is difficult for an outsider to know
where the truth lies. For it is Nike managers themselves, and not just
visiting writers, who are confronted with this difficulty of penetrating
an alien factory culture.

The American multinational does not actually own the facilities
producing its sports gear around the world; rather, it contracts out
its manufacturing to other firms, such as the one visited by the
author. And it has tried to respond to western criticism over its
alleged "sweatshop" production by setting up numerous systems for
monitoring labor practices in these factories, largely involving visits
and inspections by outsiders. But just as Cecil Rhodes' British South
Africa Company seriously misunderstood the cultural dynamics of
the indigenous societies of Southern Africa, and just as Aramco, for
all its efforts, found it difficult to predict changes within Saudi
society, so Nike has been struggling to track the conditions in its
factories. Factories are smaller than societies, of course. But even

factory life involves a relatively complex set of human interactions which mere visits, let alone long-term ethnographic studies, are unlikely to elucidate in full. And when it comes actually to engineering improvements in the lives of workers, it will be shown that this presents another layer of difficulties for Nike altogether.

Though this chapter focuses on Nike, its message is relevant to the thousands of other western multinationals who have in recent decades located their production in countries where workers are cheap, and who thereby open themselves to accusations from western campaigners that they benefit from sweatshop labor. Faced by such criticisms, some firms choose simply to deny that any problem exists. However, a number of prominent firms, including not just Nike, but also, for example, the Gap, Levi Strauss, and Adidas, have adopted an apparently more progressive stance, explicitly assuming responsibility for upholding labor standards in their factories. Some western campaign groups have welcomed these moves while others have denounced them as superficial, public-relations efforts.

Even if the efforts are genuine, however, what has in the past been little appreciated both by campaigners and by the multi-nationals themselves is that the task before the companies involves a degree of complexity, both in practical and ethical terms, and that – at least in certain respects – it may be beyond their capacity to deliver. This is a point which will come as little surprise to readers given the previous chapters in this book, but it is curiously absent from many contemporary debates on the issue.

While focusing on Nike's fumbling moves in this area, the chapter is relevant, too, to the broader subject of branding. In her hugely popular book *No Logo*, Naomi Klein rightly argues that brands, based as they are on the malleable perceptions of consumers, have left the many companies which rely on them highly exposed to public criticism from campaigners. Protestors easily can undermine a brand by associating it, for example, with images of child labor. What Naomi Klein assumes is a broadly beneficial development, however, is ambiguous in its effects. For, if a company such as Nike is genuinely to protect its brand, it needs above all to persuade the public in the west (where most consumers of its products for the time being still reside) that it is dealing responsibly with the "sweatshop" issue; and yet – as has been observed throughout this book – western

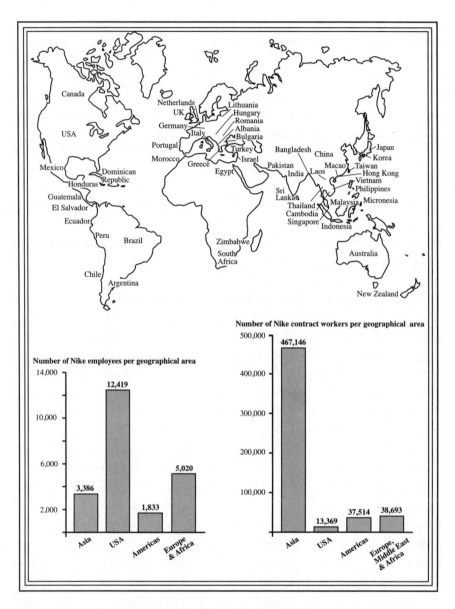

COUNTRIES WHERE NIKE GOODS ARE PRODUCED
(locations and employee/contract worker numbers based on Nike's 2001
Global Responsibility Report)

perceptions often bear only a partial relationship to the reality on the ground. The result is that some genuine, if limited, efforts by the company to improve conditions for workers have done little to slow an endless cycle of criticisms from western groups; similarly some of the company's direct responses to western criticisms have done little for, and sometimes even damaged, the interests of poverty-stricken workers. This is what is meant, in the title of this chapter, by the "contortions of corporate responsibility"; and it is a story in which both the company and its critics have engaged in self-serving spin.

Throwing up issues

The roots of Nike's current struggles with labor rights lie in the company's past, long before the sweatshop issue took off in the west. Underlying the company's commercial success, its growth from a tiny shoe business in Oregon, in America's Pacific Northwest, in the early 1960s to a $9-billion-a-year sportswear giant 40 years later, was a dependence throughout on cheap Asian production, a reliance on clever marketing to sell its goods, and, at least at first, an uproarious corporate culture. Approximating in some ways, judging by insider reports, to a drunken and immature student party, this culture left little room at the outset for subtle insights into Asian labor issues.

The founder of the company was Philip Knight, a shy, blond-haired, lanky man, just out of Stanford Business School, who worked with his former running coach, Bill Bowerman, to import shoes from Japan. Back in Oregon, Knight would load them into his car trunk, and sell them to runners at local track meetings. As the company grew, partly on the back of a jogging craze which began to sweep America during the 1970s, it drew around itself a set of young employees who shared an enthusiasm for sports, a suspicion of formality in management, and a party spirit which one manager likened to a "fraternity house in college".[2]

The corporate culture of the early days is described with relish in *Swoosh*, an unauthorized account of the company by Nike's first advertising manager J. B. (Julie) Strasser and her journalist sister, Laurie Becklund. At one management gathering (typically raucous affairs which became known in Nike irreverent parlance as "buttfaces"), for example, Knight hired some video games to amuse his employees. At the mid-morning break, "the men around the table jumped up and ran to play, infected with Pac-Man fever".[3] Parties and drinking sessions held by Nike staff were in a similar vein. At one held at an Oregon bar following a sales meeting, Nike employees – as described in the book – traded marijuana pipes, threw food around, and downed tequilas, while one Nike senior manager consumed so much spicy Tabasco "he stuck his head under a beer tap to put out the fire".[4]

Over time, and partly as a result of his regular trips to Asia to source shoes from local manufacturers, Philip Knight developed a great interest in Asian cultures. However, with the party spirit embedded in the corporate ethos, little subtlety is apparent from some of the initial forays of his managers into new countries. On a trip to Communist China in 1980, for example, Nike managers apparently saw little need to adapt their behavior to local mores. During a visit to "The People's Department Store Number One", for example, they shocked onlookers by picking up a football on sale and playing ball around the aisles. According to another anecdote related in *Swoosh*, an hour before an appointment with a senior government official in Beijing to talk business on shoe production, two Nike managers were lying flat out in their hotel room, surrounded by pools of vomit, having over-indulged in the local drink the night before.[5]

Even had Nike then thought to investigate in detail the labor conditions in the factories from which it was buying, however, this would not necessarily have been a straightforward task. For the locus of low-cost shoe production was shifting over time from one Asian country to another, each with its own different cultures and patterns of worker-employee relationship. Sneakers bought from Japan, for example, were replaced by sneakers from Korea and Taiwan, and then from China and Indonesia, a progression roughly following each country's spurt of industrialization. Moreover, within each factory, there would have been various layers of culture to penetrate. Many of the firms with which Nike did business were owned by overseas Chinese, an ethnic group which dominates South East Asia's business community (and whose commercial success is said to owe much to a Confucian management style based, for example, around personal connections and trust). These ethnic-Chinese factory bosses in turn gave orders to, say, Indonesian or indigenous Malaysian underlings, depending on where they were based (and in both Indonesia and Malaysia, the relationship between ethnic Chinese and indigenous people has a history of tension). Furthermore, in recent decades, many Asian manufacturing firms have become multinationals in their own right, operating manufacturing plants across the region and even further afield. As if to underline this layering of cultures, for example, Nike also would buy some of its sports gear from Taiwanese and Korean-owned factories in Mexico.

Where Nike did devote considerable attention and develop an expertise relatively early on, however, was in the culture and psychology of its (mostly western) consumers. In common with other companies which pushed branding to new limits in the late twentieth century, Nike has succeeded in selling ever greater quantities of its products by imbuing them with a certain aura, an association with a particular lifestyle. It was a skill viewed with distaste by some in the west, but with awe by Nike's competitors.

Through clever advertising and by paying top, charismatic athletes, such as Andre Agassi and Michael Jordan, to wear Nike gear and even (as in the case of Air Jordan shoes) to put their name to products, the company forged a link in consumers' minds between purely physical goods and such intangible qualities as achievement and rebelliousness. Simply by buying a pair of Nike trainers, consumers were able to buy into a spirit of athletic heroism, or of the "Just do it" mentality – even if they only ever wore them to walk to the shops or to watch TV. Nike's marketing also began to impart political messages – anti-racism, for example, or women's empowerment – which heightened the appeal of its products among the young and the baby-boom generation.

Driving Nike's approach appears to have been a genuine passion of many of its senior managers for sport and for what it symbolized to them. "Nike is special, not just a business but something more, something of which business is only part", Philip Knight insisted in 1993.[6] The company built for itself a verdant headquarters complex in Beaverton, Oregon, known as Nike's "World Campus", and which was equipped with a running track and fitness center for the use of its mostly young, and enthusiastically athletic employees, and whose various buildings were named after sporting heroes. "They [Nike] demonstrate the symptoms of a real cult – they isolate themselves in a compound", argued one of Nike's competitors in the sports shoe business.[7] In fact, as with other multinationals examined in this book, it may be that it was precisely the strength of Nike's corporate culture, its pride and insularity, which blinded it to the potential for criticism over its reliance on cheap foreign labor.

Labor pains

What can be said for certain about the criticisms concerning Nike's contract factories which arose in the 1990s is that – whether justified or not – they represented just one feature in a broad landscape of poverty and socio-economic change in the countries concerned. Judging solely by the allegations against the company covered in the western media, some of the factories from which it bought its shoes and apparel were the scenes of shocking labor abuses. Among these were pitifully low wages by western standards (it was pointed out that for a pair of Nike shoes retailing in America for $120, for example, Indonesian workers received just $2 a day), long hours, forced overtime, environmental hazards from toxic chemicals, physical punishments for infractions of factory rules (for example, there were reports of young female employees – and most Nike workers were indeed young, apparently exploitable, women – being forced to run around one factory in the heat of the tropical sun), and also numerous instances of child labor.

All of these accusations were indeed accurate, at least in some of Nike's contract factories. Some of the abuses appear to have been isolated examples, revealing no general pattern of cruelty to workers, but an undeniable attraction of third-world production for Nike was the low level of local wages. And the criticisms made against the company could not all be dismissed as a misguided attempt by campaigners to apply western standards to poor countries. This had been an obvious failing of anti-multinational activists from earlier periods, such as – it will be remembered – the London campaigners against Cecil Rhodes or against the East India Company. But Nike's critics – at least on some issues, such as child labor and unhealthy working conditions in the factories (even if not low wages) – were highlighting apparent wrongdoing that ought surely to have been unacceptable anywhere in the world.

However, what Nike's critics did share with these earlier campaigners was a tendency to focus their attention on the activities of the multinational they opposed, rather than the broader social context in which it operated. This is a key point in this chapter, and it is important to sketch some of this social context in Nike's case. The aim in what follows is thus not to excuse any particular labor abuses that may (or may not) have occurred, but rather to provide the background usually absent from the western criticisms – and also to set the scene for Nike's problems at a later stage in actually attempting to improve the situation on the ground.

One basic point of context, already mentioned before, is that many of Nike's factories were in countries such as Korea, Taiwan and Indonesia which were undergoing rapid industrialization. A common policy of these Asian "tigers" was to establish "export processing zones", where government duties and regulations were relaxed, in order to attract foreign companies. Arguably these countries might have found alternative ways to develop economically and without doubt there were major costs associated with the particular development path they followed, including – for a time – authoritarian regimes and devastating financial gyrations (such as the crash of 1997–98). Nonetheless, their approach resulted in dramatic declines in poverty: according to World Bank figures, for example, the number of people in the East Asian region (excluding China) living on less than a $1 a day fell from 114 million in 1987 to 54 million in 1998.[8]

Another point of context is that – whatever the precise goings on in Nike contract factories – foreign multinationals in general, by dint of their limited involvement in national economies, contribute to just one aspect of the overall exploitation suffered by workers in developing countries, and which is driven in large part by poverty. Child labor is a case in point. Of an estimated 209 million working children between the ages of 5 and 14 in developing countries, less than 5% are employed in export-related production – such as making sneakers for westerners, for example. Less reported in the west are the tens of millions of children doing back-breaking work on farms, as domestic servants, or in hazardous local industries.[9]

Judging from an array of studies and ethnographies into Asian factories producing goods for export (and excluding those studies targeted specifically at Nike, for reasons which will become clear later), the experience of employees in these factories defies simple characterization. They often find the work grueling, and poorly paid, but they usually say it is better than any alternative.[10] It is a sign of the degree of poverty in developing countries that jobs involving exhausting hours, at say $2 a day, are sometimes considered an improvement on existing conditions, which may involve even harsher toil in the fields. According to one ethnography of female factory workers in Java, Indonesia, for example:

> Although it is undeniable that factory work is exploitative, it is equally undeniable that young women prefer it to their other meager choices. Although factory work organization and discipline are strict and often brutal, female workers perceive factory employment as a progressive change in their lives, not as a gaping un-healed wound.[11]

Women's world

Why is it that workers in export factories, such as those producing Nike sneakers, tend to be young women in their late teens and early twenties? This phenomenon, too, defies a simple interpretation, springing as it does from a far-reaching process of social change in many countries in the region in which traditional values are being challenged and redefined. Certainly, in the past, some Asian governments hunting for foreign investors have been eager to play on the image of young Asian women as docile, obedient, employees. For example, an investment brochure from the Malaysian government in the late 1970s proclaimed unashamedly: "The manual dexterity of the oriental female is famous the world over. Her hands are small and she works with extreme care [...] No need for a Zero Defects program here! By nature, they [the women] will 'quality control' themselves".[12]

There are also various instances of young female factory workers in Asia being overcome by fears that they will be possessed by spirits – a puzzling phenomenon which suggests that the transition from village life to the factory floor (in effect a sudden leap from pre-capitalist to capitalist lifestyle) can prove psychologically traumatic

Industrial utopia or regimented sweatshop? Employees arrive for work at a Nike contract factory near Ho Chi Minh City in Vietnam.

for them. "Some girls started sobbing and screaming hysterically and when it seemed like spreading, the other workers in the production line were immediately ushered out [...] It is a common belief among workers that the factory is 'dirty' and supposed to be haunted by a *datuk* [the spirit of an ancestor]", as a manager at a microelectronics export factory in Malaysia which had just experienced one such "spirit possession" described the episode to reporters. Aihwa Ong, an anthropologist who studied the phenomenon in the 1980s, reported that managers of Malaysian factories themselves had hired local spirit healers to perform ritual exorcisms – slaughtering chickens or goats on factory premises, for example – in the hope that this would reassure their female employees and keep them at work.[13]

In spite of these worrying (if difficult to interpret) episodes, it is clear that for many young women, factory work has been a liberation, or at least an escape, from the restrictions and male control of traditional society. Free from the strict guidance of parents who usually remain at home in the village, for example, young female workers are able to exercise more choice over their marriage partners, to dress as they like, and to sample (what for them) is the excitement of urban life. This phenomenon has been noted by a number of anthropologists.[14]

The most striking evidence that factory work sometimes may bring about a social transformation for women, however, comes from a recent study by Naila Kabeer, a British academic, of employees in export-oriented garment factories in Bangladesh (and though the study does not look specifically at plants making Nike products, Nike does have a number of contract factories in the country). Until recently in Bangladesh, strict Muslim traditions of Purdah made it socially unacceptable for many women to work outside their homes. Now, however, the emergence of an industry relying heavily on female workers has provided many wives and daughters with a means of escape from often-tragic home lives. One of Kabeer's interviewees, called Renu, described how she was driven to seek employment in a garment factory to avoid the nastiness of a lazy, violent husband:

> He would work well for two days, digging earth, and then he would sleep for two days … I wasn't working then so I sometimes ate for two days and then I starved for the rest of the week. He used to give me a hard time, he used to beat me … I wanted to leave my husband many times but I thought I have had one son but he died, now I am going to have another and things will be better, our marriage will last. But when my daughter was born, I saw nothing changed and my heart broke and I came away.[15]

In the words of another garment worker:

> If garments had not come to Bangladesh, so many women would have had to eat by sacrificing their honor or eating off their brothers. Without these factories, they would have had no honor. Now their value has risen. Daughters whose parents used to curse them, even they get respect now. If husbands die, or don't look after their wives or bring in co-wives, the woman can come here to work. The garments have saved so many lives.[16]

Marketing causes

This, then, was some of the context missing from the attacks in the west against Nike. It does not, as mentioned before, excuse any instances of wrongdoing within the company's factories, but it does illustrate that the anti-Nike campaigners were focusing only on certain features in a broad and variable landscape – a fact which in turn will help explain the company's difficulties at a later stage in responding constructively to the criticisms. But before moving on to Nike's struggles in this respect, it will help first to understand exactly why the context was missing from western debates. For this was not due just to the desire of the western media for sound-bites, but also because, of all the multifaceted evidence available, instances of downright abuse by Nike contract factories accorded most closely with the suspicions both of many western consumers and of a broad coalition of political interests.

The tendency of westerners to pick up on those issues relating to multinationals which chime with their own preoccupations has been observed regularly in this book. In Nike's case, the company's success with branding turned it into a distasteful symbol for many western pundits of an economic system in which demand for goods is based, not on real need, but – in their view – on the psychological manipulation of consumers by advertising and marketing. At one point in the 1980s American youths famously took to mugging people for their Nike trainers – apparent evidence of the unchecked power of the brands. That Nike also was alleged to be exploiting its third-world workers fitted this perspective nicely.

Interestingly, the anti-Nike movement in America also resonated with domestic preoccupations about race and racism. The company's shoes had become popular with many African-American inner-city youths, which in turn seems to have heightened their perceived coolness among middle-class white teenagers. But foreign sweatshop allegations against Nike were taken up by some older African-American leaders at least in part because they saw apparent parallels with the exploitation they themselves had experienced. As described by Naomi Klein, for example, the director of a community center in the Bronx made explicit comparisons between Nike's Indonesian workers and her own experience as a young girl picking cotton in

Alabama for a miserly wage: "maybe a lot of Americans can't identify with those [Indonesian] workers' situations, but I certainly can", she insisted.[17]

The western political coalition which helped focus and project the attacks on Nike – like that against other major retail brands – comprised a mix of unions, environmental campaigners, church groups, student organizations, human-rights activists, and feminists. For each part of the coalition, Nike's high profile presented a good opportunity to push forward, and to raise public awareness of, their particular cause. But the unions were among the most active, perceiving in Nike's reliance on Asian and Latin American labor a symbol of the hemorrhaging of domestic jobs to low-wage economies, a trend which they were, and still are, desperate to halt. The AFL-CIO, the umbrella group for American unions, for example, funded a full-time labor activist in Jakarta who produced some of the most devastating reports on Nike factories during the 1990s. Such interest by unions in the issue was motivated partly by a genuine desire to help workers in developing countries ruled by repressive regimes to stand up for their rights. But other motives were also at work. "There is no way we can be expected to compete with these [Asian] people", a British union activist once commented in an unguarded moment. "All you have to do is throw them a handful of rice and they are prepared to work all hours of the day."[18]

The broad western coalition could call upon any number of critics of Nike within countries such as Indonesia or Mexico to create the impression in the west that the anti-Nike campaign was unambiguously in the interests of third-world workers. For a start, there was a plentiful supply of disgruntled factory employees: "a staple of many anticorporate campaigns", remarks Naomi Klein, is "inviting a worker from a Third World country to come visit a First World superstore – with plenty of cameras rolling."[19] Also available to confirm western suspicions of Nike's general unpleasantness were local economic nationalists (and as will be seen in subsequent chapters there are plenty of these still influential in developing countries), as well as local unions. Indeed in newly democratic countries like Indonesia, where dozens of new unions were competing for attention, Nike-bashing provided such groups with a means of gaining international credibility.

A point usually absent from the anti-Nike campaigns, and which would have marred the impression that they were incontrovertibly in the interests of third-world workers, was that governments of developing countries – including those democratically elected – were opposed to a principal policy tool by which western unions proposed to curb third-world sweatshops: the insertion of tough labor standards in international trade agreements. Many third-world leaders regard this as protectionism, an attempt to safeguard western jobs at the expense of their own citizens.

The rights and wrongs of this overarching, controversial issue are beyond the scope of this book. All that is relevant here is that the western coalition, together with its particular allies in developing countries, successfully teased out and dramatized one element of Nike's system of factory production. And to protect its brand, Nike had to respond to these particular attacks. The Oregon-based company, many of its managers once more interested in drunken partying than the intricacies of the global labor debate, needed both to endeavor, and above all to be seen, to behave more "responsibly". But its response – as now will become clear – has been hobbled precisely by the mismatch between the perceptions which it is trying to tackle, and the reality on the ground with which it is forced to work.

Knight's armor

The basics of Nike's approach from the late 1990s onwards was to combine practical action, with an approach to public relations involving a Maoist style of self-criticism. "Nike has become synonymous with slave wages, forced overtime and arbitrary abuse", proclaimed Philip Knight in Washington in 1998, shortly before unveiling a package of ethical reforms which he hoped might win over his company's critics.[20] This was not quite an end to Nike's rebellious, blithe, cult-like corporate culture (well into middle-age, for example, Knight maintained a penchant for fast cars and wearing wraparound sunglasses, confirmation that this was still no conservative company). But "corporate responsibility" appeared to require a serious attitude, and a new open-mindedness by the company to the views of its western opponents.

In 1996, Nike had joined Bill Clinton's "Apparel Industry Partnership", and later it signed up to UN Secretary General Kofi Annan's "Global Compact", both political initiatives aimed at reconciling the demands of multinationals and campaign groups. The company also began to pay more attention to environmental and health problems, insisting on the use of water-based solvents in its factories, for example, so as to reduce fumes inhaled by workers, and also developing shoes from recycled materials.

The most frantic effort, because that was where criticism had been the most intense, was on labor issues. At the core of the company's strategy here was its code of conduct. Among other things, this proclaimed that children under 16 were prohibited from working in its factories; it also established a maximum working week of 60 hours, and expressed support for the "right to free association and collective bargaining". To try to ensure that factory bosses were implementing this code, Nike recruited a worldwide team of compliance staff, and hired consultants to undertake factory inspections. It also helped found the "Global Alliance", an organization uniting corporations, non-governmental groups, and agencies such as the World Bank, and which began to undertake research of its own into the views of workers in Nike, and other company, contract factories.

So what exactly have been the "contortions of corporate responsibility" resulting from Nike's efforts? In what ways has the disjointed relationship between western criticism and the reality on the ground resulted in perverse outcomes both for the company and its factory workers? Two broad sorts of contortion can be pinpointed. The first is that, on the occasions that Nike has successfully and significantly altered the grassroots situation in response to western criticism, this has often had ethically ambiguous results.

The most striking example of this is in the company's handling of the controversy over child labor in football-stitching. A photo in *Life* magazine showing a 12-year-old Pakistani boy slaving over a Nike football in 1996, was just one part of a broad campaign in the west linking branded footballs (and not just Nike's but also those of other western firms) to Sialkot, a town in Pakistan which had become the world's center for cheap hand-stitched balls, and where contractors farmed out production to hundreds of small workshops and homes in which children were being unashamedly put to work.

Taken aback by an uproar over working conditions about which its own managers had been only faintly aware, Nike responded by restricting all its purchases of footballs to one, large contractor which could guarantee no children were employed in its stitching centers. Other firms took similar measures. What could be wrong with all this?

It is not just that western attention was focused on just one small aspect of a broader problem: Pakistan's entire football production industry employed roughly 6,000 child laborers in 1996, compared with 3.3 million working children in the country as a whole.[21] It is that even dealing with these 6,000-or-so children proved to be a moral quagmire, for these children were enmeshed at the local level in a social context which was neither amenable to a quick fix, nor had been sufficiently understood at first by either the western companies or their critics.

An earlier controversy in Bangladesh – though not involving Nike – had already provided some warning of the unintended consequences of western compassion. A threat by American consumer activists to lead a boycott of clothes made with child labor in the country in the early 1990s worried Bangladeshi factory owners so much that they sacked an estimated 50,000 child workers under 14. The result? Driven as these children were by abject poverty – their own and their family's – to work in the first place, they mostly sought jobs or meager earnings elsewhere, and the alternatives were generally more unpleasant still than garment sweatshops. Among the available options were scavenging for waste, street hawking, and brute physical work such as breaking bricks.[22] The following is a case study from a 1997 survey of Bangladeshi child workers:

> Delwar Hossein is 12 years old. For a year he worked in a garment factory, 12 hours a day, pressing shirts and packing them for export. As a result of the pressure of groups campaigning to stop child labor, Delwar was fired. He now sells waste paper that he picks up along the road. Delwar and his mother live with his brother's family, eight people in a one-room hovel. Lately they have been skipping meals. For two months they weren't able to pay the rent. In the garment factory, Delwar earned a wage of $20 a month. Delwar does not understand why he had to leave the factory.[23]

So were lessons learned from the Bangladesh situation? In Pakistan, Nike – in conjunction with other western firms, charities, and international agencies working on the issue – tried to ensure that children removed from work were not simply abandoned, as they had been in Bangladesh. Various education programs were established in Sialkot, for example, and Nike also demanded of its contractors worldwide that if any children were found in their employment they should pay for those children to go to school.

Yet the effects of all these efforts were still mixed, for the underlying landscape revealed contours initially unappreciated in the west. For example, the decision by Nike and other western firms to centralize football production in stitching centers and away from individual households may have tackled some abusive child labor, but it also made it more difficult for women to gain employment. Football stitching used to be one of the few jobs suitable for women in Sialkot's tradition-bound society as it allowed them to work from home (just as garment factories in Bangladesh, as Naila Kabeer documented, had provided women there with an important lifeline). A study carried out in Sialkot in 1999 found that women's workload and wages had fallen since the child-labor controversy and that with less cash to spend, many households involved in the football industry were eating fewer meals a day.[24]

Meanwhile, getting children who once stitched footballs into education sometimes proved problematic. With the quality of local teaching often poor, and continuing pressure from parents to earn a wage, many children dropped out of school and re-entered employment. "I discovered the children were being employed in much worse industries," wrote Sue Lloyd-Roberts, a BBC journalist, of a visit to Sialkot in 1998, "I visited this foul tannery – children were treating the hides of animals using quite dangerous chemicals in appalling working conditions. [...] another industry they were working in [...] was making medical equipment, scissors and steel equipment, etc. with a flare flaring out all over the place – without any eye protection at all – tiny children aged six." Lloyd-Roberts was one of the western journalists whose reports originally drew attention to child labor in Sialkot; since then, interestingly, her perspective had evolved, as she explained in 2001:

One had liberated children from high-profile [brand] names which embarrassed the Western consumer but meanwhile these children were going back and working in the indigenous industries where there were no high profile names – the West isn't interested in these kinds of industries and that's where they will stay. So the problem is more fundamental than just these headline-grabbing campaigns which myself and other journalists have been guilty of in the past.[25]

Concluding contortions

The second "contortion of corporate responsibility" illustrated by Nike's experience is related to the first. It is that its efforts to actually improve the situation on the ground have often proved too unsubtle, or too limited, for the inherently complex task at hand, and thus have done little to stem the western campaigns against it. Moreover, given that these campaigns are focused on certain features of the landscape which, abstracted from their context, will always have the potential to disturb western minds, Nike in the future faces a potentially endless cycle of attacks on its brand.

Some of the problems of penetrating alien factory cultures have already been mentioned. Nike's team of over 30 labor compliance staff is large by the standards of most multinationals and yet, even swelled by an array of consultants and local charities, is small compared with the challenge it faces: monitoring some 700 factories across the world that employ over 500,000 people in total. Compliance with safety and health standards – such as the existence of fire extinguishers in factories – is easy enough to confirm, provided the factories can be trusted not to put such equipment on display only for the inspector's visit. Less ascertainable are issues involving day-to-day human interactions where managers and employees often tell Nike inspectors different stories. Are workers being harassed for example? Are managers, as has sometimes been alleged, hiring thugs to rough up potential union organizers? Even monitoring the age of workers can be a slippery process. Checking their birth certificates, for example, is often assumed to provide some assurance, but such documents may be unreliable in countries where all sorts of forms can be procured with a bribe.

Even if the main factories manufacturing Nike goods are obeying its code of conduct, what about their suppliers, or the suppliers of their suppliers? The typical Nike shoe has around 50 components manufactured in 6–10 countries. Nike's supply chain, like those of other multinationals, resembles a river system, fed by countless small tributaries. Labor monitoring is focused on the main arteries but it is often unclear what is happening in the upper reaches, the hundreds of factories and workshops which rarely see a Nike inspector.

On the issue of wages, Nike always will be unable or unwilling to satisfy fully the demands of its western critics, unless it rethinks its entire system of production. Salaries can be raised incrementally – as they have been, for example, in contract factories in Indonesia – but any large increases would eat away at Nike's incentive to invest in such low-wage economies in the first place. Union recognition, meanwhile, creates some unavoidable political dilemmas for Nike, especially in countries such as China where the government itself keeps a lid on the formation of independent unions.

It is sufficient to cite just a few of the many controversies in which Nike has been embroiled in recent years to illustrate the endless potential for criticism. A BBC documentary in 2000, for example, uncovered suspected children working in a Nike contract factory in Cambodia, an apparent contravention of the company's code of conduct which had eluded its labor monitors. Nike says it responded by reviewing all 3,800 employee records and conducting face-to-face interviews with suspected under-age workers. But the problem of unreliable birth certificates reared its head here. "Even at the end of that process, there was no absolute assurance we had got in right", the company admitted.

Nike might have added that there was no "absolute assurance" that in another of its 700 factories, too, or at least in their myriad suppliers, some more children might not be at work, their parents having, say, procured forged documents about their age – or that in another factory, say, managers were not harassing women workers or union organizers. With the company's monitoring system struggling to pick up on such problems, there easily could be more western media scandals waiting in the wings. And certainly there were in 2001.

Early in that year, for example, the media focused on a Nike contract factory in Puebla, Mexico, owned by Koreans, where a strike had erupted, and where two unions were competing with each other to represent workers. Employees alleged that labor leaders had been fired, a charge denied by the management.[26] "Clearly, our monitoring had missed key elements of the factory labor situation", Nike later confessed.[27]

Meanwhile, around the same time in Indonesia, a report by the Global Alliance, the partnership organization of companies and non-governmental groups of which Nike itself was a member, uncovered various allegations of sexual harassment and physical and verbal abuse in local contract factories. These were issues which, again, had eluded Nike's monitoring system. Global Alliance researchers found that around 8% of employees said they had received unwelcome sexual comments. One of the factors underlying complaints of "verbal abuse" was that Indonesian workers objected to what they saw as the rude, aggressive style of ethnic Chinese and Taiwanese factory bosses. Cultural tensions were also uncovered between the Indonesians. Some Javanese assembly workers, for example, accused their Sumatran supervisors of aggressiveness too. Among the reforms Nike subsequently introduced in Indonesia, many super-visors were given training to soften their management style, as noted at the start of the chapter.

It remains to be seen whether the problems in the Indonesian factories will now be fully resolved. But all these controversies reinforce the idea that Nike has become locked into a cycle of criticism in which the opacity of local factory culture, and the company's fumbling attempts to penetrate it, have provided an almost limitless source of material for western critics who themselves are looking with relish to expose another scandal. Unless the critics simply tire of Nike-bashing, or Nike develops a far more exhaustive, detailed and sophisticated system of labor monitoring, it is difficult to foresee any exit from the cycle as far as the company is concerned.

That has not stopped Philip Knight, Nike's founder, from trying. He has begun to call publicly for a "set of generally accepted social accounting principles" by which a company's performance on "responsibility" can be measured. This certainly would make Nike's task more manageable. The man who grew a vast empire from a tiny business selling cheap Japanese sneakers from the trunk of a car is thus now attempting to reshape the terms of the global "corporate responsibility" debate. Knight argued recently:

> I know what makes for good performance when I see it on the running track. I know it when I read quarterly results from the finance department. I have to admit, though, I'm not sure how we measure good performance in corporate responsibility. I'm not convinced anybody does. Why not? Because there are no standards, no agreed-on definitions [...] If we have a scorecard that includes all of our main competitors, or a set of multinational companies, and a uniform yardstick, I'll at least have a way to frame an answer.[28]

But it would be difficult to achieve agreement from everyone concerned on such a "uniform yardstick". A consensus exists globally on such basic standards as providing safe conditions for workers. But on issues such as the ethically correct level of local wages, the perspective of many western activists remains at odds with that of companies, and indeed many local people. Moreover, even if such a yardstick could be universally agreed, it may not diminish western criticisms of Nike, for the company's capacity to ensure labor standards are upheld without exception in its factories has been shown to be limited – just as has been the ability of other companies examined in this book to understand and shape the particular local social environment in which they operate. In short, with this proposal of his, Knight – for all his marketing savvy, for all the "just do it" spirit of his company – is unlikely to be about to crack a set of problems that have bedeviled multinationals through history.

EIGHT

Trappings of power
Royal Dutch/Shell and Nigeria

This is the time my son should have been feeding me. God will never forgive Shell.

Jim Wiwa, 99-year-old father of anti-Shell activist, Ken Saro-Wiwa,
executed by the Nigerian government in 1995.[1]

Dear Shell Nigeria, you are simply wonderful. May God bless you richly.

Recent recipient of Shell educational scholarship in Nigeria, quoted in Shell
publicity.

Among the hundreds of oil towns worldwide to which Shell's
managers are sent on their postings, Warri must count as among
the least relaxing. At first sight nothing appears disconcerting from
the company's residential compound in the town, an oasis of rich-
world comforts, with manicured lawns, plush guest houses, shops,
satellite-TV facilities, and a company hospital. But a glance at the
toweringly high barbed-wire fences and police checkpoints that
protect the compound indicates that all is not well. Warri is one of
the main urban centers in the Niger Delta, a large area of swamps,
creeks, and dry land from where Nigeria's oil – the country's
principal source of wealth – is extracted. Outside the gates of the
Shell compound, the town of Warri itself – much of it a chaotic,
waste-strewn expanse of one-story buildings and shacks constructed
from wood and pieces of scrap – has a reputation, even among
Nigerians who are hardened to urban violence, as a "wild place".

Tensions run high between the three major ethnic groups in the
town – the Ijaws, Urhobos, and Itsekiris – who vie with each other

for political influence. In mid-1999, in a spate of fighting sparked by a long-running argument over the relocation of a local government office, as many as 200 people were killed, and large areas of the town were flattened.[2] But it is oil that fuels much of the violence. The youth of all three ethnic groups are angry that – in their eyes – the wealth of their land is being drained away by the oil companies, who they see as being in collusion with the federal government of Nigeria. And it is the largest of these firms, the Shell Petroleum Development Company of Nigeria, or SPDC, that is a major target of their anger. (SPDC is owned by Shell – or, to give it its formal name, Royal Dutch/Shell, the Anglo-Dutch multinational, which is why "Shell" is often used to denote "SPDC" in this chapter. The company's significance in Nigeria is not just that it has a 30% share in a colossal joint venture which controls around half the country's oil and gas reserves, but also that it manages this entire business on behalf of the other shareholders.)

There have been frequent allegations of heavy-handed tactics on the part of police and army officers protecting the company's installations and staff in Nigeria. But it is also true that Shell managers – both expatriate and Nigerian – run a high risk of being attacked or kidnapped in and around Warri, which is why the company often pays for them to be escorted by armed guards, and houses many of them in the protected residential compound. On the day of this author's visit to Shell's offices in the town, the general manager, a Dutchman called Maarten Wink, was distracted by the news that youths with speedboats had blockaded two of his off-shore rigs, holding some 140 employees and contractors hostage – but he was not panicked, for such protests occur almost weekly.

So routine is the violence that it is even a subject for light-hearted, macho, banter among some of Shell's employees. Chatting about current ethnic tensions in Warri, for example, a group of Nigerian Shell men point out that things would be even worse were it not for the fact that the Itsekiri women were so beautiful ("the other groups fight the Itsekiris by day, and love their women by night", they roar with laughter). Meanwhile the wives of many managers, including both Africans and Europeans among them, rarely venture outside the company compound, preferring the diversions it offers (these include, for example, women's aerobics classes, and a variety of other sporting and social events, rather as if this were a surreal holiday camp) to the chaos on the other side of the fence.

It was some time ago now, in 1995, that the Nigerian dictator Sani Abacha hanged Ken Saro-Wiwa, a leader of the Ogonis, another of the ethnic groups in the Niger Delta, causing an international outcry against Shell. Abacha was well known for his ruthless crushing of opponents as well as for channeling state billions into his private bank accounts. Saro-Wiwa's fame in Nigeria, by contrast, stemmed from his success as a writer and journalist. (He had even scripted and produced one of the country's most popular television soap operas, about a group of scheming, feckless wide-boys in Lagos.) But he had latterly gained global attention as a political activist, accusing Shell of causing environmental destruction, of behaving irresponsibly, and generally of putting its profits before its principles, accusations which were repeated avidly by campaigners in Europe and America. After his death, Shell's logo was shown dripping with blood, and such was the tide of disapproval that managers in Europe complained that even their children had turned against them.

The controversy over Saro-Wiwa's execution, together with another publicity disaster for Shell – over its plans to dump an old oil storage buoy, the Brent Spar, at sea – caused a major rethink within the company over its approach to social and environmental issues. As part of a self-proclaimed corporate "transformation", Shell decided that it would henceforth redouble its efforts to bring about "sustainable development", to act "responsibly", to uphold human rights, and to generate social harmony around its operations.

On one level this strategy has worked: once-noisy western campaigns against Shell's activities in Nigeria have at the time of writing softened to a whisper. As a result of the company's new-found enthusiasm for "stakeholder engagement", many, though not all, campaign groups have been persuaded that it genuinely intends to reconcile "profits and principles" (which was the title of one of its recent social and environment reports). The company has become active in a host of international initiatives on "corporate social responsibility" (or "CSR") including the UN's Global Compact. Within the corporate world, Shell – together with another oil giant BP – is now considered a model for other firms interested in CSR.

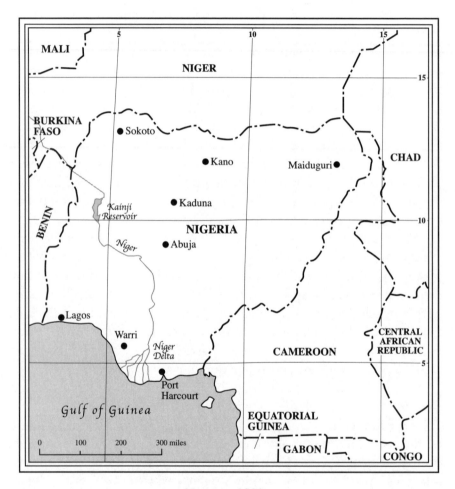

NIGERIA 1990s

Meanwhile, events in the Niger Delta these days rarely make it into western media, let alone penetrate the western conscience. And yet, as the above snapshot of Warri illustrates, the situation on the ground remains a political cauldron, in which oil still fuels tensions, in which kidnapping and the use of force are among the main forms of social interaction between the company and local people, and in which economic inequalities between these two groups are stark. What explains this discrepancy between the local situation and international perceptions? Has Shell managed to pull the wool over the eyes of its western critics?

The answer, as might be expected given the theme of this book, is more complex than that. The fact that criticisms against Shell have dropped off is not so much because of the effectiveness of its corporate PR-machine, but rather because the attention of its western critics has always been somewhat sporadic. And there has always been a degree of discrepancy between their perspective and the local situation, even at the peak of western uproar against Shell in the mid-1990s.

This chapter will show that what brought about this uproar was an unusual combination of forces. The key factor was the involvement of Ken Saro-Wiwa who, through his eloquence and political skill, packaged and communicated local problems in the Niger Delta in a way which would appeal to western environmentalist and other rich-world pressure groups. This helps explain why, since Saro-Wiwa's elimination from the scene, local people with complaints against Shell have found it more difficult to gain international attention. (It also helps explain, for that matter, why international criticisms against Nike have proved longer-lasting than those against Shell: the momentum of the anti-Nike campaign has been driven by continuing concerns in the west about the loss of jobs to sweatshops in low-wage economies, as well as by long-term support from western unions. The unifying force which Ken Saro-Wiwa – together with the obvious unpleasantness of the then dictator of Nigeria, Sani Abacha – provided for the anti-Shell coalition was altogether more fleeting.)

As for the mismatch between the western perspective and the local situation, the key point is that Shell has been – and indeed still is – less in control of the social situation in the Niger Delta than many outsiders have assumed. This is not to absolve the company of all responsibility for the problems in the region. But the limitations of its approach have been amplified by the local failures of the Nigerian state. Indeed any attempt to define "principled" or "responsible" corporate behavior in the context of Shell's operations in Nigeria is problematic, for it raises a dilemma which resonates through history: to what extent can or should a western multinational influence the government of a developing country?

The aim of this chapter is thus not to defend or attack Shell, for its record has moments of both darkness and enlightenment, but rather to provide a richer account of the genesis and aftermath of the controversy. In the period leading up to Ken Saro-Wiwa's death, the company's behavior – like that of many western firms in developing countries – was shaped by the experience of "backlash", and the perceived need to avoid antagonizing whichever indigenous government was in power. At the same time, however, this crude strategy of political non-involvement failed to prevent social problems from festering in the Niger Delta.

In the period since then, Shell's experience provides a fascinating insight for the thousands of other companies now engaging in CSR of the benefits, as well as the limitations and new risks, of that approach. Shell in Nigeria has indeed become more proactive on environmental and social issues, including community development, and has taken a more forthright stance on political matters. This is an evolutionary change, rather than a conversion on the road to Damascus, but it also raises fresh dilemmas. The company's activism is open to criticism as being neo-colonial, for example; it also may encourage dangerous arguments over the secession of various of Nigeria's fractious regions, as will be explained. Other oil and mining companies have become embroiled in similar situations in such countries as Angola, Papua New Guinea and Indonesia where internal conflict has erupted over (or has been driven by) the economic revenues they generate. Meanwhile, Shell's efforts at community development, themselves facing inherent difficulties, will count for little so long as the institutions of the state in Nigeria remain so corrupted, or, as is often the case, simply absent. It is these factors, less easily packaged as a sound-bite in the western media than a simple story of profits versus principles, which underlie the continuing anarchy around Warri.

The attractions of inaction

To flesh out this argument, it will help to explore in more detail the period leading up to Saro-Wiwa's death. As well as the company's alleged environmental sins during this period, what incensed western observers was its failure to prevent the execution of the Ogoni leader, an omission which was interpreted by many as evidence of the company's collusion with Sani Abacha's regime. Shell's role as the largest operator in an industry which provided some 80% of the government revenues and 90% of the country's export earnings, seemed to many outsiders to place it in a strong position to influence national events.

Shell claims that, in private, its managers tried to dissuade Abacha from his decision to execute Saro-Wiwa; apparently they sometimes would wait at the dictator's residence until the early hours of the morning in the hope of an audience with him (this was when Abacha bizarrely preferred to do business). Nonetheless the company made no public expressions of outrage before Saro-Wiwa went to the gallows. What explains Shell's reluctance then to speak out more? What exactly was its relationship with the Nigerian government? Part of the answer to this (though not necessarily a justification for it), lies in the period of "backlash". In the wake of Nigeria's independence from Britain in 1960, the country's quest for economic self-determination led Shell to adopt a hands-off, non-political role, and also to "indigenise" the company through increased employment of Nigerians.

In fact, Shell began operating in Nigeria well before independence, which made its actions in the post-colonial period all the more subject to nationalist scrutiny. (Through a venture originally known as Shell D'Arcy, the company was in 1937 granted an oil exploration license covering the entire expanse of the country.) Shell also had to take account of a deeper link in the minds of many Nigerians between colonialism and foreign investment, for Nigeria itself was forged from a set of distinct ethnic territories partly as a result of the activities of the Royal Niger Company in the 1890s. This was an imperial corporation with a charter from the British crown, which – much like Cecil Rhodes multinational of the same period – undertook territorial conquest as a means to secure profits (though the sought-after commodity in this case was not gold, but palm oil, the prime export of the Niger Delta region before crude oil was discovered, and which was in demand as a lubricant for the machines of industrializing Europe).

The three principal ethnic groups united within the colonially drawn boundaries of Nigeria are the Hausa-Fulanis in the north, a people once part of a large Islamic state called the Sokoto Caliphate, the Yorubas in the west, and the Ibos to the east. These groups not only felt, indeed still feel, limited identification with each other, but were themselves once divided (the Fulanis used to lord it over the Hausas, for example, while prior to colonial rule various Yoruba kingdoms were fighting among themselves). Nigeria also contains hundreds of smaller ethnic and religious groups, including the Ogonis in the Delta region. During the colonial period, British military force kept a lid on tensions between the ethnic groups, while British imperial officials dictated how revenues – such as from exports of palm oil – should be distributed among the different regions.

So the seeds of internal conflicts, in which Shell eventually would become embroiled, had been sown many decades before. In fact, the company's strategy of keeping a low political profile was put to the test shortly after independence. In 1967, Ibo leaders proclaimed that Nigeria's eastern region, which then contained much of its oil, would secede from the rest of the country, a situation which panicked many of the other ethnic groups. Thus began a bloody civil conflict – the Biafran war – in which over a million people are estimated to have lost their lives to violence or to famine. Still today, wounded old soldiers from this war, limbless, or crippled in other ways, can be seen begging for a living at street corners in Nigerian towns.

The attempted secession was eventually put down, and Nigeria restored as a unified, though still unstable, territory. But for a time, all the foreign oil companies in Nigeria had been caught between the conflicting demands of the Ibo leaders and federal politicians, each demanding control over the oil revenues. Shell was criticized by some because much of the revenue it generated ended up in the federal government's coffers (although it avoided taking any active role in the conflict). But it is important to note for later that even had Shell wanted to become more politically involved, there would have been some difficult choices to make. Support for the Ibos, for example, may well have prolonged the conflict. Union Minière's alliance with the Katangan secessionists in the Congo, it will be recalled, hastened the fragmentation of that country.

The question of secession settled for the time being, Shell opted again to keep its head down, forswearing any intention to interfere in politics, as waves of economic nationalism broke over the country in the 1970s. Nigeria's membership of OPEC had encouraged its politicians to follow the course of defiance set by Middle Eastern governments. In 1973, for example, the federal government took a 35% stake in Shell's joint venture in the country with British Petroleum, which had replaced the original Shell-D'Arcy concession; a year later the government increased its share to 55%. Nigeria then fully nationalized BP's stake in the venture in 1979, in protest at the British government's perceived softness towards white racist regimes in Rhodesia and South Africa. Today the Nigerian state owns 55% of the Shell-operated joint venture, as the concession is now known (the other partners today, apart from Shell, are Italy's ENI with 5% and France's TotalFinaElf with 10%). In the 1970s, Shell was also obliged by law to ensure that almost its entire workforce consisted of Nigerians, a process described as "Nigerianization". These were heady days of economic self confidence for the country. OPEC, argued one senior Nigerian oil official in 1979, had inflicted the "first defeat of [the] western imperial economic system in the last four hundred years".[3]

Feeling constrained from becoming involved in anything but the extraction of oil – and in many ways content simply to focus on this – Shell thus largely stood by while a succession of Nigerian governments, some civilian, most military, squandered the country's oil wealth and abused the trust of the people they were supposed to serve. This is a blunt judgment about Nigeria's rulers, but evident enough from the statistics. Since the discovery of the first significant reserves in the late 1950s, oil export revenues have exceeded $290 billion, and yet according to the United Nations Development Program nearly 70% of Nigerians live below the poverty line.

Admittedly, managing the wealth brought by oil windfalls is not an inherently easy task. Many oil-rich countries have encountered difficulties in fostering sustainable growth in economic sectors outside the petroleum industry itself. Even so, Nigeria's rulers failed in such economic challenges more than most. What should be a relatively well-off country is now one of the poorest in the world. GNP per head is now around $260 – below the level at independence four decades ago. Much of the country still lacks elementary services such as clean water, paved roads, and electricity.[4]

Local knowledge

Where a proportion of the oil money has gone is indicated by the widespread stories in the 1980s and 1990s about lavish shopping sprees in western cities by Nigerian politicians and their families, and about mysterious off-shore bank accounts containing hundreds of millions of dollars. Within Nigeria, corruption bred economic mismanagement on a colossal scale. One among a host of scandals from the 1970s occurred when military officers imported vast, unneeded quantities of cement, creating huge congestion at ports, in order to line their own pockets.[5] A more current example of waste is a giant steel mill which has swallowed some $5 billion of state investment over 20 years but has still failed, at least at the time of writing, to produce any steel.[6]

Over time Nigeria's state came to resemble a medieval system of patronage. Political office at the federal level gave access to the oil revenues, whose collection had been centralized, and which could then be dispersed to supporters and clients, a distribution which often followed ethnic lines (and since independence, the Hausa-Fulanis, the main northern ethnic group, have mostly dominated federal politics, much to the frustration of both Ibos and Yorubas). The creation of dozens of new states within Nigeria's federal structure since independence had also been partly driven by this system of patronage. State bureaucracies require funding from the federal government, and their creation thereby helps local elites attract some of the oil money downwards.

Although Shell was not simply sitting on its hands during this period – it engaged in philanthropic activities including funding research on agriculture, and also thousands of scholarships for bright Nigerians to study overseas – such projects had a basic aim. This was to embed Shell within Nigerian society, a process already accelerated by the "Nigerianization" of the company's workforce, rather than to attempt to alter radically the direction in which that society was evolving. The scholarship scheme proved particularly fruitful in this respect. As one beneficiary from the early 1970s recently wrote unblushingly in one of the company's pamphlets: "In banking, industry, academia and commerce there is invariably a fellow Shell Scholar at the other end of the phone who will go out of his way to assist another Shell Scholar and is ready as well to promote, support or project a position on any issue in the interests of Shell".[7]

It was in the Niger Delta region, however, where the company's reluctance to intervene in politics gave critics the strongest impression, fairly or unfairly, that it was working hand-in-glove with the federal government. The corruption and economic mismanagement of the country's elites was galling enough for Nigerians elsewhere in the country, but the millions living in the Delta had reason to feel particularly incensed. The oil under their land was financing the whole, rotten federal system, and yet they themselves were receiving little, if any, economic benefits, while experiencing all of the environmental impacts of oil productions (these environmental concerns will be returned to later).

At one point the dictator Abacha had unintentionally fueled locals' frustration by bussing in youths from across Nigeria to the country's capital Abuja for a stage-managed rally in his support. The youths of the Delta saw, many for the first time, a lavish city of grand federal buildings and clean, wide boulevards, quite unlike other Nigerian towns, and began to appreciate the quantities of wealth flowing from their region. Admittedly in the 1980s, in an attempt to appease growing local discontent, the federal government had allocated 1.5% of the oil revenues specifically to the country's oil-producing areas, a figure that was subsequently raised to 3%. But only a portion of that money actually benefited communities, much of it being siphoned off by local bureaucrats and politicians. This is apparent from the half-finished or abandoned projects from this era, such as water towers and electricity plants, which still dot the Delta region.

What made Shell particularly vulnerable to community anger in the Delta was the physical location and spread of its facilities. Some of the other foreign-managed oil companies ran fields off-shore, making their facilities difficult to reach. But Shell's wells – and there are now over a thousand of them – were mostly on land, or in the swamps, creeks, and inlets of the Delta's humid terrain. Like a web of capillaries and veins, some 6,000 km of Shell pipelines conveyed oil across the land of the inhabitants of the Delta region, close to and sometimes through their villages. For these local people, sabotaging Shell's facilities by, for example, drilling holes in the pipelines, was among the ways they felt they could gain the attention of those in positions of power. For any loss of oil production directly affected not just Shell, but also the federal politicians who depended so heavily on the revenues, and who, it was perceived, were keeping this economic bounty for themselves.

Shell's response to growing unrest in the Delta was partly to pump more of its own money into local development. Its funding of community projects rose from about $4 million a year in the late 1980s to $22 million in 1995. It also, tentatively, leaned on the federal government to spend more money (which was one of the reasons why the 1.5% figure had been raised to 3%). But even $22 million was a drop in the ocean given the crushing poverty of the Delta, a region of 70,000 square kilometers, with a population today of 7 million; and, as noted above, the federal money tended to disappear quickly.

Against this background of local anger, and the failure of its limited community efforts to quieten the situation, Shell thus came to depend on a short-term and basic solution to protect its facilities and employees: it turned to the forces of "law and order". In the eyes of its critics, however, this merely confirmed its collusion with the government. Allegations of brutality, including massacres of local protestors by soldiers and police in the Delta region became commonplace. Shell paid the salaries of many of the police protecting its own installations. It was obliged to do so by law (as are today many multinationals operating in developing countries where governments are strapped for cash) but this did not lessen the impression, strongly denied by the company, of collusion in human rights abuses.

As for the soldiers dispatched to the region directly on the orders of Abacha's regime, an idea of their brazen tactics can be gleaned from the fate of prominent opposition figures in this period. In 1996, for example, the wife of Moshood Abiola, a politician who had been elected Nigeria's president before being imprisoned by Abacha, was gunned down by a group of armed men in Lagos, the country's main commercial center, in an area of the city dotted with army checkpoints. A regime which allowed important figures to be dispatched in such a forthright matter had little concern about eliminating irritating local activists in the Delta.

The Ogoni flashpoint

With the situation volatile across the whole Delta region, and with Shell neither dictating the behavior of the security forces, nor able to claim it had no responsibility for their actions, it was the plight of the Ogonis which caught the attention of international campaigners. Numbering some 500,000, and occupying a small area of land, the Ogonis were one of over a dozen ethnic groups in the Delta. The reason they, unlike other downtrodden groups, successfully pricked the western conscience was, as mentioned before, the political canniness of one of their leaders.

It was Ken Saro-Wiwa, educated, eloquent, and urbane, who packaged and projected their cause globally with the help of western-based campaign groups such as Greenpeace and the Sierra Club. The former television scriptwriter understood that attacks on Shell, a brand with which European and American consumers were familiar, would focus westerners' attention better than any campaign aimed solely against the Nigerian state. And in his view, in any case, the two were in cahoots. Also, a visit to America in the early 1990s convinced him that, as he later explained, "the environment would have to be a strong plank" on which to base MOSOP, a new Ogoni political organization which he had helped found.[8] "My father always suggested often as a campaigning gambit that before the European arrived on the scene our people had lived in perfect harmony with itself and the land", noted the writer's son after his death.[9]

This is from one of Ken Saro-Wiwa's speeches in 1993, typical of his line of attack:

Since oil was discovered in the area in 1958 [... the Ogoni] have been the victims of a deadly ecological war in which no

© GREENPEACE/CORBIS SYGMA

Ken Saro-Wiwa, Ogoni leader, appeals to a crowd at a rally in Nigeria in January, 1993. His eloquence and international popularity could not protect him from Nigeria's dictator, Sani Abacha.

blood is spilled, no bones are broken and no one is maimed. But people die all the time. Men, women and children are at risk; plants, wildlife and fish are destroyed, the air and water are poisoned and finally, the land dies. Today, Ogoni has been reduced to a wasteland. [...] For a multinational oil company, Shell, to take over US$30 billion from the small, defenceless Ogoni people and put nothing back but degradation and death is a crime against all of humanity.[10]

The instinctive inclination of many westerners to believe Saro-Wiwa's claims, in spite of energetic denials by Shell, was what gave his campaign such international momentum, and thereby made him a threat to Abacha. It is not that his anger against Shell had no merit, but his tactic appears to have been to tease out, and then dramatize, a few strands that had particular resonance in the west but which, in fact, formed a part of a much larger, more complex, fabric. The result was that when his message was taken up by western groups, an impression was created that Shell controlled all events in the Delta, while the Nigerian state took a back seat. Similarly, while environmental issues were brought to the fore in western campaigns, ethnic competition for oil revenues – which was a crucial issue for local people, too – became a background detail.

What about the "deadly ecological war" claimed by Saro-Wiwa, a notion which gave rise to articles in western papers portraying Ogoniland as a Dantean inferno of explosions and oil slicks? There were significant environmental problems it was true. Past oil spills had contaminated a number of locations, and Shell would burn off natural gas as a by-product of oil production (and this practice continues at the time of writing), creating ugly flares the size of houses. But a broader context was absent from western media accounts. Often missing, for example, was the fact that the environmental standards of many Nigerian firms in the region were abysmal, that Shell's facilities covered less than 1% of the land in the Delta, or that oil was one among a host of factors – which included population growth and logging – driving land degradation. What struck this author on a recent visit to the region was not great swathes of environmental devastation – Ogoniland, for example, is a mostly lush expanse of farms and vegetation – but instead the continuing extent of poverty, the women struggling under huge bundles of wood and greenery, used for fuel, and the small children with bellies distended by malnutrition. Local people interviewed in the Niger Delta criticized Shell's environmental impacts – but rather than this being the central issue for them, it appeared to be instead a grating symbol of a deeper source of anguish: their lack of control over the oil resources under their land.

That western opinion had failed to reflect all these underlying issues may be unsurprising. For a similar phenomenon has been observed at various times in this book. It is the way in which western audiences are often moved by certain, filtered, aspects of the situation on the ground, aspects which chime with their own concerns, such as about the power of big corporations, while neglecting the broader local context. This is what made Saro-Wiwa a globally important figure, and indirectly therefore an opponent whom Abacha could tolerate no longer. In a trial which made a mockery of the principles of justice and due process, Saro-Wiwa was convicted of inciting the murder of various Ogoni chiefs (these leaders, conservatives within their community, had indeed been killed, probably by young Ogoni radicals, but the evidence regarding Saro-Wiwa's involvement in the violence was flimsy). The former television writer was hanged on 10th November 1995, together with eight other Ogoni activists, in a jail in a Delta region. "I'm mentally prepared for the worst, but hopeful for the best. I think I have the moral victory", Saro-Wiwa had written from prison shortly before his death.[11] A video tape of his execution was said to have been couriered to Abacha as proof that the Ogoni leader had been truly eliminated.[12]

The subsequent global outcry may not have made Abacha feel guilty, but it did change Shell. Shell had recently been taken aback by the degree of public outrage over its plans to sink a disused oil storage buoy in the Atlantic (an internal analysis commissioned by the company had argued that this option for its disposal would create least environmental damage, but many Europeans simply refused to believe this). Now the storm over Saro-Wiwa forced a fundamental rethink by the company of its approach to social and environmental issues across the world, not just in Nigeria. The scene is now set for Shell's present-day struggles in this field.

Better in principle

These days there are few multinationals in the world as loudly committed as the Shell group to "sustainable development", or as evangelically enthusiastic about CSR. In 1997, the parent company revised its business principles, incorporating in them a commitment to human rights. This was a revolutionary move by corporate standards; most multinationals up till then had eschewed such an explicit statement on human rights, for fear it might entangle them in political difficulties in host countries. The Shell group also produced "primers" for its managers on its policies on corruption, child labor and human rights (the author has drafted similar docu-ments for the mining giant Rio Tinto). And through a "sustainable development management framework", the company began attempting to integrate environmental and social factors within its business decisions.

Where Shell once responded to criticism defensively, it makes a point now of listening to critics, inviting them to "stakeholder workshops", and also reproducing their views, even to the point of self-flagellation. Shell managers, for example, chose to reprint this rant from an anonymous contributor in the group's social and environment report in 2000:

> This is the most obvious Greenwash [i.e. environmental white-wash] I have yet to see – well done Shell, you've sunk to new levels. It appears your PR agency have successfully managed to convince you that the bulk of the population are morons.[13]

But in fact, Shell's new-found openness, together with the resulting shifts in its behavior, have dampened criticism from western campaigners, at least at the time of writing. Many groups remain suspicious, it is true, but the recovery in the company's reputation has surprised managers, accustomed as they had become to abuse from the outside world. At a recent CSR conference in London, for example, a member of Shell's new "Social Accountability" team, described excitedly how members of the public sometimes now give him an unprovoked hug, so delighted were they to hear about Shell's "transformation".[14]

It is true that Shell's efforts involve a degree of public-relations froth. But neither can they be dismissed simply as "greenwash". Every year now the heads of Shell operations are obliged to report to headquarters in London and The Hague on how they have complied with the policies. And given the continuing public scrutiny of Shell's activities, any grievous mismatch between its policies and practices soon will become an embarrassment.

Shell's experience does, however, provide an opportunity to debunk an assumption which permeates modern discussions about CSR, and which is unthinkingly accepted both by many companies and by critics of multinationals. Once a company has genuinely decided to behave "responsibly", goes this assumption, once it has opted for real action, rather than "greenwash", then it is both clear how it should behave, and inevitable that its actions will promote general harmony in the communities in which it works.

The truth is that the situation on the ground often bears only a weak relationship with how zealously the local managers implement policies and "primers" issued by corporate headquarters; and it is far from obvious how a company should behave, and where its "responsibility" ends, and that of the state begins. This is particularly true in developing countries where state failure commonly creates a set of demands on multinationals to become involved in governmental and political issues, just as if they were old-fashioned colonial entities. Shell's struggles in Nigeria in the period since the death of Saro-Wiwa provide an ideal illustration of these problems.

Admittedly, the death of General Abacha from a heart attack in June 1998 (it was widely rumored that the sexually voracious dictator had died from overexertion in the company of two Indian prostitutes[15]) has reduced the demands on Shell in certain respects. Democracy has re-emerged in Nigeria (and, at least at the time of writing, continues): Olusegun Obasanjo, the country's military ruler in the late 1970s, was returned to power, this time in a free election to the presidency in 1999. Nigeria's regime is thus less reliant than it was on brutal tactics to quash dissent, which in turn has produced fewer human-rights outrages in the Niger Delta. It is also more receptive to popular demands. For several years now, the federal government has been returning 13% of the oil revenues to the oil-producing region (the figure was 3% previously), resulting in a relative flood of money to state governments in the Delta.

The Shell group's "transformation" has also had noticeable effects on its subsidiary in Nigeria. The latter's annual spending on community projects has risen to $60 million, a near-trebling since 1995, for example; and managers pay more attention now to how the money is spent, focusing their efforts on promoting development rather than buying off local chiefs. Emboldened by the stance of Shell headquarters on human rights and corruption, the bosses of Shell's Nigerian arm are also now exerting more "ethical" pressure inside and outside their organization. They have set up anonymous telephone lines to encourage employees to blow the whistle on corrupt colleagues, for example, and they also now urge the local police to deal non-violently with community unrest.

Most significant of all, the company has been more actively pressing the case in Abuja, the federal capital, for better treatment for the Delta region. Shell lobbying was a factor behind the rise in the revenue formula to 13%, and even with that success, the company is keeping up the pressure. Shell headquarters, meanwhile, has been sufficiently reassured by all this activity to risk more of its money in Nigeria. In March 2002, for example, in partnership with other energy companies, it approved its share of a $7.5 billion investment program in the country for the next three years.[16]

Ground forces

Beyond these headline changes, however, Shell is confronted by a set of local issues which are potentially as explosive as the crisis of 1995, and which the company often struggles to circumvent or control. A similar underlying phenomenon was observed with regard to the British South Africa Company in the 1890s or Aramco in the mid-twentieth century: the limited capacity of large organizations whose prime focus is profits to predict, let alone manage, often fine-grained political developments. And in Shell's case the problems are driven in particular by the continuing incapacity of Nigeria's state institutions.

Even at a federal level, with its concerted lobbying in Abuja, there is little Shell can do to shape national developments, which in turn affect the Delta. In spite of democracy's return, the country remains mired in poverty and corruption. According to a poll of investors and others knowledgeable about the issue undertaken by Transparency International, a campaign group, Nigeria was ranked among the world's most corrupt countries in 2001. Dozens of low-level ethnic conflicts continue to sputter across the country. For example, enmity between the Tivs and the Jukuns, small groups in central Nigeria, recently resulted in several hundred deaths after the army became embroiled in their conflict.[17] And the government has failed to paper over a larger, and potentially more dangerous, divide, between the Muslim Hausa-Fulanis in the north and the main Christian groups in the south.

In the Delta itself, there is little evidence that the 13% formula has yet had any impact. Local and state governments still fail to provide clean water, roads, or basic education to many communities. Reports of state politicians buying luxurious mansions in European and American cities indicate where much of the money is being spent. Locals also allege that some of Shell's "community liaison officers" are on the take, though Shell insists that any employees found guilty of corruption are swiftly sacked.

Certainly, any positive efforts undertaken by Shell are being undermined by state corruption, and the scramble for the limited funds actually reaching local communities is in turn feeding violence, both against the company and between and within ethnic groups. Elders who once commanded respect in their villages are being denounced by more impatient, and militant, youths. The region is awash with guns, many brought back by Nigerian soldiers who served in Liberia. In 2000, there were 176 violent attacks against Shell staff, 32 of them involving firearms. Hostage takings, such as the one mentioned at the start of this chapter, and also the continuing threats by local youths to sabotage Shell pipelines, are motivated as much by the desire to extract cash from the company, as by ideological opposition to its activities.

Where the Ogonis left off in the mid-1990s, however, the Ijaws in the Niger Delta have taken up the baton of more organized political dissent. In December 1998, a conference of some 5,000 Ijaw youths issued a declaration condemning the "enslavement" of the "Ijaw nation" in "the fraudulent contraption called Nigeria", and calling on foreign oil companies to withdraw from their land. The Ijaws also adopted the tactic used by Ken Saro-Wiwa of framing their dissent in environmental terms: "We have just taken a decision to extinguish the fierce flames of hell called gas flares on our land [...] Our people are on the receiving end of ecological violence", proclaimed one Ijaw activist.[18]

Lacking a leader of Saro-Wiwa's global repute and media savvy, however, the Ijaws have so far gained limited western attention for their campaign. Western groups also may have been deterred from uniting with them *en masse* because of the violent tactics employed by some Ijaw youths. Whatever the explanation, the international spotlight which once shone brightly, if narrowly, on the plight of the Ogoni people, has failed to transfer to other ethnic groups in the region. Meanwhile, competition between ethnic groups for a share of the oil wealth has permeated Shell's own ranks. Shell jobs – and 95% of its 4,000 local employees are now Nigerian – pay well by (meager) local standards. Ethnic groups also hope that by gaining employment within the company they will be able to direct more of the oil benefits towards their own communities. A common gripe of groups in the Delta is that too many senior managers are Yorubas (Shell's Nigerian head office is located in Lagos, which is Yoruba territory). "The Yorubas don't have oil at all. Yet they've got all the key positions", complains one Delta inhabitant.

With local needs so pressing, and state provision so lacking, it is perhaps little surprise that Shell's beefed-up community development efforts are themselves having little impact. The company now funds dozens of schools, hospitals, agricultural schemes, women's empowerment projects and the like, but these go just a small way to meeting the demands of the Delta's seven million people. Moreover, many of the projects suffer the same fate as aid schemes the world over: they create a culture of dependency, or are undermined by corruption. A team of external experts invited by Shell in Nigeria to review a sample of its projects in 2000 (and few other firms dare expose their community efforts to such scrutiny) found that only 36% of these particular projects were "fully successful" in meeting communities' needs. "We're an oil-producing company. We don't have great expertise in development", admits one Shell manager.

Shell's 170-or-so community development staff in Nigeria face another difficulty which springs from the tension between the company's commercial goals and the quasi-governmental role into which it is moving. To ensure the success of their development projects they need first to build consensus and relevant skills among local people, a long-term, delicate process. Yet they are under conflicting pressure from Shell production managers quickly to secure community approval so that, for example, new pipelines or wells can be laid without fear of attack. Cash hand-outs were once considered the solution here, but these may intensify divisions within the community. There is also the risk that the company may trigger inadvertently a cycle of violence. Paying-off youths who threaten to disrupt production fosters the impression that such tactics bring financial reward.

The company's environmental efforts have succeeded little in calming local anger. It is not that there have been no improvements on past performance. Most of Shell's facilities in Nigeria, for example, have now been certified under the International Standards Organization ISO 14001 scheme and the company has committed itself to phasing out gas flaring by 2008. In addition, the questionable safety standards of Nigerian firms were tragically highlighted in 1998 when a leaking pipeline operated by an indigenous firm blew up near Warri, killing an estimated 800 people (the original cause of the leak appears to have been sabotage, although oil had been spewing from the pipeline for a number of days). Even so, it is Shell's alleged "ecological violence" which continues to be raised in the complaints of both Ogonis and Ijaws. There is a lesson here for the many other western multinationals who seek to improve their environmental performance as a means of pacifying local people: the tactic will fail so long as the political issues, such as poverty and powerlessness, which help drive environmental perceptions, remain unresolved.

Echoes of history

Finally, some of Shell's maneuvers in Nigeria as a result of its "transformation" are creating new dilemmas and risks – or rather resurrecting old ones from centuries past. It is not that Shell is now simply ordering the Nigerian government what to do. Even if this was demanded by the human-rights and corruption "primers" issued from Shell's headquarters (and these documents are in fact delicately phrased), the fact that local personnel are overwhelmingly Nigerian, their sense of personal identity tied to their country as much as their company, limits the extent to which Shell can set itself in direct opposition to the government. "Sometimes people want me to choose between Nigeria and Shell; but I want both", proudly insists one local (and Nigerian) senior manager. And the phrase, "we do not get involved in politics" still trips off the lips of many employees, as though it were a mantra. Without doubt, however, the company's traditional political reticence – which brought upon it such opprobrium over Ken Saro-Wiwa's execution – is beginning to erode over time: as noted before, Shell is indeed taking a stronger stance on human rights and corruption, and also on the level of oil revenues flowing to the Delta. And with that erosion, new fault-lines in the landscape are being revealed.

Curiously enough, a fictional account of corporate political involvement is contained in a recent thriller by none other than Shell's head of communication and media in Nigeria, Bisi Ojediran, who is a successful writer in his spare time. The latest of his pot-boilers describes a benign plot by a set of nameless foreign investors to save an African country from "self-destruction". But the book, *Sacred Seduction*, is a fantasy in more ways than one. At one point, for example, the hero, an investigative reporter, is engaged in an argument about the country's future by a mysterious, beautiful woman:

> "Nooo, come now," she taunted. "You mean everything is going on just fine? The economy has shown no signs of recovery. Militant groups strut all over the country. And what about all the heated inter-regional ethnic rivalries that are broiling? There's so much killing – do you think everybody is happy with the government? Yet you say things are all right?" She slapped her sleek thighs in protest.[19]

But rather than devising brilliantly cunning plans to rescue the entire nation, as in Mr Ojediran's page-turner, Shell's political interventions in reality have been a series of tentative, shaky, steps. With regard to human rights, for example, the company has been able to control better the behavior of the police officers whose salaries it pays, but its attempts to restrain trigger-happy army and navy units – under direct orders from the Nigerian government to protect the nation's oil resources from community protest – have met with less success. According to one of Shell's general managers, military officers often disregard the company's entreaties: "They say: 'who are you Mr Shell, to tell us what to do?'".

Similarly, with regard to corruption, the company can root out relatively easily rotten individuals from within its own ranks. Yet there is the broader issue of how government agencies spend oil revenues, a corruption problem from which Shell, as the main oil provider, cannot entirely disassociate itself, and which is far more significant in its effects on Nigeria. But here, as with human rights, Shell's steps are tentative, restrained by the fear of being seen to meddle in government affairs. In Abuja, the company has facilitated meetings between Transparency International and government officials and it is encouraging local spending agencies such as the recently established Niger Delta Development Commission to award contracts through a process of competitive tendering. But these still are mere nibbles at a canker of corruption that has spread deep through Nigeria's state system.

What about the issue on which Shell's lobbying has actually achieved significant results, the distribution of oil revenues to the Delta states? It appears at first sight ethically unquestionable that the oil-rich regions deserve more wealth from the oil. But the development also raises a number of fuzzier, more difficult questions. How exactly should revenues be divided between each of Nigeria's ethnic groups? How much further can the Delta's share increase before the very unity of Nigeria is endangered?

Conflicting ethnic demands over oil revenues have already driven one devastating secessionist movement – the Biafran war in the late 1960s. Now Shell's lobbying has helped build a momentum for the escalating demands of the Delta groups. Though arguably too internally divided to attempt any form of secession, the Delta peoples' success in attracting more revenues for themselves (or at least for their politicians) is being watched enviously by states whose slice of the cake has diminished as a result. Given Nigeria's current ethnic tensions and its fragile origins as a colonially imposed state, oil now could fuel divisions in the country in any of a number of ways (just as conflict over Union Minière's copper mines helped divide the Congo in the 1960s). "Nigeria is a shaky, even temporary, phenomenon", says one Ijaw activist ominously.

Even if the reallocation of the oil-cake does not lead directly to conflict, the mere fact that Shell, as a foreign company, has taken a forthright position on this issue may expose it over the long run to political attack from the groups who have lost out. "If you push too hard on behalf of the Niger Delta, you may lose the friendship of people in the North [of Nigeria]", admits one of Shell's government relations managers. These fault-lines in the country's political landscape cannot be ignored. And Shell cannot rely on unquestion-ing support of its economic contribution to the country to protect it against any future backlash.

The enthusiasm of the country's politicians for foreign invest-ment has relatively shallow roots. During his last stint in power in the

1970s, for example, President Obasanjo was more keen on nationalizing industries than on privatizing them, as he is now; and many Nigerian university graduates still recall approvingly *How Europe Underdeveloped Africa*, a famous 1970s book attacking colonialism and calling for "a radical break with the international capitalist system". In fact, even some Nigerian managers at Shell still proudly admit to being Marxists.

In some respects, by promoting the interests of the Delta community, Shell is now tentatively doing what Ken Saro-Wiwa had always demanded of it. But interestingly, the hanged writer also approved of certain aspects of British colonial rule. *On a Darkling Plain*, his account of the Biafran war, for example, contains a fond description of the British-established school he attended in Eastern Nigeria in the 1950s. What he liked about the school was that his own ethnicity, and that of fellow students, was considered irrelevant:

> The British flag was flown during parade on Saturdays, we sang "God Save Our Gracious Queen" when occasion demanded, and we had a lot of fun [...] *In Unum Luceant* was our motto, and we did shine as one. Our places of origin did not matter at all.[20]

The risk for Shell today is that rather than helping to unite Nigeria, its actions in support of the Delta may intensify ethnic divisions, or at least trigger complaints of neo-colonialism on its part. As with Shell, so with many other modern-day multinationals in developing countries: what appear from the west, and from companies' headquarters, as uncomplicated, risk-free instructions to local managers to behave "responsibly" are neither as easy to define in practice, nor as removed from the old dilemmas of history as may be imagined.

NINE

The cultural revolution
Rupert Murdoch in China and India

We in the entertainment and media industries must realize that unlike many other industries, what we do has important consequences for the political, social and cultural life of the other nations in which we operate. We have to respect the culture. To act otherwise would be to act as cultural imperialists.

Rupert Murdoch, chairman and chief executive of News Corporation.[1]

To get rich is glorious
Deng Xiaoping, late Chinese leader.[2]

Rupert Murdoch, the boss of News Corporation, one of the modern world's most powerful media empires, wedded Chinese-born Wendi Deng in June 1999. The celebration was discreet, aboard Murdoch's yacht *Morning Glory* in New York harbor, with some 80 guests, and a string ensemble providing harmonious accompaniment. Deng, then 32, and with an MBA from Yale University, had been working as a manager in Star, News Corp's Asian satellite television arm, based in Hong Kong. Star was one of the most strategic assets in Murdoch's portfolio.

It was no secret that Murdoch considered China's media market alluring, just as he did that of India, the other most populous nation on earth, in which Star was also doing business. And in the years since the wedding, Wendi Deng has played a small role in her husband's ambitions of expansion. She has accompanied him on some of his trips to China to meet key local figures, advising him on the subtleties of Chinese business culture and communications (successfully building relationships – or *guanxi* – is crucial to business success in the country).

The interesting significance of the marriage from the perspective of this chapter lies in how it should be interpreted in the context of Murdoch's overall Asian business strategy. A decade or so from now – whoever is running the mogul's empire at that stage – will the marriage be looked back upon as the symbolic start of a successful melding of cultures, of his company's ability to navigate the political and social currents of the Asian media market? Or will it instead be viewed as just a mere curiosity, and an exception to a general pattern of cultural confusion and misunderstanding? (On this point, it may be useful to recall from this book's first chapter that, in the early, peaceful days of the British East India Company, before interactions between its managers and the local people degenerated into conflict, company men often would marry Indian women.)

This chapter traces the fascinating to-and-fro of Murdoch's forays in Asia, focusing primarily on China (as this has been the focus of Murdoch's attention), but also on India. It describes events up to the time of writing in early 2002, starting with an early period of relatively inflexible, blunder-prone involvement in the region. Initial local resistance to Star TV helps explain Murdoch's subsequent enthusiasm for a strategy of cultural adaptation. While this new approach – neatly summarized by Murdoch as "think globally, but act locally" – provoked accusations in the west that he was becoming too friendly with the Chinese government, it has also brought some early business successes, too.

The chapter also raises questions about the future, about how foolproof even this flexible approach will prove to be over the long term. For as was seen in the stories of Aramco and ENI, even western companies which adopt an explicitly "indigenous" or culturally sensitive mantle, may find that this offers them only limited protection against the myriad forces of change which they themselves help unleash. Star television's ventures in both China and India, it will be shown, face a parallel set of issues.

In short, the story of Rupert Murdoch in Asia, though still unfolding, contains evidence for the argument of the whole book: that multinationals, however powerful, often struggle to deal with the political and social forces underlying their operations in developing countries, responding with blunt tactics to fine-grained issues (just like the western campaigners who criticize them), and finding themselves swimming alongside potentially dangerous currents.

A novel aspect of this chapter is that it shows that these same challenges apply as much to a multinational involved in information-based and "new economy" activities as to the more traditional industrial, resource or manufacturing companies that have been featured previously. For News Corp has invested in sectors such as satellite broadcasting and the internet, as well as keeping a hand in old-style businesses such as newspapers and publishing. In fact, the problems for media concerns such as Murdoch's may prove to be more acute than for exclusively "old economy" firms. Information and entertainment – the commodities which are their stock in trade – help spread foreign ideas and new cultural values with more virulence than any other product, thus making them an obvious target of any indigenous backlash.

Think global ...

The first stage of the story, in which Murdoch's initial forays into China and India are met by a flurry of local controversies, needs to be set in the context of the overall strategy and style of the tycoon himself. These ventures, after all, were only the latest in a series of business gambles by which the son of a minor Australian newspaper proprietor had gathered around himself a $15 billion-a-year global empire spanning newspapers, television, books, films, and much else besides, demonstrating a degree of personal drive, vision, and imperviousness to opposition on a par with Cecil Rhodes (though employing rather different tactics to achieve his expansion).

Murdoch's first taste of business success was in the 1950s, when he was in his 20s, winning a local newspaper circulation war in Adelaide by jazzing up the titles he had inherited from his father. But this only whetted his appetite for further growth. Shortly after, he expanded into television and national newspapers in Australia, then bought or launched papers in both Britain (the *Sun* and *News of the World* in the late 1960s, followed by the more upmarket *Times* and *Sunday Times* in 1981), and also America (the *New York Post* in 1977, for example). He spread his tentacles into Hollywood with the

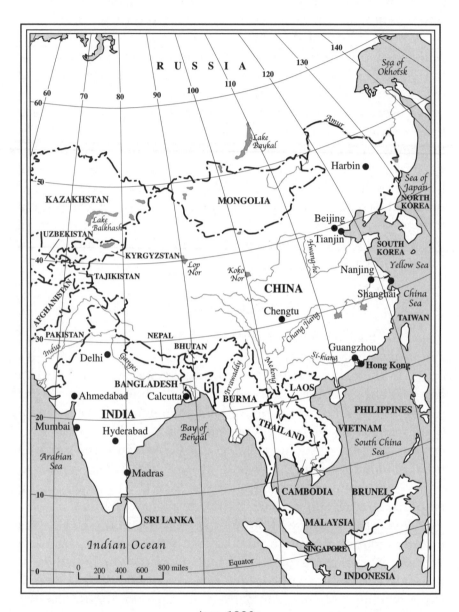

ASIA 1990s

acquisition of half of 20th Century Fox film studios in 1985, drove the creation of satellite television in Britain (with BSkyB), and, among other deals, has recently taken over a large pay-TV company in Italy. Murdoch's empire faced a temporary financial crisis in the 1990s caused partly by over-expansion, but has recovered since then, and at the time of writing neither old age nor occasional ill-health appear to have diminished the tycoon's acquisitive spirit.

Like Cecil Rhodes, Murdoch has been accused of an autocratic style of management. The fact that he has appointed his adult children to key positions within the hierarchy, certainly heightens the impression that he treats News Corp as a personal fiefdom. The following comes from Andrew Neil, a former editor of Britain's *Sunday Times* under Murdoch:

> When you work for Rupert Murdoch you do not work for a company chairman or chief executive: you work for a Sun King. You are not a director or a manager or an editor: you are a courtier at the court of the Sun King – rewarded with money and status by a grateful king as long as you serve his purpose, dismissed outright or demoted to a remote corner of the empire when you have ceased to please him or outlived your usefulness.[3]

As for the controversies aroused by Murdoch's initial forays in China and India, previous experience had given him ample preparation in dealing with criticism. Almost all of Murdoch's major ventures had sparked a degree of local fury, whether from local competitors, print-workers unions (whose power he broke in Britain in the 1980s), or moral conservatives criticizing his papers for their sometimes salacious tone. Like other media moguls, he has been accused within the west of leading a process of dumbing-down of news, of cultural homogenization (by which is usually meant the alleged evil of exporting American films and television shows across the world) and of exerting excessive influence over national politics, all allegations which he refutes but which do not appear to have wounded him personally. "You can't be an outsider and be successful over 30 years without leaving a certain amount of scar tissue around the place", he once mused.[4]

What drew Murdoch to China and India in the 1990s was precisely what also enticed other western businessmen to these countries: a newly welcoming attitude to foreign investment among their political leaders, a population of potential consumers roughly a billion strong in both countries, and rapid increases in prosperity, at least among certain sectors of the population and in certain regions. India's period of opening up to foreign investment and its dismantling of state controls over the economy had begun seriously in 1991, when the government of prime minister Narasimha Rao unveiled reforms "to unshackle the Indian industrial economy from the cobwebs of unnecessary bureaucratic control".[5] China's Communist elite opened their arms to western capital with even greater effect. By the late 1990s, foreign direct investment in China was running at around $40 billion a year, compared with some $2 billion for India.

In both China and India, the politically sensitive nature of the media businesses meant that governments were quicker to open up other sectors of industry to foreign investment. Nonetheless, the western media multinationals were eager to exploit opportunities as they became available. Though this chapter focuses on Murdoch's News Corp, both AOL Time Warner and Disney have also become swept up in enthusiasm for China. "The economic potential of China is staggering and we believe it will become one of our most important markets", said Michael Eisner, Disney's chief executive recently (and in recognition of this, a new Disneyland is planned for Hong Kong).[6]

Interestingly, western multinationals were in a similar mood of excitement about China during its previous period of opening up to foreign investment – in the nineteenth and early twentieth centuries. Towards the end of this period, in 1937, for example, Carl Crow, an American advertising agent in China, published a book alluringly entitled *Four Hundred Million Customers* (the country's then population), in which he described the techniques used by western firms to market a range of products, from cosmetics to cigarettes, to the Chinese. He did note, however, that many companies' predictions of their potential sales in the country turned out to be over-optimistic.[7]

In fact, today, as in this previous era, there exist various forces resisting capitalist penetration in both China and India. These countervailing pressures will be returned to later, but it is worth sketching them briefly here. In India, for example, the liberalization process has been complicated by the fact that decades of state interventions and "five-year plans" have spawned a bureaucracy too powerful simply to be blown away like cobwebs. And opposition to foreign involvement has long been used by Indian politicians as a tool with which to conjure up a sense of national identity or advance particular factional or ethnic goals. For India was not just once ruled by a foreign multinational; it is a country whose identity today is made fragile by a number of religious and ethnic divides (such as, for example, between Hindus and Muslims).

The way in which these political tensions within India could work against foreign firms became particularly apparent in the 1990s, when the government's economic liberalization program came under fire from right-wing Hindu nationalists (they found this line of criticism more politically sellable than their explicitly ethnic Hindu agenda). McDonald's, it may be remembered from the start of this book, was accused by Hindus in 2001 of "secretly" lacing its French fries with beef fat – a charge it denied. The 1984 Bhopal tragedy, in which a gas leak from a chemical plant owned by America's Union Carbide killed thousands of local people, had long before provided horrific evidence of the apparent evil of multinationals. When the Hindu nationalist Bharatiya Janata Party rose to form part of India's governing coalition in 1998, suspicion of western firms moved into the mainstream of the country's politics, although the overall economic liberalization program remained broadly on track.

As for China, the mere fact that a "Communist Party" regime was pursuing market reforms is evidence enough that the country's conversion to capitalism was an ambiguous – and, for western investors, potentially unstable – process. The pioneer of China's liberalization was Deng Xiaoping, a pragmatic leader who had survived the purges of Mao's Cultural Revolution. But the brutal quashing of the Tiananmen Square protests in 1989 illustrated the extent of fear among China's leaders that economic freedom might spill over into the political sphere. Indeed Deng's reforms were justified as a way of maintaining the power of the ruling Communist Party rather than diluting it. It was argued that the way to uphold popular support for the regime was by delivering rapid economic growth, even if achieving this meant allowing some "spiritual pollution" from the west. A key paper at the 1992 Communist Party Congress summarized the strategy thus: "Speed Up the Pace of

Reform, Opening and Modernization and Strive for Even Greater Victories in the Cause of Building Socialism with Chinese Characteristics".[8]

Such was the speed of economic change delivered by the reforms that they created fresh challenges for the regime. A population exodus from rural areas heightened existing social problems in China's cities, for example. The economic imbalance between China's coastal areas, which had experienced the bulk of the industrialization, and the poverty-stricken interior, grew ever wider. Many large state-owned firms, now exposed to the rigors of the market, faced potential bankruptcy. And China's entry into the World Trade Organization in 2001, whose conditions included increased market liberalization, appears likely only to intensify these problems.

The box rebellion

To return to Murdoch, Star TV was to be the spearhead of his attempted penetration of the region. He bought the company from Richard Li, the son of Li Ka-shing, a famously successful and well-connected Hong Kong businessman, in a two-stage deal in 1993 and 1995 for close to $1 billion. The company's satellite broadcasts had a vast geographical spread, or "footprint", reaching from Japan to the Middle East, covering some two-thirds of the world's population. But it was in China and India where the greatest potential appeared to lie, and where Murdoch would channel his efforts.

In this early, less culturally adaptive stage of Star's strategy – which admittedly had been put in place by Star's founders rather than by Murdoch himself – the company broadcast five channels, mostly in English (in the hope that this would appeal to Asia's wealthy elite, many of whom spoke the language). Much of its fare consisted of re-runs of American programs such as *Dynasty* or *Baywatch*, and one of the offerings was the "MTV" international channel. To add to the globalized nature of Star's output, its news was supplied by BBC World Service Television (and the BBC's coverage "contains a lot of distorted reports about China and it frequently attacks China's domestic and foreign policies", fumed one Chinese government minister[9]).

Murdoch soon would revise Star's approach. But at first he, himself, exhibited a degree of cultural inflexibility – at least as far as the Chinese regime was concerned. Commenting in 1993 on the political impact of technology, Murdoch argued that telecommunications "have proved an unambiguous threat to totalitarian regime everywhere", and that satellite TV "makes it possible for information-hungry residents of many closed societies to bypass state-controlled channels".[10]

The Chinese government's angry response to these comments lent some credence to Murdoch's view, but it also set back his business by several years. In late 1993 the government banned the sale of unauthorized satellite dishes; it also prohibited anyone from tuning in to Star TV programs. Ever since Mao's victory over the Nationalists in 1949, the Communists had been accustomed to controlling the media sector tightly, depending upon radio stations, newspapers and television to disseminate their propaganda, to reinforce a sense of national pride, and also to keep a lid on any news or ideological notions that, once unleashed, might undermine their power. By clamping down on satellite TV, the Party was now signaling its intention to defend this ideological monopoly.

Admittedly, economic liberalization had made control increasingly difficult. Already by 1993, for example, millions of well-off Chinese families had installed satellite dishes, and it was impossible to guarantee they were not surreptitiously tuning in to Star. But this just reinforced the Party's desire to prevent the upstart Australian tycoon from making further inroads. As an official at the Ministry of Radio, Film and Television commented delicately in 1996, "Mr Murdoch has a lot of beautiful dreams, but at this stage I don't think it will be possible in China for him to realize them."[11]

In India, too, Murdoch's expansion plans at first began to bump up against local obstacles. While a democracy (unlike China), India had also long treated television as an instrument of nation-building, its state-owned terrestrial broadcaster Doordarshan producing serious (and often incredibly dull) programs on such subjects as national integration, folk music, farming, and the environment, as well as more colorful soap operas and serials based around traditional Indian epics such as the *Mahabharata*. Indian intellectuals began to criticize Star for importing what they saw as crass, American culture; others condemned it for showing allegedly obscene movies (though the films in question, many of them popular hits across Asia, would hardly have raised an eyebrow among western audiences).

There were more practical problems too. While Zee, a private-sector Indian-owned television firm (in which Star also was for a time involved in various joint ventures), achieved success in the ratings, largely because of the popularity of its own Hindi-language programs, Star was finding it difficult to attract large numbers of viewers. The Indian government, meanwhile, suddenly and unexpectedly banned "direct-to-home" satellite television in 1997, an area of the business based on the use of set-top decoders, which would have allowed Murdoch to charge consumers directly for channels and programs they wanted to watch (rather than providing their content to local cable TV operators, as was the existing business model in India). The government explained that this new technology would be difficult to regulate and that it wanted to prevent any "undesirable" broadcasts.[12] It was known that Murdoch had been planning to move into "direct-to-home" television for some time.

The most striking episode of Indian backlash occurred in 1995 after the hostess of one of Star's chat shows encouraged one of her guests – a Bombay gay activist with a penchant for controversy – to repeat an insult he had previously made about Mahatma Gandhi, in which he had called India's revered independence leader "a bastard *bania*" (*bania* is a term for the Hindu merchant caste often used derogatively). Though neither Murdoch nor Star senior managers had instigated this exchange, it was appalling enough in the eyes of many Indians that they had allowed it to be broadcast. Some politicians demanded that Star be banned from India. Wanted by police, the chat show's producer and hostess were forced to leave the country. At one point a Bombay magistrate even issued an arrest warrant for Murdoch himself (though no arrest was actually carried out).[13]

For some Indians, perhaps predictably, the backlash against Murdoch was reminiscent of the struggle against the British imperialists. "In the megalomaniac media business, titans like Rupert Murdoch hardly ever eat humble pie. But then, the sun wasn't supposed to set on the British empire either, until a modest Indian dressed in his self-made clothes, de-jewelled the crown without firing a single bullet," wrote Nyay Bhushan, the editor of *Connect*, a magazine established to advance "India's Voice in the Global Village".[14]

Hobbled as it was by these cultural difficulties and the relative disinterest of many Asian viewers in its programs, Star notched up financial losses year after year in the 1990s. Admittedly, Murdoch was far from the only western businessman encountering teething problems in China and India. Few of the multinationals which had invested in either country in the 1990s had yet to turn a profit,[15] and many had faced political frictions of their own. Disney, for example, had ruffled feathers in China in the mid-1990s by producing a film called *Kundun* about the Dalai Lama and his experience of Chinese repression in Tibet. In India, the American energy firm Enron – which later went spectacularly bust – became bogged down in arguments over a big new power plant in the state of Maharashtra. Even so, Murdoch's plans for Asian expansion were encountering some serious difficulties. And this pleased his detractors across the world; the would-be conqueror of the global media system appeared finally to be having his come-uppance. But in fact it would prove much too soon to write off Murdoch's plans. For what he now was putting in place was a strategy which would dramatically resurrect Star's fortunes.

Decoding signals

What he did was to shift the company's approach from one of relative cultural inflexibility to a self-conscious adaptation to local *mores*, a change which brought some immediate commercial benefits. This strategy would once again raise the hackles of the media mogul's critics, particularly the western liberals and human-rights activists among them. But whatever the rights and wrongs of Murdoch's tactics (and as always, such ethical judgments are left to the reader), it is in the unsubtle nature of the strategy that may be detected the seeds of future problems for his business.

But first, what exactly did Star's newly flexible approach entail? Starting with the Indian market, it meant here a dramatic indigenization of the company's broadcasting output. "If you look at the changes to Star Plus [Star's flagship Indian channel] over the last

18 months", explained a Star manager in 1998, "you see it going from an all-English, primarily Western [programming] channel. It is now over 100 hours per week of locally produced programming in Hindi and English. Indian in flavor, Indian-produced, reflecting the culture of its viewers".[16] Among Star's locally produced fare was *Kyunki Saas Bhi Kabhi Bahu Thi* ("Every Mother-in-Law was Once a Daughter-in-Law"), a colorful soap opera involving improbable plots and exploring a relationship of key significance in many Indian families. Star found that such Indian-themed programs boosted its ratings considerably; by late 2001, of the top 50 television shows in India, Star Plus was broadcasting an extraordinary 36.[17]

Interestingly, it was not just Star that began to discover in the 1990s that local content could sell better than imported American fare. Other media multinationals were also busily indigenising their output. (Sony television, for example, began producing Hindi programming in India, Portuguese content in Brazil, and so on.[18]) All this suggested that the popular fear among anti-globalizers of an impending homogenization of local cultures was overdone. Nonetheless the fact that television was locally produced did not imply an absence of western, or materialistic, content. One of Star's biggest hits in India was a Hindi version of a game show format which had originally swept Britain and America: *Who Wants to Be a Millionaire?*

In China, a similar shift towards local-language content was accompanied by a succession of flattering overtures towards the Communist Party regime. This new plank of the strategy was a joint effort by Murdoch and by his son James, whom he had appointed as Star's boss in 2000. And it was this apparently cozy relationship that riled the tycoon's critics in the west.

Murdoch senior's first move in this respect was to exclude BBC News from Star's broadcasts in 1994 after it had become clear that Chinese politicians were displeased by the British corporation's repeated, and unpatriotic, references to past events in Tiananmen Square. Then, in 1995, HarperCollins, a subsidiary of Murdoch's News Corp, published a flattering biography of the early life of Deng Xiaoping by the great leader's daughter ("His smile transcends the range of time and space and is eternal", she concludes in the last line[19]). The following year, in further evidence of local relationship building, or *guanxi*, Murdoch entered into a joint venture with Liu Chang Le, a former official of the People's Liberation Army, to help establish a new Hong Kong-based Chinese satellite TV channel.

The late 1990s provided Rupert Murdoch with further oppor- tunities to signal his warm feelings towards China. In 1998, HarperCollins, having happily published Deng's biography, dropped its plans to publish Chris Patten's memoirs of his time as Governor of Hong Kong. Patten had attempted to introduce a degree of democracy in the administration of the old British treaty port before its return to China in 1997. As a critic of Beijing he had become – in the eyes of some Chinese – an "enemy of China for 10,000 years".[20] The following year, in an interview with *Vanity Fair*, Murdoch made dismissive comments about another character disliked by Beijing. Discussing the Dalai Lama, the exiled Tibetan leader, Murdoch insisted, "I have heard cynics who say he's a very political old monk shuffling around in Gucci shoes".[21] Both these incidents were greeted in British newspapers, at least those owned by competitors of the Australian tycoon, with gleeful outrage. But criticism seemed to bounce off Murdoch. And with his son James, and new wife Wendi now lending support to his approach, his words began to win converts in Beijing.

James's youth (he was aged only 27 when he was appointed Star's boss) and rebellious background (he had earlier dropped out of Harvard and launched a small, hip-hop record company with some high-school friends), made him a surprising business disciple of his father. But he proved just as enthusiastic both about tailoring broadcast content to local markets and also about making pronouncements pleasing to local politicians. His most widely reported move in the latter respect was his comments about Falun Gong, a spiritual movement involving breathing exercises and meditation, which had become so popular in China that the Communist regime regarded it as a political threat, clamping down often brutally on its adherents. In 2001, to the amazement of western human-rights activists, the young Murdoch described Falun Gong as a "dangerous", "apocalyptic cult" which "clearly does not have the success of China at heart".[22]

As for Wendi, her role in honing her husband's *guanxi* skills has been mentioned previously, but her presence must have been particularly helpful in January 2001, when she, Rupert and James Murdoch together dined in Beijing with the Chinese president Jiang Zemin. This meeting is described in a book about Murdoch's recent business ventures by Wendy Goldman Rohm, a journalist. "It was private, strictly not a business dinner," Murdoch senior noted after the meal.

> We had a meeting beforehand for half an hour, and his [Jiang's] broadcasting policy was just touched on. Then we went to dinner and had a terribly personal conversation. His only disappointment was we didn't get up and sing with him. He loves to sing. He has a very good voice. And people will go away completely charmed.[23]

Shortly before this meeting Jiang had publicly praised Murdoch and Star for their efforts to "present China objectively and to co-operate with the Chinese press".[24]

An even greater reward than official praise was soon to come Murdoch's way. Late in 2001, Star struck an agreement with the Chinese government to launch a Mandarin-language entertainment channel for the affluent southern coastal province of Guangdong. Called "Starry Sky Satellite TV", the channel would include such locally produced delights as "Woman in Control", the first male beauty contest on Chinese television, and a crime show produced in collaboration with the Chinese Ministry of Security.[25] Though over the years many Chinese homes had continued to tune in to Star surreptitiously, this was the first official opening of the television market to foreigners, an honor granted to only one other western media multinational, AOL Time Warner.

In India, at around the same time, Murdoch and his son James appeared to be gearing up for further expansion, dusting off plans to enter the "direct-to-home" market, acquiring a stake in a local cable television firm, and nosing around various potential internet investments. And to cap it all, in early 2002, after years of losses, Star announced that it had achieved its first quarterly operating profit (admittedly only $2.4 million) since Murdoch had acquired the company. In short, by this point in time, the Australian tycoon's strategy appeared to have been vindicated; certainly it was widely interpreted this way in the western press.[26]

December 2001. Respect to China: the young James Murdoch – Star TV boss and former hip-hop music entrepreneur – with Xu Guangchun, director of China's State Administration of Radio, Film and Television, after signing an agreement for the new Mandarin-language channel in southern China.

Empire or backlash?

Predicting the future is hazardous, but without doubt behind the headlines can be discerned some potential political obstacles to continued expansion in Asia by Murdoch and his successors – and indeed by many other firms investing in the region. The common theme in what follows is that the underlying situation faced by Star involves a number of complex factors which are unlikely to be solved by any simple attempt by the company to "indigenize" itself. This strategy – like those of other multinationals in this book – may be too blunt for the task at hand.

Relationships with regimes, to start with, can be only partly protected by such tactics as friendly dinners and publishing laudatory biographies of local politicians. In a fascinating study of foreign investment in China, based on off-the-record interviews with scores of managers of foreign firms and officials, Hongying Wang, an academic, shows that the reason many investors have come to rely heavily on personal contacts is the weakness of the country's formal institutions, including its legal system. But *guanxi* networks can be a precarious substitute for legal protection, the author points out. An American businessman, interviewed at the time of Deng Xiaoping's leadership, complained:

> China is a big country. Even if you have Deng's family on your side, you cannot do everything. You can never have all the connections. There is always the risk that other people may gang up and become more powerful than you.[27]

Local power structures are constantly in flux. Hongying Wang cites a number of large foreign investors with links to Deng's network, who came unstuck after his political influence waned. To guarantee it will avoid a similar outcome following the political demise of its own allies in government, Murdoch's Star will need to have developed in advance friendships with all their potential successors and rivals – a time-consuming, not to say politically dangerous, task.

In fact, even the long-term stability of the entire Communist regime in China cannot be taken for granted. Some of the changes unleashed by economic reform – the swelling ranks of unemployed in rustbelt regions such as the provinces of former Manchuria, for example, and the financially precarious situation of the country's state-owned conglomerates – pose significant threats to the government. These are among the problems that have led Gordon Chang, an experienced (if pessimistic) China watcher, to predict "the coming collapse of China", as his recent book on the subject is titled.[28]

Another potential limit to News Corp's attempts to embed itself in local societies is that, as a foreign firm, it may be unable to avoid becoming caught up in international tensions. Aramco, another high-profile multinational in its time, experienced similar pressures – at one point, it may be remembered, being asked by Saudi Arabia's rulers to try to sway American foreign policy on Israel. Television may not be a strategic industry like oil, but there are signs that the Chinese leadership are starting to treat it as such. Part of the *quid pro quo* for Star's winning permission for the new channel in Guangdong was that News Corp should broadcast CCTV-9, an English-language Chinese government propaganda channel, as part of its offerings to television viewers in America. A similar condition formed part of the deal with AOL Time Warner. Whether many Americans would tune in to the Communist Party's news and entertainment offerings is a moot question. But Jiang Zemin, who had apparently been inspired by this idea while watching television in his hotel room on a state visit to America in the 1990s, clearly thought it important that the American public should be exposed to China's spin on world events.[29]

Already, in small ways, political tensions between China and America have rebounded on foreign investors. When American planes accidentally bombed the Chinese embassy in Belgrade in 1999, for example, angry crowds surrounded American consular buildings in Beijing, creating ripples of anxiety among American investors in the country.[30] The following year, after an American spyplane collided with a Chinese fighter jet in the South China Sea, Chinese hackers bombarded American internet sites, including some government networks, with furious messages such as "Beat down American imperialists" (and American hackers in turn pasted rude messages on Chinese websites).[31]

Another international issue in which Star may find itself increasingly embroiled is human rights. Just as the Chinese regime has become increasingly nervous about the political impact of the internet (the banned Falun Gong, for example, has continued to communicate with its members using the web), western campaigners have started to push "new-economy" and media companies not to compromise with the government. AOL Time Warner, for example, has come under pressure from campaigners to uphold principles of free speech and privacy in its planned internet ventures in China – to commit, for example, not to pass data about the internet activities of political dissenters on to the government. Western information companies have a "fundamental responsibility not to be complicit in the suppression of speech", argued Tom Malinowski, Washington advocacy director of Human Rights Watch, in 2001.[32] Star may face increasing western pressures in this respect, even if its response is to try to ignore them.

There is another, more practical reason why the attempted "indigenization" of a firm like Murdoch's faces inherent limits – its commercial interests will often be at odds with those of local firms, providing further potential scope for backlash. Though Star's channels are broadcast by satellite, for example, in many countries its signals are picked up not directly by individual households but instead by indigenous cable TV operators who in turn distribute them to homes in their particular vicinity. And many of these local firms naturally prefer to keep the subscriptions they collect from customers for themselves, rather than giving them up to Star. In India, in particular, the cable industry is chaotic and loosely regulated, comprising thousands of small operators – there were estimated to be somewhere between 30,000 and 70,000 Indian cable firms in 2000.[33]

There exists, in short, potential for friction, as foreign multinationals such as Star and indigenous firms each try to maximize their share of the profits from the business in which they are jointly involved. This is a similar phenomenon to past struggles over the distribution of oil revenues in, say, Iran or Saudi Arabia or Nigeria. It may also be relevant here to recall the series of popular boycotts of foreign goods in China in the 1920s and 30s, during that country's last period of openness to western investment. These boycotts were often organized by indigenous manufacturers, irritated at what they saw as unfair competition from foreign firms.

Underlying the potential for friction today is a broader issue which may be a focus for future disagreements between western multinationals and developing countries: intellectual property rights. Information-based multinationals, such as News Corp, Disney and Microsoft, have regularly complained about the pirating of their products. This loses such firms billions of dollars of potential revenues in rich countries alone. In much of Asia, selling a bootleg video of the latest Hollywood blockbuster, for example, or a copied version of the latest Windows software, carries with it even less of a social stigma, or risk of punishment, than it does in the west. With Star now controlling over 25,000 hours of original programming a year, preventing piracy is key to protecting its profitability.

However, a common assumption of western multinationals about this problem – that it is essentially one of illegal behavior, and is therefore likely to be eradicated eventually – may only partly reflect the less clear-cut, underlying reality. For even though many governments of developing countries have committed to clamping down on piracy, notions of what constitute intellectual property rights (or IPR) may vary from culture to culture. Some Asian environmental activists, for example, have recently argued that rules on intellectual property are a western imposition, contrary to local ethical values which hold that information is a social good, to be shared.[34] This is partly perhaps a politically convenient argument with which to beat foreign firms. Nonetheless it indicates that the problem will not be easy to eradicate.

"IPR is a rather new concept in China", writes Hongying Wang. "Until recently, those using others' creative work without paying for such use did not regard this as exploitation; and those whose work was used without compensation did not feel violated." One indication that IPR is a novel idea in China is that, once introduced, it is now being tested by a minority of people to bizarre limits. In urban areas recently, some people have been "demanding compensation for allowing their picture to be taken (portrait rights) or giving directions to a location (information rights)."[35]

Even more dramatic evidence that enforcing intellectual property involves both ethical ambiguities and the potential for backlash comes from the pharmaceuticals industry. The initial reluctance by western drugs firms in the 1990s to permit their HIV drugs to be reproduced at discounted prices in Africa (where in some countries as much as a quarter of the population is infected with the virus) helped unite against them a coalition of both indigenous governments and western activists. On the one side, the drugs firms insisted that any erosion of patent protection (that is, their intellectual property) would undermine their incentive to research new treatments; on the other side, their opponents argued that such notions were irrelevant in the face of the impending death of millions. Admittedly, the pirating of television programs is a problem involving less human tragedy. But it too may be sustained by a genuine incomprehension by each side of the others' perspective.

Star struck

Finally, even if Star overcomes all these obstacles, even if it successfully navigates all the intricacies of domestic politics, avoids potential international flashpoints as well as backlash from local economic interests, and brings to an end the piracy of its intellectual property, the fact remains that its activities form a part – and an important symbolic part – of a momentous and difficult process of change in both China and India.

In both countries, although perhaps at a faster rate in China than in India, traditional economic structures, and the social traditions that envelop them, are being broken down by modern capitalist forces. As a distributor of new-style, glitzy television programs and of adverts promoting a tempting array of consumer goods, Star cannot avoid being identified as a symbol of this process of change, and of the spread of foreign values, even if it produces the programs locally and tries to "indigenize" itself in other ways. And because the industrialization of China and India is likely to create not just many economic winners, but also some losers, and a sense of insecurity among millions, it is conceivable that Star will become a focus of backlash again, a phenomenon over which, like other companies in this book, it will have little control.

In China, anti-foreigner sentiment is never far from the surface, laced as it is with historical memories. Generations of Chinese schoolchildren have been taught about the indignities suffered by their nation at the hands of foreign powers and capitalists in the nineteenth and early twentieth centuries. Among the most popular Chinese-made films in the 1990s was an epic about the Opium War, the conflict by which the aggressive British helped open up China to trade.[36] Today Chinese internet chat-rooms, for all the government's fear about the threat posed by the web to its own power, are often filled with nationalistic, rather than subversive, rantings (the 11th September attacks on America, for example, were applauded by some Chinese web users).[37]

In India, the potential for backlash lies as much in popular insecurities triggered by the process of change as by gung-ho forms of nationalism. "India's encounter with cultural and economic modernity has come at a time when it is feeling particularly vulnerable", argues the Indian writer Pankaj Mishra in an essay about Rupert Murdoch's ventures in the country, "The regular exposure, through the visual and print media, to western lifestyles, which are models for millions of Indians, has induced deep feelings of anxiety and inferiority among the modernizing class."[38]

Gurcharan Das, another prominent Indian writer, who is also a businessman, is optimistic about the country's economic prospects, particularly in high-tech areas such as the internet. But he, too, notes the considerable forces of resistance. For example, "the right wing of the BJP [the Hindu nationalist Bharatiya Janata Party] wants to close the economy to foreigners in the name of nationalism. The left-wing intellectuals in the universities continue to fill the minds of our young with postmodern, postcolonial theories of multinational conspiracies and other variants of impotence."[39]

Will these forces of resistance be overcome? Will Rupert Murdoch's empire triumph in China and India? All that can be said for sure is that it would be unwise to brush aside the risks. This was a tendency of Carl Crow, the American advertising manager, whose 1937 book *Four Hundred Million Customers* conveyed some of the excitement of the previous great wave of foreign investment in China and whose words provide a fitting conclusion to the chapter.

Crow was genuinely interested in the cultural habits and behavior of Chinese consumers, just like many modern-day foreign managers, and he describes these in some detail. However, he does not dwell in the book on the turbulent regional politics of the time. It is an indication of his relatively unworried attitude to this broader social context in which his business operated that he viewed local conflicts as a source of potential entertainment. At one point he describes taking "a couple of tourist [i.e. western] ladies out to show them what a Chinese battle was really like. Two local warlords were manifesting their hatred of each other on the shores of the Yangtsze about thirty miles away, and several friends who had been out to see the battle said it was more than usually thrilling. We drove through the war-ravaged countryside, where a terrified population was fleeing to safety, and [...] got settled in a comfortable and fairly safe position [...]".[40]

But it is not Crow's insensitivity, but his dismissal of potential political threats which parallels the faith of some modern managers in the progress of western investment in the country. "On an average once a year there is an emotional wave which hits some part of China and gives the foreign importer or manufacturer some rather serious worries, because the object of this wave is to boycott foreign goods and thereby break the foreigners' rice bowl", Crow explained. But he added, "they [the boycotts] are usually very noisy affairs, but we 'old China hands' do not take them very seriously, for we have seen too many of them fizzle out."[41]

Soon after Crow wrote these words, the "thrilling" fights between local warlords would be superseded by an all-out conflict between China and Japan (partly, it will be remembered, because of the activities of the South Manchurian Railway Company), and then later, once that war was out of the way, there would recommence a full-scale civil war between Nationalists and Communists, with both parties firmly opposed to future foreign interference in China. Then, with the triumph of Mao Tse-tung, there began a major boycott of foreign capitalists lasting several decades.

That Crow got it horribly wrong in *Four Hundred Million Customers* is not necessarily a guide to the future. But modern multinationals such as Star should draw at least a warning from his failure to understand that the conflicts and swirling social changes that he was witnessing, changes that foreign investment had helped in part to unleash, eventually might rebound on the whole project of western business in the country. For such an inability to anticipate, let alone shape, the broader social environment in which business operates has a been a weakness of multinationals noted throughout this book.

Epilogue

This book has examined the social and political interactions of some of the most powerful multinational companies that have operated in developing countries through history. These corporate giants have often wielded their power in unplanned, unco-ordinated and self-defeating ways. Time and time again, they have failed adequately to understand the social and political environment in which they operate and have thus struggled to achieve their objectives. These difficulties have arisen in varied contexts – whether the companies have been trying simply to enhance their profits and protect them from political attack, or to pursue a particular "ethical" agenda.

The problem has often been exacerbated by the nature of ideological debates concerning corporate behavior in the west which have tended to focus on simplified elements of the underlying situation. Sometimes the task of managing political issues, involving as it does understanding intricate processes of social change, tackling complex dilemmas, and overcoming deep-rooted indigenous suspicions of foreign companies, has simply exceeded the capacity of the multinationals concerned. In short, the corporate giants have shown themselves to be a particularly clumsy and fumbling breed.

It is worth briefly reviewing the evidence from each of the chapters that has led to this conclusion. The main focus throughout the book has been on the political maneuvers of the multinationals concerned, as opposed to their economic performance – although failures in the former have inevitably rebounded on the latter. Of course, in each case the situation faced by a particular multinational has not been an exact replica of another's experience – especially across eras, the forces at work and the issues have differed. However, the evidence for the conclusion runs as a common thread through the various stories.

In the case of the British East India Company, it was seen how a multinational could embark on the invasion of an entire sub-continent not because the company's bosses in its headquarters actually intended this (they had generally instructed local managers to engage only in peaceful trade), but because of the unplanned, and unexpected, embroilment of managers in local political disputes. Territorial acquisition both undermined the company's profitability over the long term, and involved it in intricate questions of administration and cultural management. Its insensitive, western responses to these issues provided one of the sparks for the Indian Rebellion of 1857.

In the case of Cecil Rhodes' British South Africa Company, the multinational was so focused on rapid expansion that it neglected, and made dangerously false assumptions about, the attitude of local societies. Many of the company's managers believed the Matabele and Shona peoples to be broadly welcoming of the occupation of their lands. Yet these tribes launched a fierce rebellion of their own in 1896, which only the company's possession of machine guns, and its managers' general indifference to mowing down Africans, allowed it to survive.

The Japanese-owned South Manchurian Railway Company, like the East India Company, became inextricably embroiled in local disputes, partly because its wealth and economic influence acted as a magnet for political controversies. These disputes were eventually settled in the company's favor by an outright Japanese invasion of Manchuria. However, the nature of the invasion also highlighted the company's – and the Japanese government's – failure to predict and control the local situation. For it was undertaken by war-mongering Japanese military units, many of whom had originally been sent to Manchuria to guard the company's assets, and who were acting in direct contravention of their orders from Tokyo.

Then came United Fruit, the hugely controversial American banana multinational, whose involvement in toppling a democratic government in 1954 in Guatemala was a no less ill-conceived (and unethical) corporate strategy. The decision by the company's bosses to support the coup, it was shown, was not an example of cunning on their part, nor a conscious choice to sacrifice their principles for the sake of profits, but rather an illustration of the blind, outdated nature of the corporate culture which informed their actions, and of the company's insulation from the social and political situation in Guatemala. United Fruit's support for the coup failed miserably to solve its long-term financial problems.

That the companies examined in the "Backlash" part struggled to comprehend and shape their respective political environments, is perhaps less unexpected given the new political climate in this era in which they were subject to deeper local hostility and found themselves bereft of protection from imperial armies. Union Minière, the Belgian giant, botched its attempt to safeguard its copper mines in the Congo: it provided support to a short-lived secessionist movement, thereby making its assets an obvious target for nationalization by the subsequent leader of the united Congo, Mobutu. Ente Nazionale Idrocarburi, the Italian energy firm, successfully wooed the Shah of Iran, but at a later stage was ejected from the oil-rich country by the militant Islamic leaders who took his place. Aramco's genuine efforts at cultural sensitivity in Saudi Arabia, meanwhile, provided only flimsy protection from the gale-force winds of social change in the country – social change which the company's oil finds had helped to unleash. The eventual result, as with Union Minière and ENI, was nationalization of its assets.

In the most recent period dealt with in "Resurgence", different factors have been in play. There has been a more welcoming attitude towards foreign investors in developing countries. But still the multinationals have found social issues profoundly difficult to resolve. Nike's efforts to deal with western ethical criticisms of its behavior (criticisms which themselves focused only on a narrow aspect of the underlying reality) failed to take sufficient account of the complexity of local factory cultures, and of the social environ-ment in which they are embedded. Shell has struggled to improve the violent and poverty-stricken social environment in the Niger Delta, a region in which its oil has contributed to many problems, but where its actions are constrained by fear of being seen to interfere in domestic politics. Finally, Rupert Murdoch's Star TV experienced an initial backlash in China and India; and in spite of his company's increased sensitivity to local social and political tastes, there remain plenty of opportunities for further unanticipated cultural collisions.

Is it possible that a different sample of multinationals would have led to a different set of findings? This seems unlikely. It is not just that the stories have pinpointed inherent problems for any large profit-making organizations that attempt to manage fine-grained social and political situations. The particular multinationals in this book were chosen either because of the sheer scale of their power or because their actions were seen at the time to be examples of political cunning or general ruthlessness and hence aroused public interest or ire. This makes the main finding – that such epicenters of power and reputed savvy have in fact engaged in fumbling, unplanned political maneuvers – all the more unexpected.

Powers of understanding

The book has generally avoided taking sides in the overall ideological debate about multinationals, precisely because its aim has been to observe their behavior objectively, undistorted by any political slant. Even so, two very basic lessons can be drawn from its findings, irrespective of one's political leanings.

The first is addressed to the bosses and managers of modern-day multinationals; it is that it is in their own interests to pay greater attention to the complexity of the underlying situations with which they are dealing. In particular, companies need to be more cognizant of potential sources of conflict with indigenous societies. For whether or not the current wave of foreign investment in developing countries leads to a second overall era of backlash, as in the decades immediately after the colonial era, localized outbreaks of hostility and friction would appear to be inevitable.

What does this mean in practice for multinationals? If the underlying situations they face are so complex and involve such potentially overwhelming political tides, is there actually any way in which companies can deal with them more effectively (except, that is, by avoiding investing in poor countries in the first place)? The answer, at least in some cases, will be yes, for merely by developing a deeper understanding of the social and political context in which they do business, by appreciating the intricate nature of problems which may arise, and also by maintaining a skepticism about any management techniques which purport to provide simple solutions, companies will be less liable to walk blindly into the sort of political quagmires which afflicted the multinationals in this book.

A natural tendency of big companies both past and present has been to focus their attention on what they consider to be core business functions – such as, say, production or marketing – while social and political problems are treated as distractions. As a result, the latter are often dealt with on a reactive, *ad hoc* basis, and companies commonly try to solve them simply by hiring public-relations people and lobbyists to present their case more persuasively to the external world. "Corporate social responsibility" can help in this respect, but sometimes it also falls into the category of a simplistic, unthinking response. CSR tends to carry with it the assumption that "responsible" corporate behavior is easy to define on the ground, and that by striving for it, companies can avoid dilemmas and political frictions (whereas – as Shell has found in Nigeria – these may remain as acute as ever). But irrespective of the precise technique used, what has invariably been lacking from companies' efforts in this area is the sort of long-term clear-sighted, analytical approach which they typically would apply to, say, financial planning or analysis of economic trends.

Judging by some of the examples from history, more forethought certainly could reap rewards. For example, had the bosses of the East India Company, or of United Fruit, developed a more accurate understanding in advance of the political dynamics in their respective regions of business, the strategies of both multinationals would likely have been less disastrous. The London directors of the East India Company would have been less credulous of the misleading, oversimplified political information fed to them by local managers and, as a result, may have acted more assertively in restraining these managers from waging their unprofitable local wars. Similarly, United Fruit's bosses would have been less convinced than they were that the government of Jacobo Arbenz posed a mortal threat to the company's commercial interests. This would have discouraged them from supporting the coup against the government, a tactic which brought the company little benefit and much opprobrium.

A more strategic, informed approach also might have helped the multinationals examined in "Resurgence" to avoid at least some of their problems. In Shell's case, for example, the company probably ought to have been able to predict some decades back that if the Niger Delta's oil wealth continued to be drained away by Nigeria's federal government, with few benefits accruing to local people, dangerous resentments would be likely to develop in the oil-producing region. Even given such foresight, the solutions would not have been obvious. But it would have inclined Shell at an earlier stage to focus less exclusively on maintaining good relations with the federal politicians, and to pay more attention to local concerns.

As for Nike, had the company been more cognizant in advance of the potential for labor abuses within its contract factories, and also of the deep chord which allegations of such abuses would strike in the west (and, again, both phenomena surely could have been predicted), it might have begun monitoring its suppliers at a much earlier stage. It also might have spotted earlier on the inherent difficulties of penetrating factory cultures – and hence devised from the start a monitoring system that applied more intensive scrutiny to the contract factories and which as a result overlooked fewer potential scandals.

The basic approach that modern multinationals might adopt to reduce the risk of such problems, in short, is clear – although its practical implications will vary from company to company and its implementation is unlikely to be easy. For what is required is no more or less than a serious attempt by companies to understand objectively the political and social context in which they operate, both at a local and international level, and to pinpoint the complexities, risks and dilemmas that may lurk initially unseen within it.

To be truly objective, such an understanding needs to be unclouded by the sort of defensive or self-justifying beliefs which envelop many companies. It also needs to permeate all levels of the organization, rather than being restricted to local management, and to inform the way in which the company conducts its business, not just how it defends itself to the outside world. Public relations, lobbying and CSR all may be useful techniques in addition to this understanding, but they cannot provide a substitute for it.

States of confusion

The second lesson springing from the book's findings relates to the world beyond the boardrooms and offices of the multinationals. For it remains unlikely that giant companies will become suddenly more adept in the way they manage their social and political interactions. And non-governmental organizations, too, have been shown to suffer from their own structural flaws and biases in their attempts to regulate corporate behavior. Given all this – and this is the basic point – the role and responsibility of western and host governments in dealing with the social context for investment becomes crucially important.

This is not to prejudge how heavily governments should regulate multinationals, nor to suggest that developing countries ought to be less welcoming of foreign firms – for such judgments depend on one's political bias. (And to conclude either way would require an overall assessment of costs and benefits brought by western firms, which has been beyond the scope of the book.) However, the evidence it contains does indicate that multinationals should be neither trusted to rectify all surrounding social problems, nor entirely blamed for them. In an era when corporate power has become a hot topic, the spotlight ought also to be shone more brightly on the important role of the state.

A crucial task for governments in developing countries is to tackle admittedly chronic, deep-rooted problems such as ethnic conflict, corruption, abusive child labor, and economic inequality, which the entry of foreign multinationals either can exacerbate or ameliorate, depending partly on the policy framework. That Nike struggled to deal with the problem of under-age workers in its Asian contract factories, for example, indicates that there is no substitute for sound, enforceable regulations against exploitative child labor by governments, underpinned by state education and anti-poverty programs (although in many countries such an outcome remains far off). Similarly Shell's struggles to promote social harmony in the Niger Delta underline the pressing need for more effective systems of social provision and for greater transparency on the part of the Nigerian government.

Governments of rich countries, meanwhile, ought not to ignore the possible political problems, and diplomatic sparks, which may be generated by waves of western investment in developing countries and the changes these bring about in local societies and power structures. It was noted that the sudden wealth and western influences brought to Saudi Arabia by Aramco exacerbated ideological tensions within that country, and contributed (if only indirectly) to the rise of Islamic extremism. The recent flood of western investment in China may lead to new geo-political frictions too. If the Chinese government ever opts to reverse its market reforms, for example, western firms no doubt will call upon their governments to help them recover their invested billions. Again, this is not an argument against foreign investment, but just a reminder that governments ought not to assume multinationals have everything under control.

Whether western governments also should impose tougher regulations on their multinationals so that they behave more "ethically" abroad, an approach advocated by many campaigners, is a less clear-cut issue, for it depends on how exactly these laws are drafted and how they define "ethical" behavior. The views of westerners as to which are the correct standards and the more important issues, as has been noted regularly, do not always coincide with the views of local people or of host governments; and the experience of the companies themselves has shown that solving complex, ethically ambiguous issues from afar is not easy.

Certainly, many of the episodes in this book could be retold from the perspective of states or regimes, both those in the west and those host to the multinationals, which placed too much trust in the companies concerned, assuming that their political interactions would follow some coherent, predictable plan. In the case of the East India Company, for example, the Mughal rulers of India who granted the multinational its first trading concessions in the country can have had little expectation that an organization whose bosses proclaimed quite sincerely that they were mere peaceful traders, would metamorphose over time, and in an almost accidental way, into a violent invasion force.

The British government's understanding of the dynamics of the situation was limited too. Few officials expected that a private enterprise eventually would saddle their country with an enormous empire, with all the economic bounty and political problems that entailed. "Nothing can be more absurd and preposterous than the present system", wrote John Robinson, a British minister, in the 1770s about the company's acquisition of Indian territories.[1] Yet the British state would struggle for decades to find a sensible way to regulate the company, only assuming full responsibility for the administration of India some 80 years later.

It may be wise to stop here, however. For exploring this subject – the confused, clumsy response of states to multinationals, as opposed to the fumbling behavior of the corporate giants themselves – would require a different book altogether.

Notes

Maps

Maps have been prepared and drawn specifically for *Empires of Profit* by Alan and Julie Snook. Map in Chapter 7 based on information available at http://www.nike.com/nikebiz/gc/r/pdf/vision.pdf.

Preface

1. August 1993 edition; article by Kirkpatrick Sale.
2. Figure for 1998, cited by D. Held 1999 p236.
3. S. Huntington 1996.
4. R. Venton 1998.
5. N. Klein 2000.

Part One: Introduction

1. Reuters news report, 8th May 2001.
2. *FT*, 8th April and 16th June 2000.
3. Quoted in C.R. Boxer 1977 p96.
4. See, for example, J. Parry and M. Bloch 1989.
5. D.A. Washbrook 1988 pp60, 66.

Chapter One

1. The Azimgarh proclamation in A. Embree 1963 p1.
2. Quoted in P. Moon 1989 p755.
3. Quoted in B.J. Gupta 1962 p40.
4. Quoted in B.J. Gupta 1962 p45.
5. Quoted in P. Turnbull p1.
6. Quoted in P. Spear 1975 p43.
7. Quoted in P. Spear 1975 p75.
8. Quoted in K.N. Chaudhuri 1978 p125.

9. R. Grove 1995.
10. P. Moon 1989 p51.
11. R. Garrett 1976 p147.
12. Luke Scrafton, *Reflections on the Government of Indostan, 1761*, quoted in P. Moon 1989 p55.
13. Quoted in P.J. Marshall 1987 p84.
14. Quoted in B.J.Gupta 1962 p126.
15. Quoted in P.J.Marshall 1987 p88.
16. P. Lawson 1987 p133.
17. Quoted in P. Griffiths 1974 p107.
18. Quoted in T. Metcalfe 1995 p19.
19. Quote from Lord Chatham in P. Lawson p120.
20. Quoted R. Vohra 1997 p72.
21. Quoted in T. Metcalfe 1995 p33.
22. Quoted in R.Vohra 1997 p76.
23. Wilberforce speech to parliament 1813. Quoted in P. Woodford 1978 p112.
24. C. Hibbert 1978 p289; P. Moon 1989 p701.
25. Quoted in C. Hibbert 1978 p59.
26. Quoted in P. Mehra 1985 p61.
27. C. Campbell 1858 p2.
28. C. Hibbert 1978 pp 210-211.
29. Quoted in C. Hibbert 1978 p316.
30. Quoted in C. Hibbert 1978 p387.
31. Quoted in C. Hibbert 1978 p387.
32. V. D. Savarkar 1947 p545.

Chapter Two

1. Maurice Gifford, quoted in J. Galbraith 1976 p307.
2. Note by Edward Fairfield, Colonial Office, quoted in J. Galbraith 1976 p23.
3. Quoted in B. Roberts 1987 pp26–7.
4. Quoted in A. Thomas 1996 p114.
5. See R. Rotberg 1988 pp406–8.
6. Quoted in R. Rotberg 1988 p397.
7. Quoted in A. Thomas 1996 p127.
8. Quoted in A. Keppel-Jones 1983 p29.
9. Quoted in A. Thomas 1996 p138.
10. D. Beach 1994 p60.
11. Roger Summers, quoted in T. O. Ranger 1967 p10 .
12. D. Beach 1994 p157.
13. Quoted in A. Thomas 1996 p184.
14. D. Beach 1994 pp132–3.
15. J. Blake-Thompson and R. Summers, quoted in T.O. Ranger 1967 p22.
16. Lord Knutsford, quoted in M. Loney 1975 p35.
17. Sir Sidney Shippard, quoted in B. Roberts 1987 p105.
18. B. Roberts 1987 p133.
19. Quoted in O. Ransford 1968 p208.

20. Quoted in J. Galbraith 1976 p292.
21. July 1896; quoted in B. Porter 1968 pp50–1.
22. Quoted in B. Roberts 1987 p116.
23. *The Economist*, 9th May 1891; quoted in B. Porter 1968 p42.
24. Quoted in B. Roberts 1987 p121.
25. See J. Galbraith 1976 p129.
26. Quoted in J. Galbraith 1976 p328.
27. Quoted in J. Galbraith 1976 p298.
28. Maurice Gifford, quoted in J. Galbraith 1976 p307.
29. A. Keppel-Jones 1983 p286.
30. Quoted in B. Roberts 1987 p187.
31. Quoted in A. Thomas 1996 p273.
32. Quoted in A. Keppel-Jones 1983 p425.
33. Quoted in B. Roberts 1987 p226.
34. Quoted in T.O. Ranger 1967 p39 .
35. Quoted in T.O. Ranger 1967 p3.
36. Quoted in T.O. Ranger 1967 p4.
37. Report of the Directors of the British South Africa Company 1897–8 p9.
38. See T. O. Ranger 1967.
39. See J. Cobbing 1977.
40. Quoted in A. Thomas 1996 p306.
41. Quoted in A. Keppel-Jones 1983 p441–2.
42. A. Thomas 1996 p312.
43. Quoted in B. Roberts 1987 p 232.
44. O. Schreiner 1897.
45. R.S.S. Baden-Powell 1897 pp131–2.
46. R.S.S. Baden-Powell 1897 pp 297 and 299.
47. Quoted in R. Rotberg 1988 p567.
48. Account drawn from V. Stent. Reproduced in F. Sykes 1897 pp217–38.
49. R. Rotberg 1988 p557; A. Keppel-Jones 1983 p529.
50. Quoted in A. Thomas 1996 p320.
51. See Lan, D 1985.
52. "Rhodesia's Last Tribute to its Founder"; Bulawayo, 1902; quoted in B. Roberts 1987 p297.

Part Two: Introduction

1. See, for example, *FT* 30th November 2000 – "Chinese victims win war payout".
2. Quoted in F. Ninkovich 2001 p47.
3. W. G. Beasley 2001 p125.
4. D. Landes 1998 p379.
5. Quoted in D. Landes 1998 p335; and J. Roberts 1995 p801.
6. See, for example, J. Roberts 1995 p800.

Chapter Three

1. Quoted in R. Myers 1989 p129.
2. Quoted in Takehiko Yoshihashi 1963 p159.
3. Quoted in G. McCormack 1977 p250.
4. See G. McCormack 1977 pp16–17.
5. Sources for last two paragraphs: Yoshihashi 1963 pp45–60; Dull 1952 pp455–6.
6. Quoted in Shinkichi Etō 1986 p76.
7. Figure cited in A. Feuerwerker 1983 p117.
8. Source for previous two paragraphs: A. Feuerwerker 1983 pp193–8.
9. Quoted in A. Feuerwerker 1983 p133.
10. Quoted in A. Feuerwerker 1983 p155.
11. Quoted in A. Feuerwerker 1983 p162.
12. Quoted in Itō Takeo 1988 p77.
13. Quoted in Ikuhiko Hata 1988 p290.
14. See Yoshihisa Tak Matsusaka 2001 p90.
15. See M. Peattie 1988 p251.
16. Quoted in R. Myers 1989 p106.
17. Quoted in Itō Takeo 1988 pviii.
18. See, for example, M. Peattie 1988 pp237–44.
19. Quoted in P. Duus 1989 pxx.
20. Figures cited in L. Young 1998 p32.
21. R. Myers 1989 p122.
22. W. M. Holmes. *An Eye-Witness in Manchuria* (1933). Quoted in R. Myers 1989 p124.
23. Nakamura Yūjirō. Quoted in Yoshihisa Tak Matsusaka 2001 p191.
24. Ueda Kyosuke. Quoted in R. Myers 1989 p117.
25. Itō Takeo 1988 pviii.
26. R. Myers 1989 p125.
27. Itō Takeo 1988 p12.
28. Source for paragraph: J. Fogel 1988 pvii–xxxi.
29. Quoted in W. Gardner 1999.
30. W. Gardner 1999.
31. W. G. Beasley 2001 pp159–69.
32. W. G. Beasley 2001 pp168–9.
33. Quoted in Yoshihisa Tak Matsusaka 2001 p261.
34. Quoted in P. Dull 1952 p455.
35. Quoted in P. Duus 1989 pxxv.
36. Sources for paragraph: R. Myers 1989 pp127–8; H. Kingman 1932 p28.
37. H. Kingman 1932 pp30–1.
38. Quoted in Takehiko Yoshihashi 1963 p50.
39. *The Economist* 27 October 2001 p127.
40. Quoted in H. Kingman 1932 p29.
41. Quoted in Takehiko Yoshihashi 1963 p129.
42. W.G. Beasley 2001 pp171–2.
43. Quoted in Ikuhiko Hata 1988 p295; also see Takehiko Yoshihashi 1963 pp158–9.
44. See Takehiko Yoshihashi 1963 pp153–4.

45. Takehiko Yoshihashi 1963 pp2–3.
46. Quoted in Nakagane Katsuji 1989 p141.
47. Itō Takeo 1988 pp xvii–xx.
48. See R. Harvey 1994 p227.
49. Obituary of Chang Hsüeh-liang *The Economist* 27 October 2001; *People's Daily* 15 October 2001.
50. Itō Takeo 1988 p210.

Chapter Four

1. Quoted in North American Congress on Latin America 1974 p128.
2. S. May and G. Plaza 1958 p232.
3. See, for example, P. Gleijeses 1991 pp185–9.
4. Quoted in S. Schlesinger and S. Kinzer 1983 p52.
5. Quoted in J. Handy 1984 p141.
6. Quoted in T. McCann 1976 p54.
7. T. McCann 1976 p56; J. Handy 1984 p139.
8. J. Handy 1984 p143.
9. T. McCann 1976 pp59–60.
10. M. Ydígoras Fuentes 1963.
11. M. Ydígoras Fuentes 1963.
12. J. Handy 1984 p145.
13. See, for example, F. Adams 1914; C. Wilson 1947.
14. See F. Adams 1914 Chapter 4.
15. C. Wilson 1947 p59.
16. M. Angel Asturias 1976 *Viento Fuerte*. Quoted in J. Handy 1984 p78.
17. F. Adams 1914 p53.
18. Quoted in F. Adams 1914 p205.
19. F. Adams 1914 p203.
20. Quoted in J. Handy 1984 p84.
21. T. McCann 1976 p34.
22. C. Wilson 1947 p262.
23. Quoted in C. Kepner and J. Soothill 1935 p107.
24. Quoted in L. Langley and T. Schoonover 1995 p128.
25. P. Dosal 1993 p141.
26. See T. McCann 1976 pp21–3.
27. T. McCann 1976 p23.
28. T. McCann 1976 p22; P. Dosal 1993 p184.
29. Quoted in R. Woodward 1999 p216.
30. K. Grieb 1979 p7.
31. R. Woodward 1999 p175.
32. Quoted in P. Dosal 1993 p41.
33. P. Dosal 1993 pp45–51.
34. See, for example, P. Dosal 1993 p109.
35. C. Kepner and J. Soothill 1935 p328.
36. Quoted in J. Handy 1984 p99.
37. Quoted in J. Handy 1984 p91.

38. I. Read 2000.
39. H. Long 1996 p214.
40. C. Kepner and J. Soothill 1935 p336 and pp342–3.
41. G. Joseph *et al.* 1998 p356.
42. S. May and G. Plaza 1958 p188.
43. T. McCann 1976 p143.
44. Victor Cutter, quoted in P. Dosal 1993 p161.
45. T. McCann 1976 p30.
46. T. McCann 1976 p67.
47. S. Braden 1971 p411.
48. N. Cullather 1999 p88.
49. Quoted in S. Schlesinger and S. Kinzer 1983 p199.
50. Quoted in North American Congress on Latin America 1974 p68.
51. S. Schlesinger and S. Kinzer 1983 p232.
52. Afterword by Piero Gleijeses in N. Cullather 1999 pxxxii.
53. S. Schlesinger and S. Kinzer 1983 p184.
54. M. Bucheli 1998 p26.
55. Quoted in M. Bucheli 1998 p13.
56. See T. McCann 1976 p205.
57. United Fruit Historical Society website.
58. T. McCann 1976 p175.
59. T. McCann 1976 p209.

Part Three: Introduction

1. See *FT* 19th May 2001.
2. See, for example, *FT* 2nd March 2001.
3. Quoted in Oil Ministry Newsletter, Aug 2000; downloaded from: http://www.netiran.com/Htdocs/Clippings/DEconomy/200819XXDE01.html
4. Source for paragraph: M. Falcoff pp199–212.
5. Quoted in P. Sigmund 1977 p193.
6. W. Rodney 1988.
7. Cited in J. Dunning 1993 pp135–6.

Chapter Five

1. P. Lumumba 1972 p44.
2. Quoted in F. Fesharaki 1976 p69.
3. See L. De Witte 2001 p141; also C. O'Brien 1962 p104.
4. P. Frankel 1966 p141.
5. Figures in S. Hempstone 1962 p53.
6. T. Marvel 1949 pp275–7.
7. Quoted in C. Young 1965 p61.
8. Figures in S. Hempstone 1962 pp62–3.
9. See T. Marvel 1949 p283.
10. J. Latouche 1945 p24.

11. C. O'Brien 1962 p167.
12. C. Young 1984 p706 and p718.
13. P. Lumumba 1972 pp220–4.
14. Source for paragraph: S. Hempstone 1962 pp67–72.
15. Belgian parliamentary inquiry 2001 p520.
16. C. Young 1965 p503.
17. Belgian parliamentary inquiry 2001 p521.
18. Belgian parliamentary inquiry 2001 p555.
19. Belgian parliamentary inquiry 2001 p523.
20. Belgian parliamentary inquiry 2001.
21. Quoted in L. De Witte 2001 pp184–5.
22. See S. Weissman 1974 pp190–1.
23. M. Wrong 2000 p91.
24. See M. Wrong 2000 p109; C. Young and T. Turner 1985 pp298–301
25. C. Young and T. Turner 1985 p293.
26. J-P. Peemans 1980 p280.
27. Source for paragraph D. Votaw 1964 pp7–14.
28. D. Votaw pp17, 23.
29. D. Votaw 1964 p15.
30. P. Frankel 1966 p48.
31. A. Sampson 1975 p148.
32. C. Dechert 1963 pp84, 85, 90.
33. Quoted in C. Dechert 1963 pp65–66.
34. Quoted in C. Dechert 1963 p89.
35. P. Frankel 1966 p101; D. Votaw 1964 p33.
36. See, for example, J. Bamberg 2000 pp16-17 and J. Bamberg 1994 p519.
37. F. Fesharaki 1976 p70–1.
38. D. Yergin 1991 p505.
39. D. Votaw 1964 p80.
40. L. Grayson 1981 chapter 5.
41. D. Yergin 1991 p530.
42. Quoted in Keesing's Contemporary Archives 4th June 1982 pp315–21; the nationalization is also mentioned in an article by Luca Rodari on ENI's website: www.eni.it
43. F. Hoveyda 1980 p111.

Chapter Six

1. Quoted in A. Brown 1999 p219.
2. Account of kidnapping drawn from: C. Dobson and R. Payne 1977 pp92–128; J. Robinson 1988 pp152–72.
3. Quoted in C. Dobson and R. Payne 1977 p98.
4. A. Brown 1999 p310.
5. US Senate *Multinational Hearings* 1974 Part 7 p457.
6. Aramco Handbook 1960 p136.
7. H. Philby 1964 p125.
8. M. Cheney 1958 p149.

9. A. Sampson 1975 p10.
10. See H. Larson *et al.* 1971 chapter 24.
11. M. Cheney 1958 p54.
12. Aramco Handbook 1960 p1.
13. *Aramco World* Nov 1966 pp26–35.
14. A. Brown 1999 p362.
15. A. Brown 1999.
16. M. Cheney 1958 p148.
17. A. Brown 1999 p71.
18. A. Sampson 1975 p104.
19. See, for example, M. Cheney 1958 pp158–60.
20. A. Brown 1999 p15.
21. M. Cheney 1958 pp197–8.
22. A. Brown 1999 p242.
23. A. Brown 1999 p202; US Senate *Multinational Hearings* Part 7 p169.
24. A. Brown 1999 p284.
25. Quoted in A. Brown 1999 p284.
26. M. Cheney p240.
27. P. Terzian 1985 p88.
28. See, for example, *Multinational Hearings* 1974 Part 7 pp219–20.
29. See A. Brown 1999 pp207–14.
30. *Multinational Hearings* 1974 Part 7 pp122–34.
31 M. Cheney 1958 p214.
32. M. Cheney 1958 pp260–72.
33. Quoted in A. Brown 1999 p247.
34. L. Mosley 1973 p233.
35. Quoted in L. Mosley 1973 p237.
36. D. Holden and R. Johns 1981 p203.
37. Quoted in J. Robinson 1988 p52.
38. Source for last two paragraphs A. Brown 1999 chapter 12.
39. Quoted in A. Brown p363.
40. Quoted in P. Terzian 1985 p150.
41. Quoted in D. Yergin 1991 p640.
42. L. Mosley 1973 p331.
43. Jungers memo, 3rd May 1973, reproduced in *Multinational Hearings* 1974 part 7 p507.
44. Letter reproduced in *Multinational Hearings* 1974 part 7 p547.
45. Quoted in D. Yergin 1991 p657.
46. E. F. Schumacher 1974 p117.
47. Figure cited in A. Brown 1999 p298.
48. Y. Bodansky 1999 p4.
49. See J. Robinson 1988 chapter 11.
50. Account of kidnapping drawn from C. Dobson and R. Payne 1977 chapters 8–9; J. Robinson 1988 chapter 12; A. Brown 1999 chapter 14.
51. See, for example, BBC online news 24th December 1997.
52. Quoted in J. Robinson 1988 p69.
53. Figures from A. Brown 1999 p360.
54. Quoted in J. Robinson 1988 p69.

55. Quoted in A. Brown 1999 p367.
56. See Y. Bodansky 1999 pp29–30.
57. J. Robinson 1988 p279.

Part Four: Introduction

1. See, for example, article on Mexico in *The Guardian* 10th February 2001.
2. Figures cited in D. Held 1999 p245.
3. Figures cited in H. Anheier 2001 p286.
4. This is based on the author's own experience. A variant of this argument is made by Clifford Bob in an article in *Foreign Policy* March/April 2002.

Chapter Seven

1. Nike's Corporate Responsibility Report.
2. Quoted in J. Strasser and L. Becklund 1993 p302.
3. Quoted in J. Strasser and L. Becklund 1993 p341.
4. Quoted in J. Strasser and L. Becklund 1993 pp271–3.
5. Quoted in J. Strasser and L. Becklund 1993 ch 27.
6. Quoted in D. Katz 1994 p310.
7. Quoted in D. Katz 1994 pp105–6.
8. Figures from World Bank website.
9. Figures from ILO 2002; World Bank 1999 p62.
10. See J. Rigg 1997 chapter 6 for a good survey of such studies.
11. Quoted in J. Rigg 1997 p236.
12. Quoted in N. Kabeer 2000 p4.
13. Source for two paragraphs: A. Ong 1987 chapter 9; see also D. Wolf 1992 p129.
14. See, for example, J. Rigg 1997 pp210–11.
15. N. Kabeer 2000 p103.
16. N. Kabeer 2000 p185.
17. N. Klein 2000 p372.
18. Quoted in N. Kabeer 2000 p12.
19. N. Klein 2000 p350.
20. Quoted in *FT* 21st December 2000.
21. Figures from Clean Clothes Campaign 1999.
22. See Clean Clothes Campaign 1998.
23. Rahman 1997, quoted in Clean Clothes Campaign 1998.
24. Cited in Clean Clothes Campaign 1999; see also BBC News Online "Football child labour lives on", 16th April 1998 and *The Guardian* "Football ban sends child workers into worse jobs", 25th April 2001.
25. BBC News website, Correspondent, "Ask Sue Lloyd-Roberts", 15th November 2001.
26. See *FT* 19th January 2001.
27. Nike's Corporate Responsibility Report pp28–9.
28. Philip Knight's introduction to Nike's Corporate Responsibility Report.

Chapter Eight

1. Interview with author 24th March 2002.
2. See *FT* 24th June 1999.
3. P. Asiodu 1979 p2.
4. Figures cited in World Bank website; K. Maier 2000 pxxi; *FT* survey on Nigeria 9th April 2002; NewsAfrica 25th March 2002.
5. Cited in P. Lewis, P. Robinson, and B. Rubin 1998 p37.
6. *FT* survey on Nigeria 9th April 2002.
7. "SPDC Scholarship Scheme" – SPDC pamphlet.
8. Quoted in K. Maier 2000 p91.
9. K. Wiwa. Public lecture given at Sheffield. 22nd November 2001.
10. K. Saro-Wiwa 1994 p14.
11. Quoted in A. Na'Allah 1998 p55.
12. Cited in Harvard Business School report.
13. Shell *People, Planet & Profits* 2000 p34.
14. Author's recollection.
15. See, for example, K. Maier 2000 p4.
16. *FT* 12th March 2002.
17. *BBC Focus on Africa* magazine Jan–Mar 2002.
18. Quotes from document "The Kaiama Declaration", Ijaw Youth Council, 1999.
19. B. Ojediran 2000 pp14–15.
20. K. Saro-Wiwa 1989 p44.

Chapter Nine

1. Quoted in W. Goldman Rohm 2002 p157.
2. Quoted in BBC News Online 24th September 1999.
3. A. Neil 1996 p160.
4. Quoted in W. Shawcross article in *Time* magazine 25th October 1999.
5. Quoted in V. Mathur 2001 p156.
6. Quoted in *Asia-inc* February 2002. www.asia-inc.com
7. C. Crow 1937.
8. Quoted in J. Studwell 2002 p62.
9. Quoted in Y. Zhao 1998 p173.
10. Quoted in W. Goldman Rohm 2002 p117.
11. Quoted in Y. Zhao 1998 p178.
12. See, for example, "Rediff on the Net Business News" 17th July 1997: http://www.rediff.com/business/jul/17dth.htm
13. See W. Goldman Rohm 2002 pp195–211.
14. *Connect* Magazine January 1999.
15. See, for example, *FT* 15th April 2002.
16. Quoted in Steve Barth, article in *World Trade Magazine*, March 1998.
17. Article in *Business Week*, 17th September 2001.
18. Steve Barth, article in *World Trade Magazine*, March 1998.
19. Deng Mao-Mao 1995 p471.
20. Quoted in *FT* 29th May 2001.

21. *Vanity Fair* 1999.
22. *China News Digest* 25th March 2001.
23. W. Goldman Rohm 2002 p116.
24. *China News Digest* 25th March 2001.
25. Star Press Release 29th March 2002; *FT* 15th April 2002.
26. See, example, *Guardian* 19th December 2002; *FT* 20th December 2002.
27. H. Wang 2001 pp167–8.
28. G. Chang 2001.
29. See, for example, *FT* 6th September 2001.
30. See, for example, G. Chang 2001 pp187–9.
31. CNN.com report 3rd May 2001.
32. *International Herald Tribune* 21st April 2001; see also *Washington Post* 29th August 2001.
33. Cited in *The Economist* 25th May 2000.
34. See, for example, article by Roberto Verzola, "Globalization: The Third Wave", http://glocal.peacenet.or.kr/training/global1.htm
35. H. Wang 2001 p79.
36. G. Chang 2001 p157.
37. See *The Economist survey of China* p15.
38. *FT* 23th June 1997.
39. G. Das 2002 p347.
40. C. Crow 1937 pp133–4.
41. C. Crow 1937 p136.

Epilogue

1. Quoted in J. Keay 1993 p363.

Bibliography

Preface

Held, David, Anthony G. McGrew, David Goldblatt and Jonathan Perraton, *Global Transformations: Politics, Economics and Culture*, 1999, Cambridge, UK: Polity Press; 1999, Stanford, CA: Stanford University Press.

Klein, Naomi, No Logo, 2000, London: HarperCollins; 2000, New York: Picador USA (2001, London: Flamingo, paper; 2002, New York: Picador USA, paper).

Huntington, Samuel P., *The Clash of Civilizations and the Remaking of the World Order*, 1996, New York: Simon and Schuster (2002, New York: Free Press, new edition).

Vernon, Raymond, *In the Hurricane's Eye*, 1998, Cambridge, MA: Harvard University Press (2000, Cambridge, MA: Harvard University Press, paper).

Part One: Introduction

Boxer, C. R., *The Dutch Seaborne Empire 1600–1800*, 1977, London: Hutchinson.

Parry, J. and M. Bloch, *Money and the Morality of Exchange*, 1989, Cambridge, UK: Cambridge University Press.

Washbrook, D. A., "Progress and Problems: South Asian Economic and Social History" in *Modern Asian Studies*, 22,1. 1988.

Chapter One

Campbell, Sir Colin, *Narrative of the Indian Revolt*, 1858, London: George Vickers.

Chaudhuri, K. N., *The Trading World of Asia and the English East India Company 1660–1760*, 1978, Cambridge, UK: Cambridge University Press.

Embree, Ainslie T. (ed.), *1857 in India: Mutiny or War of Independence*, 1963, Lexington, MA: D. C. Heath and Company.

Fisher, Michael H., *The Politics of the British Annexation of India 1757–1857*, 1994, New Delhi: Oxford University Press (1997, New Delhi: Oxford University Press, paper).

Garrett, Richard, *Robert Clive*, 1976, London: Arthur Barker Limited.

Griffiths, Sir Percival, *A History of the English Chartered Companies*, 1974, London: Ernest Benn Limited.

Grove, Richard H., *Green Imperialism: Colonial Expansion, Tropical Island Edens and the Origins of Environmentalism*, 1995, Cambridge, UK: Cambridge University Press (1996, Cambridge, UK: Cambridge University Press, paper).

Gupta, Brijen K., *Sirajuddaullah and the East India Company, 1756–1757*, 1962, Leiden: E. J. Brill.

Hibbert, Christopher, *The Great Mutiny*, 1978, London: Allen Lane.

Keay, John, *The Honourable Company*, 1993, London: HarperCollins.

Lawson, Philip, *The East India Company: a History*, 1987, London: Longman.

Marshall, P. J., *Bengal: the British Bridgehead*, 1988, Cambridge, UK: Cambridge University Press.

Mehra, Parshotam, *A Dictionary of Modern Indian History (1707–1947)*, 1985, Oxford, UK: Oxford University Press (reprinted 1987).

Metcalf, Thomas R., *Ideologies of the Raj*, 1995, Cambridge, UK: Cambridge University Press (1997, Cambridge, UK: Cambridge University Press, paper).

Moon, Sir Penderel, *The British Conquest and Dominion of India*, 1989, London: Duckworth; 1989, Bloomington, IN: Indiana University Press.

Savarkar, Vinayak Damodar, *The Indian War of Independence 1857* (according to copyright page, first published in England in 1909 and immediately proscribed), 1947, India: Phoenix Publications (1970, India: New Delhi).

Spear, Percival, *Master of Bengal: Clive and his India*, 1975, London: Thames & Hudson (also 1975 Purnell Book Services).

Tuck, Patrick (ed.), *The East India Company: 1600–1858*, 1998, London: Routledge.

Turnbull, Patrick, *Clive of India*, Folkestone, UK: Bailey Brothers & Swinfen.

Vohra, Ranbir, *The Making of India*, 1997, Armonk, NY: M. E. Sharpe (2000, Armonk, NY: M. E. Sharpe, 2nd edition, paper).

Wild, Anthony, *The East India Company*, 1999, London: HarperCollins (2000, London: HarperCollins, paper).

Woodford, Peggy, *Rise of the Raj*, 1978, Tunbridge Wells, UK: Midas Books.

Chapter Two

Baden-Powell, R.S.S., *The Matabele Campaign 1896*, 1897, London: Methuen.

Beach, D.N., *War and Politics in Zimbabwe 1840–1900*, 1986, Zimbabwe: Mambo Press.

Beach, D.N., *The Shona and their Neighbours*, 1994, Oxford, UK: Blackwell.

British South Africa Company Directors' Report 1897–1898.

Cobbing, J., "The Absent Priesthood: Another Look at the Rhodesian Risings of 1896–7" in *Journal of African History*, XVIII (1), 1977.

Galbraith, John S., *Crown and Charter*, 1974, Berkeley, CA: University of California Press.

Keppel-Jones, Arthur, *Rhodes and Rhodesia*, 1983, Montreal: McGill-Queen's University Press.

Lan, David, *Guns and Rain*, 1985, Berkeley, CA: University of California Press.

Loney, Martin, *Rhodesia: White Racism and Imperial Response*, 1975, London: Penguin Books.

Porter, Bernard, *Critics of Empire: British Radical Attitudes to Colonialism in Africa*, 1968, London: Macmillan.

Ranger, T.O., *Revolt in Southern Rhodesia, 1896–7*, 1967, London: Heinemann.

Ransford, Oliver, *The Rulers of Rhodesia*, 1968, London: John Murray.

Roberts, Brian, *Cecil Rhodes, Flawed Colossus*, 1988, New York: W.W. Norton.

Rotberg, Robert T., *The Founder: Cecil Rhodes and the Pursuit of Power*, 1988, New York: Oxford University Press.

Schreiner, Olive, *Trooper Peter Halket of Mashonaland*, 1897, Boston: Roberts Brothers; 1897, London: T. Fisher Unwin.

Sykes, Frank W., *With Plumer in Matabeleland*, 1897, London: Archibald Constable.

Thomas, Anthony, *Rhodes: the Race for Africa*, 1996, London: BBC Books; 1997, New York: St. Martin's Press.

Part Two: Introduction

Beasley, William Gerald, *The Rise of Modern Japan*, 2001, New York: Palgrave Macmillan; 2001, London: Phoenix.

Landes, David, *The Wealth and Poverty of Nations*, 1998, New York: W.W. Norton; 1998, London: Little, Brown and Company (1999, New York: W.W. Norton, paper; 1999, London: Abacus, paper).

Ninkovich, Frank, *The United States and Imperialism*, 2000, Oxford, UK: Blackwell.

Roberts, John M., *The Penguin History of the World*, 1995, New York: Penguin USA; 1995, London: Penguin.

Chapter Three

Beasley, W.G., *The Rise of Modern Japan*, 2001, London: Phoenix.

Dull, Paul S., "The Assassination of Chang Tso-lin", in *Far Eastern Quarterly*, Vol. XI, 1952.

Duus, Peter, Ramon H. Myers and Mark R. Peattie (eds), Introduction to *The Japanese Informal Empire in China, 1895–1937*, 1989, Princeton, NJ: Princeton University Press.

Etō, Shinkichi, "China's international relations 1911–1931" in *The Cambridge History of China, Vol. 13, Part 2* (John K. Fairbank and Albert Feuerwerker, eds), 1986, Cambridge, UK: Cambridge University Press.

Feuerwerker, Albert, Chapter 2 ("Economic trends") and Chapter 3 ("The Foreign Presence in China") in *The Cambridge History of China, Vol. 12, Part 1*, 1983, Cambridge, UK: Cambridge University Press.

Fogel, Joshua, "Introduction: Itō Takeo and the Research Work of the South Manchurian Railway Company" in *Life Along the South Manchurian Railway* by Itō Takeo, 1988, Armonk, NY: M.E. Sharpe.

Gardner, William O., "Colonialism and the Avant-Garde: Kitagawa Fuyuhiko's Manchurian Railway" in *Stanford Humanities Review*, Vol. 1.1, 1999.

Harvey, Robert, *The Undefeated: the Rise, Fall, and Rise of Greater Japan*, 1994, London: Macmillan.

Hata, Ikuhiko, "Continental Expansion, 1905–1941" in *The Cambridge History of Japan, Vol 6* (Peter Duus, Ed), 1988, Cambridge, UK: Cambridge University Press.

Itō, Takeo, *Life Along the South Manchurian Railway*, 1988, New York: M. E. Sharpe.

Kingman, H., *Effects of Chinese Nationalism upon Manchurian Railway Developments, 1925–1931*, 1932, Berkeley, CA: University of California Press (also published as University of California Publications in International Relations Volume III, No. 1, 1954).

McCormack, Gavan, *Chang Tso-lin in Northeast China, 1911–1928*, 1977, Folkestone, UK: Dawson; 1977, Stanford, CA: Stanford University Press.

Matsusaka, Yoshihisa Tak, *The Making of Japanese Manchuria, 1904–1932*, 2001, Cambridge, MA: Harvard University Asia Center.

Myers, Ramon H., "Japanese Imperialism in Manchuria: The South Manchuria Railway Company, 1906–1933" in *The Japanese Informal Empire in China, 1895–1937* (Peter Duus, Ramon H. Myers, and Mark R. Peattie, eds), 1989, Princeton, NJ: Princeton University Press.

Nakagane, Katsuji, "Manchukuo and Economic Development" in *The Japanese Informal Empire in China, 1895–1937* (Peter Duus, Ramon H. Myers, and Mark R. Peattie, eds), 1989, Princeton, NJ: Princeton University Press.

Ogata, Sadako N., *Defiance in Manchuria*, 1964, Berkeley, CA: University of California Press.

Peattie, Mark R., "The Japanese Colonial Empire 1895–1945" in *The Cambridge History of Japan, Vol. 6.* (Peter Duus, ed.), 1988, Cambridge, UK: Cambridge University Press.

Yoshihashi, Takehiko, *Conspiracy at Mukden*, 1963, New Haven, CT: Yale University Press (reprinted 1980, Westport, CT: Greenwood Press).

Young, Louise, *Japan's Total Empire*, 1998, Berkeley, CA: University of California Press (1999, Berkeley, CA: University of California, paper).

Chapter Four

Adams, Frederick Upham, *Conquest of the Tropics*, 1914, New York: Doubleday, Page & Co.

Braden, Spruille, *Diplomats and Demagogues*, 1971, New Rochelle, NY: Arlington House

Bucheli, Marcelo, "United Fruit Company in Latin America: Institutional Uncertainties and Changes in its Operations, 1900–70", paper presented at the American Anthropological Association in December 1998, Philadelphia (also in forthcoming *Bananas, Conflict and Capitalism in Latin America and the Caribbean*, Duke University Press).

Cullather, Nick, *Secret History: the CIA's classified account of its operations in Guatemala, 1952–1954*, 1999, Stanford, CA: Stanford University Press.

Dosal, Paul, *Doing Business with the Dictators: a Political History of United Fruit in Guatemala, 1899–1944*, 1993, Wilmington, DE: Scholarly Resources Books.

Gleijeses, Piero, *Shattered Hope: the Guatemalan Revolution and the United States, 1924–1954*, 1991, Princeton, NJ: Princeton University Press.

Grieb, Kenneth, *Guatemalan Caudillo: the Regime of Jorge Ubico*, 1979, Athens, OH: Ohio University Press.

Handy, Jim. *Gift of the Devil: a History of Guatemala*, 1984, Toronto: Between the Lines (1985, Boston, MA: South End Press, paper).

Joseph, Gilbert M., Catherine C. LeGrand, and Ricardo D. Salvatore (eds), *Close Encounters of Empire*, 1998, Durham, NC: Duke University Press.

Kepner, Charles David and Jay Henry Soothill, *The Banana Empire: a Case Study of Economic Imperialism*, 1935, New York: The Vanguard Press.

Langley, Lester D. and Thomas Schoonover, *The Banana Men: American Mercenaries and Entrepreneurs in Central America, 1880–1930*, 1995, Lexington, KY: The University Press of Kentucky (1998, Lexington, KY: The University Press of Kentucky, paper).

Long, Huey, *Every Man a King: the autobiography of Huey P. Long*, 1996, New York: Da Capo Press.

May, Stacy and Galo Plaza, *The United Fruit Company in Latin America*, 1958, Washington DC: National Planning Association.

McCann, Thomas P., *An American Company: the Tragedy of United Fruit*, 1976, New York: Crown Publishers Inc.

North American Congress on Latin America. *Guatemala*. 1974.

Read, Ian, "The Rise and Fall of the United Fruit Company: Reinterpreting the Role of the US Government and American Popular Opinion", 2000, Stanford, unpublished paper.

Schlesinger, Stephen and Stephen Kinzer, *Bitter Fruit: the Untold Story of the American Coup in Guatemala*, 1983, New York: Anchor Press/Doubleday (1999, Cambridge, MA: Harvard University Press, expanded paper edition).

United Fruit Historical Society Website: www.unitedfruit.org

Wilson, Charles Morrow, *Empire in Green and Gold: the Story of the American Banana Trade*, 1947, New York: Henry Holt and Company.

Woodward, Ralph Lee, *Central America: a Nation Divided* (3rd edn), 1999, Oxford, UK: Oxford University Press.

Ydígoras Fuentes, Miguel, *My War with Communism*, 1963, Englewood Cliffs, NJ: Prentice-Hall 1963.

Part Three: Introduction

Dunning, John, *Multinational Enterprises and the Global Economy*, 1993, Wokingham, UK: Addison-Wesley Publishing Company.

Falcoff, Mark, *Modern Chile 1970–1989*, 1989, New Brunswick, Transaction Publishers (1990, New Brunswick: Transaction Publishers, paper).

Rodney, Walter, *How Europe Underdeveloped Africa*, 1988, London: Bogle L'Ouverture Publications Ltd.

Sigmund, Paul, *The Overthrow of Allende and the Politics of Chile, 1964–1976*, 1977, Pittsburgh, PA: University of Pittsburgh Press.

Chapter Five

Belgian parliamentary inquiry. *Enquête Parlementaire, visant à déterminer les circonstances exactes de l'assassinat de Patrice Lumumba et l'implication éventuelle des responsables politiques belges dans celui-ci*. Chambre des Représentants de Belgique. 16th November 2001.

Dechert, Charles, *Ente Nazionale Idrocarburi*, 1963, Leiden: E. J. Brill.

De Witte, Ludo, *The Assassination of Lumumba*, 2001, New York: Verso.

Fesharaki, Fereidun, *Development of the Iranian Oil Industry*, 1976, New York: Praeger Publishers.

Frankel, Paul H., *Mattei: Oil and Power Politics*, 1966, London: Faber and Faber.

Grayson, Leslie, *National Oil Companies*, 1981, Chichester, UK: John Wiley & Sons Ltd.

Hempstone, Smith, *Katanga Report*, 1962, London: Faber and Faber.

Hoveyda, Fereydoun, *The Fall of the Shah*, 1980, New York: Simon & Schuster; 1980, London: Weidenfeld and Nicolson.

Latouche, J., *Congo*, 1945, New York: Willow, White & Co.

Lumumba, Patrice, *Lumumba speaks: the speeches and writings of Patrice Lumumba* (translated by Helen R. Lane, edited by Jean van Lierde), 1972, New York: Little, Brown and Company.

Marvel, Tom, *The New Congo*, 1949, London: Macdonald.

O'Brien, Conor Cruise, *To Katanga and Back: a UN Case History*, 1962, London: Hutchinson; 1962, New York: Simon & Schuster.

Peemans, Jean-Philippe, "Imperial Hangovers: Belgium – the Economics of Decolonisation" in *Journal of Contemporary History*, 15, No. 2, 1980.

Sampson, Anthony, *The Seven Sisters*, 1975, London: Hodder and Stoughton; 1975, New York: Viking Press.

Votaw, Dow, *The Six-Legged Dog*, 1964, Berkeley, CA: University of California Press.

Weissman, Stephen, *American Foreign Policy in the Congo, 1960–1964*, 1974, Ithaca, NY: Cornell University Press.

Wrong, Michela, *In the footsteps of Mr Kurtz*, 2000, London: Fourth Estate; 2001, New York: HarperCollins (2002, London and New York: Harper Perennial).

Yergin, Daniel, *The Prize: the Epic Quest for Oil, Money and Power*, 1991, New York: Simon & Schuster (reissued 1993, New York: Touchstone Books; 1993, London: Simon & Schuster).

Young, Crawford, *Politics in the Congo*, 1965, Princeton, NJ: Princeton University Press.

Young, Crawford, "Zaire, Rwanda and Burundi" in *The Cambridge History of Africa Volume 8: from c1940 to c1975*, J.D. Fage and Roland Oliver (general eds), 1984, Cambridge, UK: Cambridge University Press.

Young, Crawford and Thomas Turner, *The Rise and Decline of the Zairian State*, 1985, Madison, WI: University of Wisconsin Press.

Chapter Six

Aramco Handbook. Arabian American Oil Company, 1960.

Aramco World magazine, 1966.

Bodansky, Yossef, *Bin Laden: The Man who Declared War on America*, 1999, Rocklin, CA: Prima Publishing (2001, New York: Prima Publishing/ Random House Inc., paper).

Brown, Anthony Cave, *Oil, God, and Gold: the Story of Aramco and the Saudi Kings*, 1999, New York: Houghton Mifflin Company.

Cheney, Michael Sheldon, *Big Oilman from Arabia*, 1958, London: Heinemann.

Dobson, Christopher and Payne, Ronald, *The Carlos Complex: a Study in Terror*, 1977, London: Hodder and Stoughton; 1977, New York: Putnam.

Holden, David and Richard Johns, *The House of Saud*, 1981, London: Sidgwick and Jackson; 1982, New York: Holt, Rinehart and Jackson (1982, London: Macmillan, paper).

Larson, Henrietta, Evelyn Knowlton and Charles Popple, *History of Standard Oil Company (New Jersey)*, Volume 3, 1971, New York: Harper & Row.

Mosley, Leonard, *Power Play: the Tumultuous World of Middle East Oil 1890–1973*, 1973, London: Weidenfeld and Nicolson; 1973, New York: Random House (1974, New York: Viking Press, paper).

"Multinational Hearings". *Multinational Corporations and United States Foreign Policy*. Subcommittee on Multinational Corporations, Senate Committee on Foreign Relations, US Congress. Washington DC, 1975.

Philby, Harry St. John Bridger, *Arabian Oil Ventures*, 1964, Washington DC: Middle East Institute.

Robinson, Jeffrey, *Yamani: the Inside Story*, 1988, London: Simon & Schuster.

Sampson, Anthony, *The Seven Sisters*, 1975, London: Hodder and Stoughton; 1975, New York: Viking Press.

Schumacher, E. F., *Small is Beautiful*, 1974, London: Sphere Books.

Terzian, Pierre, *OPEC: the Inside Story*, 1985, London: Zed Books.

Yergin, Daniel, *The Prize: the Epic Quest for Oil, Money and Power*, 1991, New York: Simon & Schuster (reissued 1993, New York: Touchstone Books; 1993, London: Simon & Schuster).

Part Four: Introduction

Anheier, Helmut, Marlies Glasius and Mary Kaldor (eds), *Global Civil Society 2001*, 2001, Oxford, UK: Oxford University Press.

Held, David, Anthony G. McGrew, David Goldblatt, and Jonathan Perraton, *Global Transformations: Politics, Economics and Culture*, 1999, Cambridge, UK: Polity Press; 1999, Stanford, CA: Stanford University Press.

Chapter Seven

Clean Clothes Campaign. *Unstitching the Child Labour Debate*. 1998. Weblink: www.cleanclothes.org/publications/unst1.htm

Clean Clothes Campaign. Report by Samuel Poos. *The Football Industry, From Child Labour to Workers' Rights*. 1999. Weblink: www.cleanclothes.org/publications/child_labour.htm

International Labour Office. *Every Child Counts, New Global Estimates on Child Labour*. ILO, Geneva, 2002.

Kabeer, Naila, *The Power to Choose*, 2000, London: Verso (2001, London: Verso, paper).

Katz, Donald, *Just Do It*, 1994, New York: Random House (1995, Avon, MA: Adams Media Corporation, paper).

Klein, Naomi, *No Logo*, 2000, London: HarperCollins; 2000, New York: Picador

USA (2001, London: Flamingo, paper; 2002, New York: Picador USA, paper).

Lim, Linda Y. C., "Women's Work in Export Factories: the Politics of a Cause" in *Persistent Inequalities*, Irene Tinker (ed.), 1990, New York: Oxford University Press (1991, New York: Oxford University Press, paper).

Ong, Aihwa, *Spirits of Resistance and Capitalist Discipline: Factory Women in Malaysia*, 1987, Albany, NY: State University Press of NY.

Rigg, Jonathan, *Southeast Asia: the Human Landscape of Modernization and Development*, 1997, London: Routledge.

Strasser, J. B. and Laurie Becklund, *Swoosh: the Unauthorized Story of Nike and the Men Who Played There*, 1993, New York: HarperBusiness.

Wolf, Diane Lauren, *Factory Daughters: Gender, Household Dynamics, and Rural Industrialization in Java*, 1992, Berkeley, CA: University of California Press.

World Bank. *World Development Report 1999/2000*, 1999, Oxford: Oxford University Press.

Chapter Eight

Asiodu, P., *Nigeria and the Oil Question*, 1979, Lagos: Nigerian Economic Society.

Harvard Business School Case N9-399-127, *Royal Dutch/Shell in Nigeria*.

Lewis, Peter M., Pearl T. Robinson and Barnett R. Rubin, *Stabilizing Nigeria*, 1998, New York: The Century Foundation Press.

Maier, Karl, *This House Has Fallen: Nigeria in Crisis*, 2000, London: Penguin Books; 2000, New York: PublicAffairs (2002, London: Penguin Books, paper).

Na'Allah, Abdul-Rasheed (ed.), *Ogoni's Agonies*, 1998, Eritrea: Africa World Press.

Okonta, Ike and Oronto Douglas, *Where Vultures Feast: Shell, Human Rights, and Oil in the Niger Delta*, 2001, San Francisco: Sierra Club Books.

Ojediran, Bisi, *Sacred Seduction*, 2000, Lagos: BusyCrafts Books.

Saro-Wiwa, Ken, *On a Darkling Plain*, 1989, Port Harcourt, Nigeria: Saros International Publishers.

Saro-Wiwa, Ken, *Ogoni: Moment of Truth*, 1994, Port Harcourt, Nigeria: Saros International Publishers.

Chapter Nine

Crow, Carl, *Four Hundred Million Customers*, 1937, London: Hamish Hamilton; 1937, New York: Harper & Brothers.

Chang, Gordon G., *The Coming Collapse of China*, 2001, New York: Random House (2002, London: Century, paper).

Das, Gurcharan, *India Unbound: From Independence to the Global Information Age*, 2002, London: Profile Books; 2002, New York: Anchor Books.

Deng Mao-Mao, *Deng Xiaoping, My Father*, 1995, New York: BasicBooks (1996, New York: BasicBooks, paper).

Goldman Rohm, Wendy, *The Murdoch Mission*, 2001, New York: John Wiley & Sons, Inc.

Mathur, Vibha, *Trade Liberalisation and Foreign Investment in India, 1991–2001*, 2001, Delhi: New Century.

Neil, Andrew, *Full Disclosure*, 1996, London: Macmillan (1997, London: Pan, paper).

Studwell, Joe, *The China Dream*, 2002, London: Profile Books; 2002, New York: Atlantic Monthly Press.

Wang, Hongying, *Weak State, Strong Networks*, 2001, Hong Kong: Oxford University Press China.

Zhao, Yuezhi, *Media, Market, and Democracy in China*, 1998, Champaign, IL: University of Illinois Press.

Epilogue

Keay, John, *The Honourable Company*, 1993, London: HarperCollins.

Index

About TEXERE

TEXERE seeks to become the most progressive and authoritative voice in business publishing by cultivating and enhancing ideas that will illuminate the global business landscape. Our name defines the spirit of our vision: TEXERE is the ancient Latin verb "to weave". In an increasingly global business community, we seek to create an intersection where authors and readers can share the best thinking and the latest ideas. We want to leverage the expertise and insights of leading thinkers by weaving them with TEXERE's capability to deliver them to the marketplace. To learn more and become a part of our community visit us at:

www.etexere.com

and

www.etexere.co.uk

About the typeface

This book was set in 11/14pt Baskerville. The Baskerville typeface was created in the 1750s by John Baskerville of England. Credited with originating the English tradition in fine printing, John Baskerville was appointed printer to Cambridge University in 1758. This typeface is known for its delicate and simple style.